The Routledge Introduction to the American Novel

The Routledge Introduction to the American Novel provides a comprehensive and engaging guide to this cornerstone literary genre, reframing our understanding of the American novel and its evolving traditions. This volume aims to engage productive classroom discussion, including:

- What differentiates the American novel from its European predecessors and traditions from other parts of the world?
- How have the related myths of the American Dream and the Great American Novel affected understanding of the tradition over time?
- How do American novels by or about women, racial and ethnic minorities, immigrants, and members of lower social classes challenge the American cultural monomyth?
- How do experimental novels and eco-conscious novels alter the American novel tradition?

Rethinking historical trends and debates surrounding the American novel, this text delivers a persuasive case for why it's important to reevaluate the American novelistic tradition. *The Routledge Introduction to the American Novel* offers a much-needed update to the history and future of this literary form.

D. Quentin Miller (Ph.D. in English, University of Connecticut) is Professor of English at Suffolk University, where he teaches courses on American literature, African American literature, and fiction writing. He is the author, editor, or co-editor of more than a dozen books, most recently *James Baldwin in Context*, *The Compact Bedford Introduction to Literature* (13th edition), and *African American Literature in Transition 1980–1990*.

Routledge Introductions to American Literature
Series Editors: D. Quentin Miller and Wendy Martin

The *Routledge Introductions to American Literature* series provides critical introductions to the most important topics in American Literature, outlining the key literary, historical, cultural, and intellectual contexts. Providing students with an analysis of the most up-to-date trends and debates in the area, they also highlight exciting new directions within the field and open the way for further study.

Volumes examine the ways in which both canonical and lesser known writers from diverse class and cultural backgrounds have shaped American literary traditions, addressing key contemporary and theoretical debates, and giving attention to a range of voices and experiences as a vital part of American life. These comprehensive volumes offer readable, cohesive narratives of the development of American Literature and provide ideal introductions for students.

Available in this series:

The Routledge Introduction to Native American Literature
Drew Lopenzina

The Routledge Introduction to American Renaissance Literature
Larry J. Reynolds

The Routledge Introduction to American Drama
Paul Thifault

The Routledge Introduction to American Life Writing
Amy Monticello and Jason Tucker

The Routledge Introduction to the American Novel
D. Quentin Miller

For more information on this series, please visit: https://www.routledge.com/Routledge-Introductions-to-American-Literature/book-series/ITAL

The Routledge Introduction to the American Novel

D. Quentin Miller

Routledge
Taylor & Francis Group
NEW YORK AND LONDON

Designed cover image: Getty

First published 2024
by Routledge
605 Third Avenue, New York, NY 10158

and by Routledge
4 Park Square, Milton Park, Abingdon, Oxon, OX14 4RN

Routledge is an imprint of the Taylor & Francis Group, an informa business

© 2024 D. Quentin Miller

The right of D. Quentin Miller to be identified as author of this work has been asserted in accordance with sections 77 and 78 of the Copyright, Designs and Patents Act 1988.

All rights reserved. No part of this book may be reprinted or reproduced or utilised in any form or by any electronic, mechanical, or other means, now known or hereafter invented, including photocopying and recording, or in any information storage or retrieval system, without permission in writing from the publishers.

Trademark notice: Product or corporate names may be trademarks or registered trademarks, and are used only for identification and explanation without intent to infringe.

ISBN: 978-1-032-18103-5 (hbk)
ISBN: 978-1-032-18102-8 (pbk)
ISBN: 978-1-003-25286-3 (ebk)

DOI: 10.4324/9781003252863

Typeset in Sabon
by MPS Limited, Dehradun

Contents

	Acknowledgments	vii
	Introduction	1
1	The Long, Annoying Shadow of Europe and the Search for Greatness	14
2	The American Dream: A Myth of Upward Mobility and Middle-Class Happiness	35
3	Domestic Discontentment: The Marriage Plot Anti-Dream	62
4	"Not a Story to Pass On": Slavery and the American Novel	86
5	Class, Race, and the Anti-Dream Narrative	113
6	Multiethnic America	137
7	Old (and New) Weird America: Experimentation and Voices from the Margins	161

8 Our Fragile Earth: Eco-Consciousness and the
   American Novel   185

   Works Cited   212
   Index   215

Acknowledgments

I imagined and developed this book during the COVID-19 pandemic and the cultural turbulence of the Trump presidency. Reflecting on its composition, I'm understandably disoriented, and my jumbled memory suggests that I was entirely cloistered as I read and wrote about the scores of novels discussed in these pages, but that's of course untrue. No academic book is a solo effort, and I'm grateful to everyone who gave me suggestions and listened to my rambling. Initial thanks go to Michelle Salyga, Bryony Reece, and the rest of the Routledge crew for their patience and encouragement.

This list will be woefully incomplete, but I've had some great conversations about American literature with the following colleagues at conferences or over coffee (and stronger beverages) over the past few years, all of which have fired and rewired my synapses to produce this book. In alphabetical order, I'd like to acknowledge: Peter Bailey (St. Lawrence University, emeritus), Marshall Boswell (Rhodes College), Jackson Bryer (University of Maryland, emeritus), Soyica Diggs Colbert (Georgetown University), Kirk Curnutt (Troy University), John Drabinski (University of Maryland), Marc Dudley (North Carolina State University), Michele Elam (Stanford University), Ernest Gibson (Auburn University), Tracie Church Guzzio (SUNY Plattsburgh), Gary Holcomb (Ohio University), Hannah Hudson (Suffolk University), Justin Joyce (Washington University), David Leeming (University of Connecticut, emeritus), Bridget Marshall (University of Massachusetts Lowell), Sylvie Mathé (Université Aix-Marseille, emerita), Dwight McBride (Washington University), Michael Meyer (University of Connecticut, emeritus), Ed Pavlic (University of Georgia), Leslie Petty (Rhodes College), Jim Plath (Illinois Wesleyan University), Jim Schiff (University of Cincinnati), Matthew Shipe (Washington University), Tony Szczesiul (University of Massachusetts Lowell), Bryan Trabold (Suffolk University), Peggy Wright-Cleveland (Florida State University), and Magdalena Zaborowska (University of Michigan).

My rambling rantings have fallen disproportionately on my immediate family: thanks to Julie Nash, Brennan Miller, and Owen Miller for putting up with me.

I dedicate this study to my mother Sylvia and to the memory of my father Robert who encouraged my obsessive novel reading from a young age. Thanks, dear parents, for recognizing that nothing meant more to me than a good book!

Introduction

Literary histories, like all histories, reflect as much about the present as about the past they are analyzing. They are inevitably marked by the individual perspective of the literary historian, a critic who might be an excellent reader, but who cannot claim to be objective because there is no such thing as an objective critic. Literary critics are the products of a lifetime of accumulated habits of mind, the training we receive, the biases we carry, and the reactions to life and art that we can't always predict or control. When Harold Bloom published his lengthy list of great books in *The Western Canon* (1994), arranged by country and time period, he claimed, "I have neither excluded nor included on the basis of cultural politics of any kind" (548). An authoritative statement like this one suggests objectivity, and Bloom didn't seem aware of or bothered by the irony that the very creation of a list such as his was the ultimate expression of cultural politics. By contrast, when Jane Smiley in *Thirteen Ways of Looking at the Novel* (2005) selects one hundred novels to read as representatives of the novel tradition, she is aware of the arbitrariness of any such list; she writes, "My list is not and was never intended to be a 'Hundred Greatest,' only a list of individual novels that would illuminate the whole concept of the novel – and almost any list of a hundred serious novels would illuminate that concept" (270). Her list was not necessarily comprised of the "greatest," but the novels had to be "serious," and also "important," and the list had to be somewhat organized: "not only did I have to start somewhere (with *The Tale of Genji*) and go somewhere (to lots of different countries), I also had to stop somewhere" (270) – hence one hundred novels. She acknowledges that her round number is arbitrary, or merely convenient. Bloom speaks as an oracle who presents his list as fact; Smiley reveals anxiety about her project but also manages to produce a list while apologizing for what didn't make it, and perhaps why. Both Bloom's and Smiley's lists are organized chronologically.

Literary histories are more than chronologically organized lists, but that methodology tends to provide the skeletal structure that supports them.

DOI: 10.4324/9781003252863-1

They are written to mark a moment of assessment – an attempt to understand and define a tradition – but they are also arguments with and affirmations of the way a tradition has been understood and defined in the past. Contained in the pages of this book is a new literary history of the American novel, written a quarter way into the twenty-first century. It is a crossroads moment in the history of the American novel and American narrative culture more generally. The twentieth century saw the flowering of the American novel tradition as a curious and literary-minded public embraced works by daring authors who built upon the sporadic advances of the nineteenth century. In the twentieth century, the core topic of American identity as a unique and fluid concept was addressed with unprecedented sophistication and innovation by authors whose works became required reading for all Americans: Wharton, Fitzgerald, Hemingway, Hurston, Steinbeck, Ellison, Baldwin, Pynchon, DeLillo, and Morrison, to name a few. The American novel tradition flourished despite the formidable force of America's most prominent medium of cultural production: the movies. Television was never regarded with the same cultural seriousness as film in the twentieth century. The small screen was intent on entertainment much more than art, and its relatively brief and tame products, frequently interrupted by advertisements, did not provide the same immersive experience as a novel or a movie. In the twenty-first century, though, so-called peak television – which happened to peak around the same moment a global pandemic kept Americans in their homes – has threatened the hegemony of cinema in visual culture. The novel tradition has survived, though it certainly cannot be considered to have the cultural impact it enjoyed in the mid- to late-twentieth century. Narrative is being explored in a variety of new forms, from podcasts to video games, that make lengthy fictional books seem quaint.

And yet, novels are a crucial part of our cultural history. On June 17, 2023, *The New York Times* asked seventeen of its veteran columnists to choose one American book, song, movie, or television show that collectively "capture so much of a country's essence that they can practically be read as foundational texts" (Editorial Board). Four out of seventeen chose novels, including classic ones by authors who are considered at length in this study (Horatio Alger, William Dean Howells, and F. Scott Fitzgerald). As the *Times* piece strove to be topical and hip by including visual and musical works like *Pulp Fiction*, *South Park*, and Sugar Hill Gang's "Rapper's Delight," roughly a quarter of the columnists turned to nineteenth- and twentieth-century novels. There is an enduring sense that whatever it means to be an American has been thoroughly explored – if never fully grasped – in our novel tradition. There is also an enduring sense that we haven't yet reached our novelistic peak, that the "Great American Novel" is yet to be written, and we eagerly wait for it to arrive even as we know we'll never agree on it. Any understanding of the American novel tradition has to come to terms with this mythical great one and with the concept of the American Dream. These are the persistent myths that guide this inquiry, and both are related to the unwavering notion that ours is a land of opportunity that rewards hard work and ambition. This study will consider both concepts which act as weights – either as anchors that hold the tradition in place, or sandbags that prevent it from soaring free.

Past Approaches to American Literary History

Some of the earliest literary histories in the United States attempted to establish American themes, concerns, and tropes, usually as they related to evolving notions of nationhood in the nineteenth century. It stands to reason that the main figures from the American Renaissance – also labeled the Transcendentalists – were chosen as the Olympian figures of our literary history, for (1) they were indisputably a concentrated group of superb writers, (2) they were writing to advance similar ideas, (3) they were mutually influential, (4) each had a unique style, and (5) they collectively advanced a new vision that endures to this day. The American fiction writers who preceded the Renaissance and/or who didn't fit into this category – Rowson, Brockden Brown, Irving, Cooper, Sedgwick, Poe, Fern, and Alcott – were certainly influential and are worth reading for many reasons. They aren't, however, identified as the true origin point of our novelistic tradition for various reasons (including the fact that Irving and Poe were committed to the short story form). For all their merits, their works individually or collectively do not carry the weight of the American Renaissance authors including Hawthorne and Melville as well as those known primarily as poets (Dickinson and Whitman) or nonfiction prose writers (Emerson, Fuller, and Thoreau).

Fuller was one of the first critics to write substantially about the American literary tradition even as she identifies it as something "which has as yet no existence … . Books which imitate or represent the thoughts and life of Europe do not constitute an American literature" (37). Her project in this 1846 essay entitled "American Literature: Its Position in the Present Time and Prospects for the Future" is to hold up the American authors who have been praised and widely read, to point out their shortcomings, and finally to show how the glimmerings of an original American genius can be discerned in her time and can offer great promise for the future. (Not surprisingly, the two authors she particularly admires are associated with her own movement, Emerson and Hawthorne). She is eager for a national literature reflective of our diversity rather than just the parent/child relationship of England and America. She states, "an original idea must animate this nation and fresh currents of life must call into life fresh thoughts upon its shores" (37–8). Though vague, the words "original" and "fresh" are important markers of something distinctly American; she adds, in contrast to England, that our culture must "develop a genius wide and full as our rivers, flowery, luxuriant, and impassioned as our vast prairies, rooted in strength as the rocks on which the Puritan fathers landed" (38). Although she is speaking figuratively, the American landscape is clearly an important feature in limning the American literary imagination.

It would seem Fuller was peering into a crystal ball in this formative essay, but she was actually attempting a definition and a set of criteria with which to establish and identify a national literature. True works of American literature, she argued, should "prize moral and intellectual no less highly than political freedom"; they should be "original" and not imitative; they should reflect a "purity of spirit" as Emerson's work does; they should not be "artificial" (a word she applies to Longfellow); they should be deep, and soaring, and complex (40–6). By calling for a "fusion of the races" (42) she also implies that American literature should reflect our diversity as well as our commitment to democracy, which are impossible goals in the glaringly unequal pre-Civil War period in which she penned the essay.

Since Fuller's time, many critics have built on some of her premises, and they had the advantage of surveying a substantial body of published literature rather than speculating about what was yet to develop. Idealism certainly informed Fuller's thinking, and the challenge for later critics was to sort out the differences between what American literature actually *is* and what one *wants it to be*. No one in the twenty-first century, or even at the end of the nineteenth, would ever claim, as Fuller did, that American literature does not yet exist, yet it is possible to look back on the tradition and perceive qualities in it that are not as soaring and praiseworthy as what Fuller imagined a "glorious" future in which authors, "seeking the sun, challenge its eagles to an earthward flight" (48). It may well be that American literature is not glorious after all, that it demonstrates the ugliness and contradictions and injustices that are as much a part of American life as our landscape that reflects our wide genius, passion, and strength. Put differently, American literature can uphold our mythology, or it can reflect our reality. Rare are the works that do both, although Ellison's *Invisible Man* (1952), especially in its prologue and epilogue, seeks to expose that contradictory tension.

More recent literary histories have tended to subdivide the tradition, either concentrating on a certain time period or on authors of a single race or ethnicity or regional writers. Frederick Karl, in his comprehensive study *American Fictions 1940–1980*, attempts to generalize the movement of

American fiction beginning roughly with World War II and lasting through the rise of postmodernism; he writes, "In all its diversity, the postwar novel has striven ... to defamiliarize the familiar, to make the reader reinvent the world, and while moving human experience to the margins, to move the margins toward the center" (xi). The same could not be said of novels from other periods of literary history, so it behooves the reader to put together ideas like this one about a certain narrow but fruitful period of literary history with ideas about earlier and later periods. Karl's study and others like it do not attempt to assemble the jigsaw puzzle of literary history, but rather to provide a key piece for others who may be attempting to do so.

Since the so-called "canon wars" of the late twentieth century in which defenders of the hallowed list of required American reading written almost exclusively by heterosexual white men of English descent squared off against critics who realized that that list did not reflect American diversity, literary historians have become especially sensitive to the politics of exclusion. Founding father Thomas Jefferson denigrated the work of Phillis Wheatley, an enslaved poet who caused a sensation with her first published book in 1773, arguing that her race prevented her from producing real poetry. In the nineteenth century, Hawthorne infamously railed about the "damned mob of scribbling women" who were competing for his readers. His comment may seem like ancient history, but American literary histories published relatively recently barely considered women writers. For example, in Marcus Klein's 1969 collection *The American Novel Since World War II*, all twenty of the critics (many of them novelists) whose essays appear in the volume are men. Christof Wegelin's 1972 study *The American Novel: Background Readings and Criticism* contains two initial chapters in which all twelve of the critics are men, then focuses on fourteen representative American novels, only one of which (Edith Wharton's *The House of Mirth* [1905]) was written by a woman. By the 1980s, the imbalance of such studies would have been glaring, and critics like Paul Lauter were busy shining a spotlight on the important works that had been in the shadows; he writes, "standards of literary merit are not absolute but contingent ... in seeking to teach 'the best' – as we should – of the various literatures that constitute our national culture, we need constantly to reexamine our cultural yardstick" (107).

My study, covering a lengthy literary history in a compressed space, cannot claim equal representation by authors whose perspectives were not considered in early literary histories, and yet I am conscious of the importance of reexamining our cultural yardstick, in Lauter's terms. Following his understanding that our literary tradition is comprised of "various literatures," I have attempted to include as wide a variety of perspectives as possible, not merely to check off identity boxes, but rather to illustrate that diversity is an extremely important hallmark of American literary history without ignoring the fact that it was not always considered so. Some works that were once prominent in the eyes of American readers and critics have a place here alongside works that would have been left out of studies written before the 1980s when the canon wars changed irrevocably the way we understand the American novelistic tradition. My hope is to achieve some level of balance between historical and contemporary critical perspectives as a way of assessing the entire tradition.

Approach and Methodology

The Routledge Introduction to the American Novel represents a somewhat unorthodox approach to literary history, one that does not plot its points along a boring old timeline, though the argument of each chapter is sometimes arranged chronologically to demonstrate call-and-response, theme-and-variation, tradition-and-innovation, or other ways of describing thematic and stylistic influence. Part of my aim is to depart from a conventional understanding of American literary history predicated on the notion of a single renaissance, i.e. a period in which the best works were produced, creating a kind of bell curve representing the supposedly lesser works produced before and after. My resistance to the timeline structure that teeters on the fulcrum of a renaissance is related to my impulse to move the study away from the search to define a single American novel as the "great" one and to place all others in its shadow, which is the subject of the first chapter. Like Jane Smiley, I want to avoid the notion that the novels I discuss in this study are meant to be a list of the "greatest" and that the many, many, many novels I did not have room to discuss are in any way less important. At the same time, I depart from her premise that *any* set of novels could work to illustrate the tradition I'm trying to outline. The adjective "American" when placed before the noun "novel" must mean something, even though both terms are slippery and expansive, and my approach to the subject is topical and thematic. I want to underscore that literary histories are subjective and incomplete by nature. What I hope to communicate is some insight into the long, rich, varied tradition that might not have been evident in earlier literary histories about the American novel while acknowledging that my literary history won't be definitive a half-century from now.

I also want to emphasize that these pages constitute an *introduction* to the American novel. To use a jigsaw puzzle metaphor, I have done what many people do when they sit down to that task: sorted out the edge pieces and put them together so that the reader has an outline that can then be filled in. I don't provide a bullet point list of what constitutes a significant

American novel, for such a list would diminish the expansive tendencies of the American novel tradition, and often of American novels themselves. There's no consistent formula. We tend to pay special attention to the enormous, grandly ambitious ones that swell and reach out to our shores and beyond, like Melville's *Moby-Dick* (1851), Dreiser's *An American Tragedy* (1925), Stein's *The Making of Americans* (1925), Ellison's *Invisible Man*, Pynchon's *Gravity's Rainbow* (1973), or Wallace's *Infinite Jest* (1996). The assumption behind this impulse is that the vastness of America calls for a tome, and yet some of our most cherished novels – Fitzgerald's *The Great Gatsby* (1925), Larsen's *Passing* (1929), and Salinger's *The Catcher in the Rye* (1951) – are notably brief. We admire ambition, but we aren't averse to restraint.

One characteristic these novels and the majority of others discussed in this study have in common is the basic conflict of the individual at odds with society. Although the same could be said of almost any novel tradition, in the American version that tension is approached with a special intensity. The reason is twofold: (1) American culture privileges the concept of the individual above virtually all else. Our great philosophers Emerson and Thoreau found countless ways to define and elevate the concept of selfhood, the individual as a nearly sacred concept that earned its merit through a constant reckoning with society. And yet, (2) American society is a frequently unacknowledged force. Our national mythology works hard to persuade its citizens that society is hardly worth mentioning and that our individual freedom is limitless. Look at our slogans: from many individuals come one nation, rendered in Latin as *e pluribus unum*. We were all "created equal." We were founded as an anti-monarchy that rejected the notion of class hierarchy. Nothing can stop our "pursuit of happiness." All these tenets and many more suggest that American society should barely register in the individual's consciousness. Our legends – John Henry, Paul Bunyan, Johnny Appleseed – are men (notably) who strive and work hard in accordance with their talents. The reality, of course, is that American society is and always has been strongly hierarchical and strident when it comes to articulating and enforcing norms. The difference between American culture and many others is that we deny the truth of these facts.

The chapters in this study are thematic rather than chronological. In the name of coherence, and after much scowling, cutting-and-pasting, and staring into the middle distance, I ultimately came upon a core theme that the other themes orbit around. That theme is the well-worn but often misunderstood American Dream. It is our culture's monomyth, the structure that has informed the way we regard the triumphs and failures of individual Americans throughout history. Year after year I ask students to define it, and inevitably they begin with illustrations that come from the rise of the suburbs in the mid-twentieth century, clichés such as a picket fence and a garage containing two cars that are rooted in homeownership and white, heteronormative fantasies of domestic stability. The Dream might have spiritual dimensions for some, but for most, it is thoroughly materialistic. It is also a dream at odds with the most fundamental idea of the Transcendentalists who believed, as Emerson put it in "Self Reliance," "Whoso would be a man, must be a nonconformist" (87). The American Dream, at least as it became cemented in the post-World War II era, is a dream of conformity as well as prosperity. Its roots may be traced to Benjamin Franklin's *Autobiography* (1791) or Thoreau's *Walden* (1854) – nonfiction works in which the authors demonstrate how self-reliance and individual genius lead to a richer life, in divergent ways – but its trunk, branches, and leaves are by now firmly in the world of social respectability, capitalistic competition, and hierarchy (sometimes taking insidious forms like sexism, racism, xenophobia, and class prejudice).

The themes that organize this study, then, generally respond to the recurrent Dream theme in American novels. Chapter 1, The Long, Annoying Shadow of Europe and the Search for Greatness, considers the pursuit of the Great American Novel as a warm-up to the main theme. The belief in and search for greatness is, after all, the energy that powers the Dream. The mythical Great American Novel indicates our cultural preference for winners and also our yearning for some spectacular future, which is a goal at odds with the conservative strain of our culture that locates our best era deep in the past, when the "Founding Fathers" created a series of sacred texts in the form of the Constitution, the Declaration of Independence, and other utopian documents at odds with the realities of American existence. The Great American Novel idea ensures that we will keep arguing, and it puts us back into the so-called canon wars beginning in the 1970s and 1980s when the standards of greatness in the assessment of our literary heritage were called out for their inherent biases. Like the American Dream, though, the Great American Novel remains a cultural myth we cannot shake. Chapter 1 considers its critical history and irreverently considers a novel that no one has ever before named as the candidate: James Baldwin's *Another Country* (1962). Recasting this unlikely choice as the Great American Novel is a way of opening up the rest of the study to expansive thinking, and also of undermining the debate as a trite, arbitrary distraction from a true understanding of the tradition.

Chapter 2, The American Dream: A Myth of Upward Mobility and Middle-Class Happiness, is the foundational American Dream chapter in which the Dream is both defined and dismantled beginning with a novel that does both: John Updike's *Rabbit, Run* (1960). This chapter returns to the naïve novelistic origins of the Dream, Horatio Alger's *Ragged Dick* (1868). Updike's novel showcases an antihero Harry "Rabbit" Angstrom who unconsciously believes in the Dream but can't figure out how to achieve it. Alger's novel – unique in this study for its lack of critical thinking or aesthetic merit – illustrates without irony how the Dream can easily be achieved through pluck and a little luck. The remaining novels considered at length in this chapter by William Dean Howells, F. Scott Fitzgerald, James Weldon Johnson, Nella Larsen, and Philip Roth demonstrate characters who, at least for a time and in the view of the public eye, succeed in "making it" – that is, advancing financially and socially, often with an emphasis on homeownership. The protagonists, unlike Updike's Rabbit, are willing to work for and sacrifice for the Dream, but the achievement of it proves unfulfilling or hollow and is frequently accompanied by tragedy or at least a material or moral downfall.

Chapter 3, Domestic Discontentment: The Marriage Plot Anti-Dream, probes further at a dimension of the American Dream that should be apparent, namely that it is largely a male-centered fantasy and that its achievement depends upon the willingness of women to assume the stereotypical female supporting roles of wife, mother, and homemaker. This chapter considers how the pressures of marriage have controlled and limited the freedom of women throughout American literary history. The primary authors considered in this chapter – Susanna Rowson, Kate Chopin, Edith Wharton, Mary McCarthy, Zora Neale Hurston, Alice Walker, and Elizabeth Strout – illustrate how female protagonists throughout the tradition have responded to the pressure to become the invisible support system of the American Dream. The struggle for women's rights throughout American history becomes an important context for considering viable alternatives as characters respond variously to this pressure.

Chapter 4, "Not a Story to Pass On": Slavery and the American Novel, considers the premise that novels about slavery might be considered in stark contrast to the Dream narrative. The long, ugly history of slavery in the United States denied basic rights to its victims, and the materialistic dimensions of the Dream would appear far removed from the much more basic goals of freedom and equality. Though this is true on one level, it can also be argued that, just as the Dream conceals the fact that it depends on the invisible labor of women as considered in Chapter 3, it also has historically depended on the white acquisition of wealth acquired through the invisible labor of the enslaved. Though the Dream is deferred for African Americans, as Langston Hughes memorably argued in the poem "Harlem" (1951), we can consider how the idealistic Dream is in conversation with the system that created its deferral. This chapter begins with a consideration of the foundational importance of slave narratives and their influence on two popular and enduring novels by white authors from the nineteenth century – Stowe's *Uncle Tom's Cabin* (1852) and Twain's *The Adventures of Huckleberry Finn* (1885) – before turning to some of the many great novels set in the era of slavery by Black authors from the twentieth and twenty-first centuries, namely Toni Morrison, Ishmael Reed, Octavia Butler, Sherley Anne Williams, and Colson Whitehead. These novels interrogate the way history requires and catalyzes new contexts for and imaginative approaches to this crucial topic.

Chapter 5, Class, Race, and the Anti-Dream Narrative, expands the assumptions of the chapter that precedes it. Two of slavery's lingering aftereffects that not only defer but deny the Dream to many Americans are poverty and class discrimination. In this chapter, the Dream is exposed as a fantasy only available to the white middle class. The novels considered here – by Stephen Crane, John Steinbeck, Richard Wright, Dorothy Allison, Ralph Ellison, Paule Marshall, and Imbolo Mbue – showcase characters who are denied the Dream not because they are not hard-working or fortunate in the mode of an Alger hero, but because they are victims of race and class discrimination, sometimes compounded by gender bias. These characters want to believe in the Dream, and their struggle invariably ends in disillusionment or worse.

The last two novels studied in Chapter 5 by Marshall and Mbue are about immigrants from Barbados and Cameroon who are discriminated against based on the color of their skin. Chapter 6, Multiethnic America, examines additional forms of discrimination in ethnic communities whose ancestry is not necessarily traced to Africa. Many of the novels considered in this chapter – by Henry Roth, Julia Alvarez, Jhumpa Lahiri, and Joseph O'Neill – examine the lives of immigrants and the experience of immigration. Frequently (though not always), American immigration stories map directly onto the American Dream narrative, born of the notion that America is a land of economic opportunity where prosperity is readily available to those willing to work hard. This dimension of the Dream obscures the very real discrimination immigrants face based on their native language and customs. Novels of immigration starkly illustrate how the Dream demands conformity and the willingness to lose connections to one's heritage in the name of assimilation. The other novels discussed in this chapter by Maxine Hong Kingston and Rudolfo Anaya consider how these pressures remain for Americans who were born in this country yet are still caught in a tug-of-war between their ancestral ethnic heritage and the demands of mainstream American culture.

Most of the novels that define the backbone of the tradition discussed in the earlier chapters are realism, with a few variations. Perhaps the strong influence of the American Dream plot is related to a stylistic conservatism related to the inherent cultural conservatism of our monomyth. One way to break free from the hegemony of the American Dream plot is to experiment with literary style. The novels considered in Chapter 7, Old (and New) Weird America: Experimentation and Voices from the Margins, represent alternatives to the thematic through-line of the other chapters. They push the boundaries of the American novelistic tradition outward by unlocking fresh perspectives and ideas accessed through unique approaches to imaginative narrative. The nineteenth century saw some novelists willing to break free from straight realism; novels by William Wells Brown and Herman Melville are considered here as foundations in this tradition. The period of high modernism – reflected in novels by Gertrude Stein, Jean Toomer, and William Faulkner – saw a more concentrated commitment to artistic experimentation in the American novel. In the latter half of the twentieth century into the twenty-first, American novelists felt confident to move further away from realism, and their topics and themes were even less tied to standard notions of the American Dream. Novels by Jack Kerouac, Thomas Pynchon, and Jennifer Egan provide an outline of the possibilities afforded by postmodernism and other divergences from the main line of American novelistic inquiry.

The final chapter, Our Fragile Earth: Eco-Consciousness and the American Novel, puts the Dream narrative aside to consider the pressing issue of the fragility of our planet. The Dream is made possible only if we consider that the bounties of nature in the United States exist primarily to fuel a ravenous economy. The earth is finite, vulnerable, and exhausted. Though the novels analyzed in this chapter are primarily from our current century, we first consider precursors by Leslie Marmon Silko, James Fenimore Cooper, and Ernest Hemingway, all of whom warned about the costs of abusing nature for human gain. Twenty-first-century novelists speak with even more urgency as concerns over the earth's imminent destruction have reached a crisis. The novelists selected for deep analysis to conclude this study include Barbara Kingsolver, T. Coraghessan Boyle, Richard Powers, Cormac McCarthy, Don DeLillo, and Jesmyn Ward.

Selection and Omission

I want to reiterate that this study is defined in its title: *an introduction*. I have no doubt that, if I were reading this study rather than writing it, I would immediately scrutinize the novelists left out as well as those who are included. I will own any errors in judgment that lead to an imbalance that might indicate a poorly drawn road map to American novelistic history, and yet the decisions I have made are based on deep contemplation and broad reading. First, I will fully admit that the mission I accepted here is an impossible one. When friends and colleagues asked me what I've been working on lately, I tended to look away in embarrassment and mutter, "Not much, just an introduction to the American novel." It's too big a topic for any single book, much less one with a specific word limit. I've left out major writers. I've included not-so-major writers. I've chosen some writers that I think are worth reading who haven't entered the canon and others who have fallen out of it. I'm sure if I were reviewing someone else's introduction, I would have similar gripes. At the end of each chapter is a list of suggested additional works that could have been included. Even these are brief and incomplete, but taken together, the novels discussed in detail combined with the suggestions for further reading should yield a reading list that would keep any scholar seeking to understand this subject productively occupied for many years.

As our novel history is approaching its 250-year mark, think about the mind-boggling number of novels that could be part of this study. What I've attempted to do is not to "cover" the whole mess, but rather to gesture toward it in a meaningful way. Despite the considerable labor involved, this has been a tremendously pleasurable and stimulating project, and I hope the reader has a similar experience. I chose to discuss roughly eight books per chapter in some detail rather than to speak abstractly and vaguely about many more. My assumption is that the reader has heard of many of these works, read fewer, and is encountering some titles for the first time. Under that assumption, I discuss the novels in such a way as to give the reader something to absorb, which combines plot summary, character analysis, and indications of the author's style. These elements (as well as others such as setting and theme) are illustrated through quotations from the texts. I'm certain that the balance I've endeavored to strike is not uniformly successful: I may have relied too much on plot summary (including spoilers), for instance, in some cases and not enough in others. My hope, of course, is that the outline I have provided is inspiration for the reader to study the works under consideration here in more depth, as it could never be a substitute for a direct encounter.

Regarding what other critics have said about these works, I have kept it to a minimum. The primary reason is, of course, space. Roughly eighty novels are surveyed in these pages, and there are countless critics who have interpreted many of them brilliantly over the years. My readings of and connections between these novels are original, though I have certainly been guided by other critics over time. I have occasionally included a word or two by some of them, but critical voices other than mine are largely absent from this volume, except in one case where criticism is the primary topic (Chapter 1). In other cases, my primary goal was to make sense of a novel's inclusion within the thematic framework of the chapter, but along the way, I hope I have managed to advance some insight that might be valuable to other scholars and teachers. That said, there is much more to say about every novel considered here, and I urge readers to seek out as many insights as they can find. This introduction, in other words, is not intended as a substitute for deep reading or research, but rather a catalyst for them.

1 The Long, Annoying Shadow of Europe and the Search for Greatness

Ernest Hemingway's gruff comment on American literary history echoes down the corridors of history: "All modern American literature comes from one book by Mark Twain called *Huckleberry Finn* ... it's the best book we've had" (*Green Hills* 22). Like many of Hemingway's pronouncements, it's spare, pithy, and has the weighty confidence of a fact even though it's clearly an opinion. Yet it is the opinion of an author who, when he uttered it, was considered to have changed the trajectory, the style, and the reputation of American fiction more than any writer alive. Hemingway was not effusive in his praise of other writers, to put it mildly. When he said something this gushing, it was regarded as factual wisdom. It sounds like a one-off comment, but he was participating in an ongoing debate. For over 150 years readers and critics have been arguing about what should be regarded as the Great American Novel. That debate – that search for something that is mythical, something that is elevated to the status of superiority and even sacredness, something that can be assumed to set a standard that all other works must try (and fail) to replicate – is a telling inroad into the study of the American novel. What is fascinating is not that Americans have failed to agree on the greatest, but that we continue to try. As the novelist Frank Norris observed, "the Great American Novel is not extinct like the Dodo, but mythical like the Hippogriff" (89). It is American nature to reach for what we wish we could have and to mythologize it. That very quality infuses our novelistic tradition, regardless of whether it produces novels that would be considered "great" in any other nation's tradition.

Let me put it another way. The fact that no one will ever agree upon "the Great American Novel" (GAN hereafter) coupled with the romantic notion that one exists or will someday exist is related to the thesis of this book, which is that the American novel tradition consistently depicts individuals in pursuit of a societally defined Dream yet who are paradoxically at odds with their society. A state of unresolved tension

DOI: 10.4324/9781003252863-2

The Long, Annoying Shadow of Europe and the Search for Greatness

fuels the plots of many American novels as well as critical conversations about the best of them. The protagonists of American novels, taking their cue from the common wisdom that the United States is a land of opportunity in which individuals are more important than crowds, consistently follow their subjective visions only to find themselves limited or even steamrolled by larger, often abstract forces. The myth of the Great American Novel is one such force, and it allows the pageant between individual choice and societal status quo to play out.

Even if a survey of one hundred literary critics somehow revealed a near-unanimous decision – if ninety-nine picked *Beloved* (1987) – the real American story would be about the one who did not, the one who argued vociferously for *The Great Gatsby* (1925) while the other ninety-nine waited out the argument with smug patience. This is not necessarily to say that the American novel tradition champions nonconformists, contrarians, or individualists, but rather to acknowledge the thematic importance in our culture of the individual at odds with society – not necessarily above, below, or even outside of society, but at odds with it even while they buy into a shared definition of the American Dream. The American novelistic tradition grows out of this very basic idea. Note the phrase "grows out of," for it would be limiting to suggest that all American novels worthy of consideration followed the same pattern. Consider the Dream script as the seed that grows and branches out into the full tradition.

A Slow Start: The Early American Novel Through the American Renaissance

Before digging into the knotty issue of the Great American Novel, it's worth considering how critics over time have defined what makes a novel American. What are its unique characteristics, and how do they relate to other novelistic traditions? The connection between nationhood and our break from England is important as we consider the origins of the American novel tradition, which are, for better or worse, contiguous with the English novel tradition. It's worth noting that the novel was slow to develop in the so-called New World. Early residents of the English colonies produced sermons and conversion narratives as well as some poetry and travel writing, but novels were considered immoral by the dominant Puritan culture. England had been producing novels since the early eighteenth century, and yet the novel considered America's first, *The Power of Sympathy* by William Hill Brown, did not appear until 1789, and it generally isn't read, studied, respected, or appreciated today. Susanna Rowson's *Charlotte Temple* (see Chapter 3), published in 1793, was the first enduring novel written in America, and yet its structure, its thematic concerns, and even much of its setting are British. Charles Brockden Brown's *Wieland* (1798) established itself as an origin point of the national tradition, including the phrase "An American Tale" in its subtitle. The early nineteenth century saw tentative additions to this foundation, but the most celebrated American fiction writer to emerge in the first two decades of that century was Washington Irving who wrote short stories rather than novels. The 1820s are recognized as a decade when the American novel started to come into its own with continued contributions from Rowson and Brown as well as the rise of Catharine Maria Sedgwick and James Fenimore Cooper. Hawthorne's first novel, *Fanshawe*, was published in 1828, anonymously, and although it is not one he is remembered for, it's clear that major American novelists were establishing the tradition in the 1820s that would flourish in the mid-nineteenth century.

It is significant, though, that the 1820s was a full century after the origins of the novel in England (Defoe's *Moll Flanders* in 1722) and a half-century after the revolution that established American nationhood. As they were defining their country, Americans did not embrace the novel as a primary means to illustrate that definition in literature. Indeed, some of the most essential works of early American prose were nonfiction: *The Federalist Papers* (1788), Franklin's *Autobiography* (1791), Douglass's *Narrative of the Life* (1845), Thoreau's *Walden* (1854), and Jacobs's *Incidents in the Life of a Slave Girl* (1861) are works that students of early American literature are likely to encounter before any early novel, save perhaps Sedgwick's *Hope Leslie* (1827) or Cooper's *The Last of the Mohicans* (1826) or *The Deerslayer* (1841). When two prime candidates for the GAN award arrived in the early 1850s – Hawthorne's *The Scarlet Letter* (1850) and Melville's *Moby-Dick* (1851) – a discernible novel tradition began to take shape. Finally.

We can only speculate why American writers took so long to warm up to the novel as a form. It was undoubtedly the most popular literary form in England in the mid-nineteenth century: Dickens was churning out a lengthy novel annually by the time Hawthorne and Melville announced their presence. Could there have been some anxiety over the applicability or adaptability of this form to the New World? Were American writers tentative about merely imitating the most popular cultural product from the country they had violently rejected? Even Cooper, the first superstar American novelist, is widely considered to have followed closely the fictional formula of Sir Walter Scott, even while setting his Leatherstocking Tales firmly in the fledgling United States. The invisible pressure to produce the GAN might have been in place long before the phrase was first used in the late nineteenth century. *Moby-Dick*, panned upon publication, represented an urge to create something enormous, mysterious, profound, and unique that would merit attention, that wouldn't be confused with or overshadowed by anything produced in England. Whether or not Melville intended to, it set a benchmark and a lofty list of expectations. "Top that," he might have said, even as he was reading the savage reviews.

A highly literate American middle class was evolving in the mid-nineteenth century as Hawthorne and Melville published astonishing novels of literary merit during the period that would be come to known as the American Renaissance. Their enduring colleagues who specialized in other genres – Fuller, Thoreau, Whitman, Emerson, Dickinson – were also writing complex works with philosophical and/or artistic merit that were recognizably different from writers who were satisfying other readerly desires, including the desire to be entertained, or perhaps the desire to escape. The American Renaissance remains an impressive, compressed outpouring of literary genius that cannot be sidestepped by students seeking to understand the American tradition, and yet its status as the pinnacle of our literary history is fraught. Many of the troubles and contradictions of canon formation can be traced to this moment. For instance, Hawthorne's enduring quip in a letter to a friend about the "damned mob of scribbling women" suggests a troubling gender divide between "popular" fiction written by and for women and "literary" fiction written by and possibly also for men. The Renaissance occurred before slavery was outlawed and before waves of global immigration further diversified our population. Additionally, in the terms I use above (*enduring, literary, philosophical, artistic, genius*), there are biases that favor a certain style of writing that is layered, complex, difficult, and weighty over a style that many critics have historically considered inferior because it is – to paraphrase – *entertaining, formulaic, derivative, sentimental, imitative,* or *simple*. These aren't terms I've invented or consciously adopted in my own critical approach to literature, but they should be acknowledged as we consider the difference between the works critics regard as great and the "lesser" ones in their shadow. It's simplistic – if not fully inaccurate – to dismiss the whole history of literary criticism as intellectual snobbery, and yet terms like *pulp fiction, chick lit, genre fiction,* or even simply *pop culture* are at least slightly pejorative.

Another noteworthy point as we consider the American Renaissance's centrality or foundation of a long tradition is its timing. There are a host of highly significant ruptures in American cultural history that occurred after Hawthorne located his GAN candidate in a Puritan past obsessed with sinfulness and Melville located his on a whaling ship populated exclusively by men. After the 1850s the American novel had to contend with enormous changes that reflect monumental shifts in our actual and cultural history, changes that hadn't yet arrived in the early 1850s. Here's a short, incomplete list:

- The Civil War and the end of slavery
- Massive waves of immigration from countries other than England
- Westward expansion and neo-colonization (from the South Pacific to the moon)
- The establishment of the world's biggest economy
- The development of extreme differences in social class
- The struggle for gender equality
- The rise of new technologies (from the cotton gin to electricity, to automobiles, to television and the movies, to smartphones and everything in between)
- The Great Migration, urbanization, the development of the modern suburb, and other demographic shifts
- The Great Depression
- The Civil Rights Movement
- Two world wars, a Cold War, and a host of other global skirmishes in which the U.S. participated
- Gun violence and terrorism
- Ecological destruction and climate change
- The development of nuclear weaponry and space exploration
- The rise of the middle class and the construction of the American Dream myth.

There could be a hundred more bullets here representing significant, even monumental shifts in the trajectory of American culture that did not exist in the early 1850s and that were thus not available to the impressive novelistic imaginations of Hawthorne and Melville. The full American story, in short, had not even begun to be told in their time, which is not to say that they weren't capable of penning what might be called the Great American Novel, but which is to say that context is as important as text, and the context for this particular debate expands over time. If one were to insist that a GAN exists, one would do well to consider American novels that account for at least some of the developments contained in the above list before going back to Hawthorne and Melville and claiming, after all, that one of their masterpieces deserves the title.

Yet the point of debating the GAN – or at least my point – is not to crown an American novel as number one, but rather to demonstrate the Americanness of perpetually trying to do so, and to indicate how that attempt affects how we read American novels. Americans are especially fond of "top ten" and "best of" lists, which reflects a competitive spirit that is baked into our culture. What is gained by such lists is a sense of order and priority. What is lost is a sense of nuance, deep understanding, nimble thinking, and, ultimately, true appreciation of a tradition. To be more provocative, what is lost is democracy, which may be an American ideal no less naïve than the notion of the Great American Novel. (Consider that the term "Great American Novel" was first coined in 1868 when the United States crowed about democracy long before women and African Americans were given the right to vote, and just a few years after the end of slavery). This is not to say that some novels aren't more worthy of our attention than others. If I believed that all novels were more or less the same and that each contributes equally to an understanding of the tradition, I wouldn't have the self-confidence to write a book like this one, nor the desire to read one. This is to say, however, that definitions of greatness should be understood as expressions of ideology, subjectivity, taste, individual experience, and implicit bias as much as declarations of enduring merit. To that end, I turn now to the evolution of the understanding of the GAN and its primary candidates before arguing, provocatively, for a novel that I know will certainly never be widely considered the GAN, James Baldwin's *Another Country* (1962).

"The Great American Novel": Origins and Arguments

The "Great American Novel" label is attributed to William De Forest, a Civil War Union soldier turned writer whose novelistic efforts over the course of the last half-century of his life have not withstood the test of time, to be blunt. He is remembered more for inventing this term, advanced in an 1868 essay of the same name, than for any of his twenty books, many of them novels. De Forest argues that the GAN had not been written at the time he wrote the essay and that it *might* be written someday, but he was "very doubtful" that his generation would produce it. He runs through a list of possible candidates and dismisses them. Washington Irving "was too cautious." James Fenimore Cooper, with "the same consciousness of incapacity," failed to produce "a tableau of American society" (156). He briefly considers W. Gilmore Simms, a politician, apologist for slavery, and sometime novelist whose name is probably completely unfamiliar to readers of this volume. He considers Hawthorne in more depth, praising him as "the greatest of American imaginations," but arguing that he "staggered under the load of the American novel" (156). He brushes over a now-forgotten author named Robert Trail Spence Lowell (great-grandfather of the renowned poet) as well as Oliver Wendell Holmes, Sr. (father of the renowned Supreme Court justice) but faults them for one of the same reasons he dismisses Hawthorne, arguing that their tales "are not

American novels; they are only New England novels; they are localisms" (158). Melville isn't mentioned. The novel that comes closest to GAN status in De Forest's estimation is Stowe's *Uncle Tom's Cabin* (1852). As discussed at length in Chapter 4 of this study, Stowe's novel is not a likely candidate for this title in the twenty-first century. It would not even likely top many current lists of "most important American novels about slavery."

But why did De Forest claim that *Uncle Tom's Cabin* came closest in his time? He argues, "there was a national breadth to the picture, truthful outlining of character, natural speaking, and plenty of strong feeling" (157). Contemporary readers might easily disagree with all these assessments of *Uncle Tom's Cabin* except the last (which is often a trait that is faulted in novels rather than praised), but my point is not to argue with De Forest's evaluation of individual novelists so much as to get at the heart of his compound adjective Great American. National breadth has much to do with his implied definition as he dismisses works that are bounded by their regions (especially New England, his home). He also values realism, as indicated by the words "picture," "truthful," and "outlining" in his praise of Stowe. Painting metaphors abound throughout the essay. He defines the task of the would-be Great American Novelist as "painting the American soul within the framework of a novel" (156) and admires in Lowell's novel "portraits of rustic souls" and "landscape pictures" alike (157). By contrast, he says Hawthorne's novels "have no sympathy with this eager and laborious people, which takes so many newspapers, builds so many railroads, does the most business on a given capital, wages the biggest war in proportion to its population, believes in the physically impossible and does some of it" (156). The GAN, according to De Forest, should be down to earth and should present "a single tale which paints American life so broadly, truly, and sympathetically that every American of feeling and culture is forced to acknowledge the picture as a likeness of something which he knows" (159). In this conception, America is not to be created in its novels but rather reflected.

Two other features of De Forest's foundational definition are worth considering. The first is that he arrives at his standards by looking back at Europe for models of greatness that the American novel has not yet accomplished. He returns to the classical era before novels even existed to argue that Homer's *Iliad*, Virgil's *Aeneid*, and Dante's *Divine Comedy*, among other epic poems, were produced in response to long histories that the United States has not yet endured. He also name-checks contemporary European novelists such as William Thackeray, Anthony Trollope, Honoré de Balzac, George Sand, and Dickens to highlight their broad, sustained novelistic accomplishments that eclipse American ones.

Again, he uses a painting metaphor to argue that America may just be too young to have produced its GAN: "Ask a portrait-painter if he can make a good likeness of a baby, and he will tell you that the features are not sufficiently marked nor the expression sufficiently personal" (159). The second noteworthy feature, related to this one, is that American society is too volatile to be captured in any enduring way; he asks, "Can a society which is changing so rapidly be painted except in the daily newspaper?" (160). Great English novelists like Trollope, he contends, are "perplexed by no such kaleidoscopic transformations" (160) nor by the regional identities of the United States. In some ways, according to De Forest, the very things that make America unique – its capacity for change, its vast size, and its newness – are what prevent it from producing a novel worthy of the "Great" title. He ends with a desperate plea for "more talent" and a question as to whether the time will ever be right for the mythical creature he's conjured.

In trying to create an ideal, De Forest created a problem. His definition reaches for an idyllic future when the United States will become stable enough to generate some novelistic hybrid of a portrait and a landscape. Yet the essence of the United States, one might argue, is that it resists stability and homogeneity. Also implicit in his definition is the imperative that American novels isolate something called American character which he believes to be tangible, but which is in fact part of our mythology. To reiterate, he believes Americans are "eager and laborious people" who pride themselves on industrial expansion, capitalism, warmongering, and a can-do spirit (Kerouac's *On the Road* [1957] is one GAN candidate that cheerfully opposes virtually all these qualities; *Huck Finn* is another). De Forest holds imagination suspect as an essential quality of the GAN; Hawthorne's works are too romantic, too "spiritual … characterized by only a vague consciousness of this life" (156). Hawthorne's characters speak "the language of men who never expressed themselves but on paper, and on paper in dreams" (156). The bottom line is that De Forest's definition is conservative even as it looks toward a murky future for its holy grail. He is a champion of the high realism that dominated the late nineteenth and early twentieth centuries, a movement or mode that would produce some prodigious candidates for greatness over the next few decades, including James, Howells, Chesnutt, Wharton, Twain, and Chopin. Yet De Forest's definition, arrived at through a careful examination of what he admires and does not admire, would not hold long enough to crown any of these novelists who, it could be argued, succeeded where others had failed. All De Forest's essay really does is critique some of the American novelists of his time and/or a few decades earlier while pointing to the existence of a mythical creature swimming invisible in the depths of our cultural ocean. Great white whales need not apply.

Thomas Sergeant Perry, a prominent editor, writer, and academic, continued the conversation in an 1872 essay titled "American Novels" in which he immediately points out some of the problems caused by the hunt for the GAN. The critics embroiled in this debate, clearly including De Forest, have "stood in [the novelist's] way by setting up before him a false aim for his art, and by giving the critical reader a defective standard by which to judge his work" (160–1). Part of his gripe is the pressure of the word "American" in the middle of the phrase; he believes that the "human nature underlying" so-called American nature should be the primary concern of the novelist (161). Above all else, a novel should be "true": "That is what is of importance; it is that alone which makes the novel great, which causes it to be read in all times and in all countries" (161). This sounds convincing enough until one realizes that "true" can be understood in many different ways – constant, authentic, real – and it's also difficult to measure or even identify. Sniffing out De Forest's agenda, Perry scrutinizes the popular mode of the day: "It is the bane of realism, as of all *isms*, to forget that it represents only one important side of truth" (161). He doesn't favor novels that are merely realistic, by which he means novels that are obsessed with facts and accuracy at the expense of the deeper currents of the truth. His first target is none other than De Forest, in whose novels "we find a great deal that is American, but not so much that goes to the making of a really great novel" (162). He develops his definition of the true as opposed to the merely realistic: "In the true novel the scene, the incidents, are subordinated to the sufferings, actions, and qualities of the characters" (162). In terms of the elements of fiction, he's suggesting that plot and setting should take a back seat to character.

Perry makes a number of convincing points with clear illustrations and an amusing dose of archness, but he falls into some of the same patterns as De Forest, wondering where our American Byron is, or Shakespeare, or Fielding, or Thackeray, alluding to a recognized pantheon of familiar literary names from across the pond even as he says that there is no clear consensus on the great British (or French) novel while wondering aloud why we expect a GAN to be named. (Norris reiterates this point almost verbatim in his 1903 essay [86]). Perry is more aligned with De Forest than he might want to admit. They agree, for instance, that "The great [American] novel is yet unwritten"; they use painting analogies to make their point; they argue that too many American novelists are bound by their regions; and they point out the "more obvious faults of some of our popular writers" as a way of arguing why greatness has not yet been achieved (167). Both critics snub Melville. Both praise Stowe and suggest that she's come the closest to the ideal. Perry is troubled by the way the term might cause future writers to try too hard: "The less conscious he is of trying to be American, the more truly will he succeed in being so" (167). The two critics diverge here, and also on the centrality of principles of realism; Perry writes, "The real novelist, he who is to write the 'great American novel,' must be a poet; he must look at life, not as the statistician, not as the census-taker, nor yet as the newspaper reporter, but with an eye that sees, through temporary disguises, the animating principles, good or bad, that direct human existence ... he must idealize" (167–8). He puts a fine point on it as he concludes: "The idealizing novelist will be the real novelist. All truth does not lie in facts" (168). The debate is clearly underway with such distinctions, but without clear examples (save *Uncle Tom's Cabin*) of what either critic considers the exemplar of this legendary being, the definition isn't much clearer than it was at the outset. Also, Perry's belief that the adjective "American" is the problem indicates that the Great American Novelist should be someone who writes a great novel who happens to be American; he writes, "there will be of course a flavor of the soil, which is to be desired, but the epicure does not want his coffee muddy" (161). He implies an ideal balance between American and universal, but the recipe is vague.

A third voice that adds significantly to the debate is Robert Herrick, a novelist and academic critic whose 1914 essay "The American Novel" extends and departs from some of the premises of the earlier two arguments. Like them, he is overly anxious about how contemporary English novels are superior to American ones: he praises H.G. Wells, Arnold Bennett, and John Galsworthy and an unnamed "half a dozen others almost as distinguished as these three" in contrast to their American counterparts: "one would have to strain patriotism to the point of absurdity to name any [American] novelist of similar performance" (168). (Looking back, one wonders if he somehow in 1914 hadn't heard of Henry James, Edith Wharton, Theodore Dreiser ...). Unlike his two predecessors, he deliberately does not spend too much time finding fault with individual American writers in favor of speaking more broadly, but he does name a few, and, again, denigrates many of them for writing "local literature" that is "in no sense national" (168–9). It is difficult to know what these critics mean, exactly, by national literature, but the constraint of regionalism is something they all react to. There is also a persistent question about the relationship between novels and journalism, which is nearly an obsession for Herrick; he defines journalism as it applies to literature as "the thing done for the immediate moment" and contrasts it with "perforce literature" which "must absorb journalism and transcend it" (169). The yet-to-be-written great work must capture a national character, must not be content with harnessing a zeitgeist, and must also be big, a "large, organic form ... epic in size and in purpose" (170). He wants novels to be revelatory rather than merely reflective, and he is wary of the effect of magazine fiction on the American taste, claiming it has made us soft and complacent: "neither journalism nor commercialized fiction is an adequate medium for interpreting life deeply – for realizing ourselves and our country" (170). This formulation is clear, but it still relies on defining something by what it is not.

Herrick identifies four specific "reasons for the inferiority" of American novels: (1) they are "weakly sentimental"; (2) they "avoid altogether the religious side of life"; (3) they reflect "prudery in the sex realm"; and (4) they are more reflective of "aristocratic" life than of the broad experiences of multiple classes. He goes deeper into each of these points, a couple of which are worth addressing here. By "the religious side of [American] life" he does not suggest that American novels should be doctrinaire or ideological, and he mentions multiple versions of faith in his discussion. Rather, he suggests that American novelists tend to shy away from this persistent feature of American culture altogether, and, in his time, are much more taken with the world of business and finance than with anything like spirituality. In terms of sex and our obsession with aristocracy, he makes a statement or two that could be seen as sexism if taken out of context, for he claims that "our novels are written largely by women and for the entertainment of women" which "is in itself a weakening element in our literature" (173). He pulls out quickly from this nosedive by stating "our literature should represent both sexes and interest both sexes" (173) which is a point that perhaps connects to his desire to have all classes represented, but he's skating on thin ice with such statements.

Nearly a half-century after De Forest's initial foray into the topic, Herrick's essay is instructive in a few ways. He faults not only novelists but the reading public, the publishing industry, and literary critics for the problem at hand, a problem that involves intellectual laziness, in his opinion. Like Perry, he wants to get away from the idea of a single GAN because of the cultural damage it causes: "I say our novels – not *the* American novel, which is a figment of the newspaper critic's imagination" (177). And yet, he still clings to belief in this fanciful beast: "The truth is that we are not yet ready for the masterpiece, if we ever shall be, – if, indeed, one epic, no matter how splendid, will ever serve for the complete record" (177). In his mind the masterpiece both theoretically exists (*"not yet ready"*) and possibly never will exist. He calls for Americans to lose "that excessive consciousness of our individualism that characterizes us now" in favor of embracing nationalism: "Then we may speak of the American novel" (177). Here he is idealistic and skeptical at the same time. The Transcendentalists implied that the perfection of each individual was an essential precursor to the perfection of the nation whereas Herrick sees the two entities as antagonistic.

The novel Herrick cites as coming closest to his ideal is not *Uncle Tom's Cabin* but rather Edith Wharton's *The House of Mirth* (1905), which "came near being the women's epic of our day" (173) but fell short because of the fourth pitfall of the American novel, namely its preoccupation with the aristocracy. (Since he calls it "the women's epic of our day," it would also seem to violate the principle that it should appeal equally to men and women, and the phrase "of our day" could be an equivocation based on what he calls journalism). Wharton herself weighed in on the debate in a 1927 essay called, again, "The Great American Novel." Of these four critics, she is the one whose name is still widely recognized in the twenty-first century, and she is undoubtedly one of our most enduring novelists. What she adds to the debate is a complication that results from the development of American culture in the twentieth century, namely the ability to travel the world with relative ease.

For Wharton, whose novels often featured wealthy Americans traveling abroad or even expatriating themselves (as she did), the unstated mandate to set the GAN or any American novel on U.S. soil rankles. Responding to the popularity of Sinclair Lewis's *Main Street* (1920) – a novel she admires for its satirical qualities – she writes,

> The American novelist must submit to much narrower social and geographical limitations before he can pretend to have produced *the* (or *the greatest*, or even simply *an*) American novel ... the novelist's scene must be laid in the United States, and his story deal exclusively with citizens of those States; furthermore, if his work is really to deserve the epithet "American," it must tell of persons so limited in education and opportunity that they live cut off from all the varied sources of culture which used to be considered the common heritage of English-speaking people. The great American novel must always be about Main Street, geographically, socially, and intellectually. (178)

She of course resists such a formula which limits the scope of the novelist's imagination artificially. Perhaps bristling at Herrick's suggestion that her novels don't fit the bill because they're too aristocratic, she advances a critique that might be regarded as anti-middle class. She corrects that interpretation: "It is not because we are middle-class but because we are middling that our story is so soon told" (179). By "middling" she means that Americans, at least in the first decades of the twentieth century, have become tame, uniform, complacent, and homogenized. She is reacting to the suffocation of what would come to be known a few decades later as the American Dream with its suburban fantasy that respectability, mild prosperity, civic engagement, and heteronormative domestic bliss were enough to make Americans happy. For her, this is a damaging fantasy that produces inferior art. She is much more interested in cultural "growth" which she defines in terms of "an ever-increasing complexity" (180). Her conclusion suggests a crucial difference between any novel that might be deemed the greatest for a short time but that will quickly fade because of the limiting, superficial, provincial tendencies of American culture, traits she satirizes in her fiction. She claims that there are a handful of "really great novels" in the American canon circa 1927 – "perhaps half a score" – but she doesn't name them (182). Her criteria are clear enough, but like the other critics, she imagines that the greatest is yet to come. As a way of throwing us off balance, though, she concludes, "When it [arrives], it will probably turn out to be very different from what the critics counsel, the publishers hope, or the public is accustomed to" (182). This assessment posits that the GAN will be original, unexpected, pathbreaking, or mold-breaking. While Wharton doesn't tell us exactly what it will look like, she clearly hopes for a work that does not pander to tastes nor bow to tame formulas or critical regulations.

The debate rages on today, but this concentration of opinions from the late nineteenth and early twentieth centuries clarifies some of the key issues that readers in search of the GAN – or even of candidates that could be considered the GAN – must come to terms with. Are we doomed to be forever looking over our shoulder at England and Europe as we define our own traditions? Does the mythical GAN have to be representative of a national character, a national story, or a national idea or can it just be a great novel that happens to be written by an American? Should it be a faithful, accurate portrait of life in America or an imaginative departure from that life? Should it isolate a key moment in time, or should it be transcendent? Does it need to be big, vast like America itself, epic in scale and scope? Does it come out of one author's individual genius and vision, or should it respond to a very specific need on the part of the reading public, the need for a cultural product that will be held up as the yardstick by which all others are measured? Finally, will it endure the oft-cited "test of time," and how will anyone know that it can if it has not already done so?

These questions are unanswerable, individually and collectively, and they exacerbate the tension around the evaluation of the American novel tradition more generally, but they have to be considered and aired out as we locate and identify that tradition's main currents. As I've mentioned, these early critics cite novelists who are not much read anymore, which is not to say they won't be again, but only to show how the tradition is not stable over time. One doesn't have to go back to 1868 to find lists of novelists once considered essential who are now passé or even completely forgotten. Through much of America's literary history, male white authors dominated the canon, and although this trend has reversed course in recent decades, it is clear that a literary tradition does not change entirely even when its foundations are severely shaken. This study is simply a record of one critic in 2024, looking back on similar earlier records and shifting the premises to advance a new argument with old roots.

The Great American Novel Over Time: The Usual Suspects

What follows is a brief list of some novels that have once been held up as the possible GAN since the debate began with a brief overview of how they align with the criteria established in the critical debate above. These are not, again, my candidates, but rather the works that have entered the critical consciousness over time. Four have already been mentioned: *The Scarlet Letter*, *Moby-Dick*, *Uncle Tom's Cabin*, and *The Adventures of Huckleberry Finn* are certainly nineteenth-century novels that all serious students of the tradition should have read. It's striking how different they are, though, and thus how difficult to compare. Hawthorne's novel looks back to what he considers the dark beginnings of a certain persistent strain of American culture based on the severe ideology of the Puritans. It's an origin story in many ways, the scarlet "A" on Hester Prynne's chest signifying not only Adultery but America itself, a nation born out of judgment and social regulation. In some senses, though, it's a *pre-American* novel, concerned not with nationhood but with an enduring facet of our national character inherited from Puritan Europe that Hawthorne saw as damaging. Yet it does illustrate the core American story of a character at odds with her society, a mother considered a sinner who is punished and overtly labeled by the stewards of conformity.

Moby-Dick travels to a philosophical space that explores ideas and psychological conditions that would not be available in a smaller, more conventional novel. For the critics discussed above who wanted versions of the news – who celebrated the domestic quotidian as the core of American experience – it was not destined to fit the bill. Not only does it delve deeply into a set of experiences that weren't shared by the vast majority of its readers, but it also seems to float us out onto a new plane of consciousness that cuts us loose from the American world we thought we knew. It's a novel of the mind, and it's famously enormous, encyclopedic even, satisfying the realm of critical thought that would insist that the GAN be "epic" in scope and "complex" (two words Wharton uses in her essay). Ahab, as the character at odds with his society, is a compelling type, obsessive, driven, competitive, and vengeful according to a solid private code of ethics. The narrator Ishmael expands the intellectual appeal of the novel considerably as he tries to scrutinize and solve the mystery that is Ahab just as Ahab, Ishmael, and the reader all try to scrutinize the elusive white whale. Nothing less than the furor and meaning of existence are at issue here. As a novel that contributes to a national mythology, it highlights the spirit of exploration and conquest as the root of the American story.

"Great" can mean "large," and *Moby-Dick* is certainly large, like the whale and like the burgeoning country, or perhaps like the expansive mind of its author. Its publication set an unwritten standard that the GAN should reach for the infinite. *Uncle Tom's Cabin* (discussed in Chapter 4) is also a large novel, but one whose size derives from interwoven plot lines in the manner of the English Victorian novel rather than the ever-expanding plane of the mind and of experience represented in Melville. As a novel about slavery published before the Civil War, Stowe's novel is much more in the category of the real than of the imagination, and yet its hallmark frameworks of sentimentality and Christian ideology are part of why the early definers of the GAN were reluctant to award it the blue ribbon. There are moments of humor in *Uncle Tom's Cabin* despite its grim subject, and yet it is a very different type of humor from what we find in Twain's novel, also discussed at length in Chapter 4. *The Adventures of Huckleberry Finn* – Hemingway's pick for the origin point of all great modern American literature – satirizes a specific dimension of the American character, namely a deficiency of critical thinking that cannot discern the differences between fake and real, between culture and confidence scheme, or especially between slavery and normal human social relationships. Published decades after the Civil War, Twain's intent was not, like Stowe's, to convince readers that slavery should be abolished, but rather to illustrate the long-term damage it inflicted on American society as embodied in a neglected, unambitious boy who loses his innocence and ignorance simultaneously while in the company of an escaped enslaved man.

The latter three of these four novels center on exploration and adventure, and these are enduring traits of the American literary tradition. As Wharton indicates, the modern era afforded opportunities for the wealthy to travel abroad, and a number of subsequent candidates for the GAN involve Americans abroad. Henry James's *The Portrait of a Lady* (1881) is largely set in England and Italy and weighs the values of the so-called Old World against the New World, a dynamic we also see in some of Wharton's best work, including *The Age of Innocence* (1920), discussed in Chapter 3. Hemingway's *The Sun Also Rises* (1926), discussed in Chapter 8, is another highly regarded GAN candidate that follows the debauchery of a crass mob of American and British expats in France and Spain as its alienated narrator chases his own elusive objects of happiness in the form of meaningful work, commitment to understanding and living the good life, and mutually satisfying friendships and love relationships.

Like the protagonists of James's and Wharton's novels (and arguably Melville's), Hemingway's Jake Barnes is a romantic in the sense that he desperately wants what he can never have. This trait is one he shares with Jay Gatsby, the central figure of another beloved and enduring GAN candidate from the 1920s, Fitzgerald's *The Great Gatsby* (1925), discussed in Chapter 2. Although its characters do not travel around Europe, this novel does contain a great deal of frenzied motion, a restlessness that wants to turn into adventure but ends up producing frustration, as well as a fatal car accident. Gatsby is, like Melville's Ahab, obsessed with control, specifically the desire to recoup the lost love of his life, and his reach toward infinity takes the form of complete identity reformation, another recurrent trait of the American novel tradition. Hemingway's and Fitzgerald's novels do not have the massive scope of Melville's or Stowe's and are, like Wharton's and James's, centered on a privileged class of Americans in contrast to Twain's ragged and "unsivilized" hero.

Other early twentieth-century novelists reached for narratives that would satisfy the size expectation as well as the appeal to a readership whose social class was somewhere between the poles of Twain and Wharton. Theodore Dreiser's *An American Tragedy* (1925) even embedded the word "American" in its title perhaps as a way of signaling his awareness of the pressure to produce a book large enough to match its nation's vastness. Fatalistic forces appealed to novelists like Dreiser, Frank Norris, Jack London, and Hamlin Garland who helped define the literary historical category of naturalism which showcased characters who often turned to desperate acts to define themselves in vain attempts to overcome the limiting forces of their environment. John Dos Passos's *U.S.A.* trilogy (three novels, published 1930–1936), like Dreiser's novels, took its cue from the newspaper headlines of the time to craft works that were of their time but that would swell in significance (and size) to become enduring tales. John Steinbeck's *The Grapes of Wrath* (1939) is another ponderous work that reflected the grim realities of migrant workers during the Great Depression, addressing nagging issues of social class while questioning the American myth of equal opportunity. Richard Wright's *Native Son* (1940) told a similar story in which race constituted a limiting factor to the individual dreams of its anti-hero, Bigger Thomas. As in Dreiser's novels, Wright's protagonist is driven to desperate measures by the society that hates and persecutes him, and the only recourse he feels he has is to commit crimes that will lead to lifelong persecution. In various ways, these four naturalistic novelists created sprawling texts – Wright's protagonist is even named "Bigger" – as a way of recasting the American story in terms that were both realistic and tragic with regard to the differences between American reality and American mythology. Of the four, Wright's and Steinbeck's (both discussed in Chapter 5) continue to be read widely, but most GAN-minded critics would not tend to champion any of these, partly, I suspect, for their relentlessly bleak rendering of American experience, and partly for the unspoken criterion that a GAN should showcase a refined original aesthetic. Hemingway's restraint, Fitzgerald's charm, and Wharton's and James's precision and eloquence aren't reflected in the hefty works of these later writers whose prose is relatively blunt.

The mid-twentieth century saw American writers experimenting with the trope of the anti-hero or with heavily burdened heroes. The 1950s and early 1960s saw the rise of some literary titans, including James Baldwin, Saul Bellow, Ralph Ellison, Jack Kerouac, Mary McCarthy, Norman Mailer, Philip Roth, and John Updike. Ellison's *Invisible Man* (1952) stands out as a work that would fulfill the criteria of virtually all the early definers of the Great American Novel, and then some. It is a vast novel, riveting from the first word to the last, hyperconscious of the underlying divisions (notably race and class) that belie the American Dream narrative, and fully aware of the literary tradition that it built upon. As discussed in Chapter 5, *Invisible Man* seemed to be what everyone had been waiting for, and it remains highly relevant, profound, and essential nearly three-quarters of a century after its publication. From the title on, though, the primacy of masculine experience is a blind spot in a novel that uses blindness and invisibility as persistent metaphors. Women aren't really in it, except as sex objects and one mother figure (pointedly named Mary). Kerouac's *On the Road* (1957), beloved for its impassioned style, its embrace of taboo subjects, its enthusiasm, and its unfiltered approach to adventurous experience, is also confined to male sensibilities. Like Melville and Hemingway before them, Ellison and Kerouac were unwilling or unable to account for the rich possibilities of women's experiences in their candidates for the GAN. A commitment to understanding the world from multiple perspectives (including gender and nonnormative sexualities) was not a criterion of the initial definers of the Great American Novel, but it has certainly become important to a readership that has had a century and a half to grow.

The late twentieth century saw a new generation of literary stars whose novels remain essential reading. Postmodernists including Thomas Pynchon, William Gaddis, John Barth, Donald Barthelme, Kurt Vonnegut, Ishmael Reed, Don DeLillo, John Edgar Wideman, and David Foster Wallace, to name a few, produced some works that matched Melville in terms of creative energy, interpretive mystery, and enormous scope. Not all have endured, but noteworthy in this regard are Pynchon's *Gravity's Rainbow* (1973), Wallace's *Infinite Jest* (1996), and DeLillo's *Underworld*

(1997). The critic looking for the unfathomable zaniness of American life would be likely to consider these books as serious candidates, but like *Moby-Dick* their challenges to the average reader would violate the idea that the GAN should appeal to the common reader: these works demand committed, sophisticated readers. Other great novelists arrived and endured in the last decades of the twentieth century and first decades of the twenty-first in numbers too great to list fully, though it bears mentioning some names of novelists held in high popular and critical regard: Joan Didion, Alice Walker, Richard Ford, Colson Whitehead, Richard Powers, Louise Erdrich, Jhumpa Lahiri, Joyce Carol Oates, Jane Smiley, Jonathan Franzen, Sandra Cisneros, Cormac McCarthy, and of course Toni Morrison.

Morrison's *Beloved* is currently the novel that would top most lists. There is no denying its power, its inventive use of language, its profundity, its complexity, and its willingness to look America's worst historical sin – slavery – straight in the eye in order to uncover its enduring damage to our collective psyche. Its heroine Sethe is deeply troubled and flawed, and her quandary, taken from the historical record, cannot be simply resolved, explained, or understood: the choice between allowing one's daughter to be returned to slavery or to kill her is one that should never have to be faced. The reader is gradually encouraged to rise above the judgment that Sethe receives from other characters in the book – including her lover and fellow enslaved sufferer Paul D – and to gain a broader and heftier understanding of the chronic destruction a system like slavery unleashes. That understanding can only come through a deep, historically informed journey into the heart of the problem.

Beloved is also a perfectly composed novel. Morrison had evolved as an artist to the point that her most important book was an aesthetic masterpiece, followed closely by the novel most critics consider her second-best, *Song of Solomon* (1977). Her narrative technique, often linked to Virginia Woolf and William Faulkner – the subjects of her master's thesis – had become fully her own by 1987 after a lifetime of reading, writing, and editing professionally. This quality sets *Beloved* apart from all the other candidates for the Great American Novel I have mentioned, save perhaps *The Great Gatsby*: not a word is out of place. *Moby-Dick* sprawls; *Huckleberry Finn* reveals its seams; *On the Road* deliberately digresses, trying to capture everything without the artifice of conventional novels; *Invisible Man* builds on its own centrifugal energy until it and its protagonist do not know how to go on. Many Great American Novel candidates, to be frank, are unholy messes. I don't mean to suggest that Morrison's masterpiece should not be lifted up because it is in some senses too good, but rather to acknowledge that some readers have preferred the energy of works that are as unruly and as full of surprises as America itself.

Baldwin's *Another Country* Considered

In the spirit of that observation, and as a way of adding to the conversation about what might trouble (rather than resolve) the debate about the Great American Novel, I offer a brief discussion of a novel that has never before and will likely never again be regarded in this context, James Baldwin's *Another Country*. Again, my intent is not to crown a champion as I think the term itself is misleading, foolish, unnecessary, and fraught, but rather to get readers to consider new perspectives that can reframe the debate and expand the canon. Every novel I mention above – indeed, I hope, nearly every novel discussed in this study – is well worth reading for anyone attempting to understand the essence of the tradition. Readers seeking the Great American Novel might just want to know which ones to read first. I have spent much of my career analyzing Baldwin's work, and I probably wouldn't even recommend *Another Country* to anyone asking which of *his* novels to read first. (*Giovanni's Room* [1956] and *Go Tell It on the Mountain* [1953] are the more likely candidates). Baldwin's third novel is undeniably imperfect, in contrast to a precisely constructed work like *Beloved*. In 1962 he had risen to meteoric fame throughout the previous decade through the strength of two essay collections, a play, and two novels, and he was about to publish a landmark nonfiction work that became a cornerstone of the civil rights movement, *The Fire Next Time* (1963). He was suddenly the most prominent African American writer alive, displacing Wright and Ellison, and *Another Country* was his first and only novel to make the top ten of *The New York Times* bestseller list. It's a tale of bohemian Greenwich Village filled with booze, weed, and lots and lots of sex, including interracial sex and homosexual sex (both largely taboo subjects at the time of publication). It features a huge cast of characters, all of whom are connected somehow to the character assumed to be the protagonist until he commits suicide at the end of the book's first section. There is no single protagonist, just a gathering of loosely affiliated characters who are all at odds with society, and with one another. There is nothing neat or tidy about this novel. And yet, there is something so passionate, intense, and daring that it deserves to be considered in light of the criteria that had begun to be articulated nearly a century before its publication.

Baldwin's argument about the potential greatness of American novels is implicit in the text. One character, Richard Silenski, has published a commercially successful murder mystery, and those closest to him – his wife Cass and his former student Vivaldo, who is struggling with writer's block – are privately critical of the venture. Cass thinks, "the book he had written to make money represented the absolute limit of his talent. It had not really been written to make money – if only it had been! It had been written because he was afraid, afraid of things dark, strange, dangerous, difficult, and deep" (112). Cass's judgment defines Baldwin's aesthetic as it is represented in *Another Country*. It is not as though novels shouldn't make money, but if a book is not willing to take risks, to avoid the illusion of safety, it is not worth the paper it's printed on. Art consists of a willingness to confront "things dark, strange, dangerous, difficult, and deep," though not necessarily to make sense of them. Vivaldo also keeps his criticism to himself, but the narrator reveals his thoughts: "He had not liked the book. He could not take it seriously. It was an able, intelligent, mildly perceptive *tour de force* and it would never mean anything to anyone. In the place in Vivaldo's mind in which books lived, whether they were great, mangled, mutilated, or mad, Richard's book did not exist" (157). For novels to "mean" something, they need to have more passion than manners; they need to be *alive*.

There are very few novels that don't engage with one or both of the novel's favorite topics (death and love). The death of Rufus in *Another Country* is followed by a quest to redefine and understand love. If Rufus had felt loved, he would not have felt suicidal despair. The passion and fearlessness Cass and Vivaldo crave in novels fuels the narrative as its benighted characters struggle to define and experience love, often mixing it up with anger, sexual pleasure, admiration, possessiveness, and companionship. For Baldwin, love is a complex, active, and not always pleasant pursuit. In *The Fire Next Time* he defines it as "quest, and daring, and growth" (109). Vivaldo and a character named Eric, both of whom are in the process of ending love affairs with women, are longtime friends who temporarily become lovers. They are able to define how their fleeting relationship is closer to love than what they have experienced with others; Vivaldo realizes, "Eric really loved him and would be proud to give Vivaldo anything Vivaldo needed" (383). He realizes that their moment is ephemeral, but that doesn't diminish it; he tells Eric, "I don't, really, dig you the way I guess you must dig me. You know? And if we tried to arrange it, prolong it, control it, if we tried to take more than what we've … stumbled on, then I'd just become a parasite and we'd both shrivel. So what can we really do for each other except – just love each other and be each other's witness?" (396). This understanding of love is hard-earned in *Another Country* and it builds on the novel's explicit arguments of what novels should attempt. Turning away from passivity, romanticism, and a false belief in order and safety, Baldwin believes that novels should engage with the deep, important questions of where Americans should expend their energies. Artists and lovers throughout the novel are caught in the trap of believing in prosperity and eternal happiness in place of nobler pursuits: sacrifice, witnessing, and commitment. Crucially, Vivaldo realizes, "life isn't ever that tidy" (392), and neither should novels be. To reach for greatness, American novels must be willing to disturb, disrupt, and make a mess of things. The best ones – including *Another Country*, even if it is not the GAN – disrupt our mythology, beginning with the foundational one, the American Dream.

2 The American Dream
A Myth of Upward Mobility and Middle-Class Happiness

In tandem with the Great American Novel myth, the myth of the American Dream is a persistent cultural phenomenon that has profoundly affected the novel tradition. The two myths are united by the cultural spirit of competition and the belief in striving for improvement. I label them myths because they're fictions that American culture largely believes in, and stories that both guide and distort our cultural efforts and individual quests. The American Dream myth may be hackneyed and clichéd, but that doesn't mean it's not widely recognized and deeply felt. As an inroad into the novel tradition, its importance is foundational.

It is something of a paradox: the "American" adjective makes the Dream sound collective and shared, but it can only be achieved by individuals at the expense of others. It's connected to some of the hallowed beliefs in popular definitions of America that have held steady over time, namely that America is a land of opportunity, that it is founded on principles of equality and democracy, and that success within its borders is separate from the social class into which one is born. Subsequent chapters in this book highlight obvious fallacies in the American Dream narrative. To be clear from the outset, as the novel tradition reflects, the American Dream fantasy as represented in novels adheres to white, middle-class, heterosexual, Christian, English-speaking, male protagonists. The American Dream is worth exploring at the outset of this study in order to come to terms with its persistence as a cultural monomyth that has both defined and limited the American novel tradition.

Post-World War II Victory Culture

Though the definers of American nationhood in the eighteenth and nineteenth centuries laid the foundation for this dimension of its mythology, current popular conceptions of the American Dream

DOI: 10.4324/9781003252863-3

were cemented in the 1950s, the decade after World War II that saw the ascendancy of the suburban middle class. There are many possible explanations why the version of the American Dream that remains most prominent in the twenty-first century was designed in the Fifties. A primary one is the rise of "Victory Culture" which cast the U.S. as one of two global superpowers with nuclear weaponry and a neocolonial hankering for space exploration. America's nationalistic swagger following its emergence as vanquisher of fascism and savior of capitalism was palpable. The nation's development of planned suburbs created an appealing model for middle-class families and gave its citizens a prefabricated model of the Dream: homeownership with a picket fence, two cars in the attached garage, a monogamous heterosexual couple with two cheerful children, and a small lawn to mow. In addition to homeownership, this distinctively middle-class Dream involves prosperity, higher education, religious affiliation, civic engagement, and domestic harmony. When everything is added up, happiness is the presumed outcome of this equation. The construction of Eisenhower's Interstate Highway System fostered the mobility that enabled Americans to relocate to pursue the Dream wherever suited them, linking geographic mobility to upward class mobility. As much as any other factor, the television placed at the center of the modern suburban home standardized the Dream. American families saw idealized versions of their lives displayed on the small screen with wholesome, family-oriented shows like *Leave it to Beaver* and *The Donna Reed Show*. For many, these anodyne sit-coms were seductive versions of the lives they wanted to lead or imagined they were already leading.

All dreams can veer unpredictably into nightmares, and the monsters lurking under the surface of this one are evident. It doesn't require much scrutiny to see the Dream as an exclusive and exclusively materialistic fantasy, with the goal of "freedom" obscured by the accumulation and display of wealth. The uniformity of the suburbs, often codified by local regulatory bodies that limit any superficial changes to houses and mandate standards for their upkeep, contradicts another cultural myth, namely the American desire to express individual identity. The tilt toward conservatism in the 1950s accelerated by prominent crusades against communism might have rankled Americans who embraced ideologies that ran counter to the mainstream, and yet the unprecedented pressure to conform tended to overwhelm the spirit of rebellion. The result of this pressure was a culture that seemed to believe strongly in a collective Dream while repressing any simmering discontentment under the surface. That dichotomy is part of what fuels this dimension of the American novel tradition over time. In contrast with those early television sit-coms, novels of the 1950s – a marquee decade for the genre – tended to rip the veneer off the American suburb to reveal repressed psychological damage (Sloan Wilson's *The Man in the Gray Flannel Suit* [1955]), rampant infidelity (Grace Metalious's *Peyton Place* [1956]), and alcohol abuse, self-destruction, violence, and every other imaginable threat to domestic harmony (Richard Yates's *Revolutionary Road* [1961]). The Beat Generation of the 1950s and the counterculture of the 1960s pursued alternative lifestyles and narrative methods, leading to the rise of postmodernism (discussed in Chapter 7).

While television provided a steady diet of saccharine scripts for the middle class to swallow, the novel refused to comply. The 1950s are thus a good entry point for looking at the Dream's promise as well as its failures. Moving backward and forward in the tradition shows both the origins of the narrative prior to the Fifties and developments afterward. It should be noted that the novels in this chapter and their counterparts in Chapters 3–6 tend to be works of realism, and the anti-realistic novels in Chapter 7 are often deliberate attempts to break away from the persistent American Dream template, using experimental narrative techniques to arrive at alternative themes. American Dream novels collectively demonstrate the individual at odds with society in evident ways, pitting struggling individuals either swimming against the tide of conformity, giving in to it, or being crushed by it.

John Updike's *Rabbit, Run* (1960) is the first of his celebrated tetralogy of novels examining the crabbed life of Harry "Rabbit" Angstrom, one of the most memorable and loathsome antiheroes in modern American fiction. Updike wrote it in response to Kerouac's *On the Road* (1957) with the idea that the drifting behavior of Kerouac's heroes ignored the realities of many young American men who felt rooted to their domestic obligations and thus could not roam around the country in search of "kicks." Rabbit expresses a passionate desire to do exactly what Kerouac's road-chums Sal and Dean do – to explore his country in search of his identity, to have sex with multiple partners, and to glory in the freedom of the open road – but his self-gratifying desire is thwarted by duties to his pregnant wife, to his infant son, and to a dead-end job that barely pays the bills. A former standout high school basketball player, Rabbit locates all the hope and promise of his life in the past and dreads that his unfulfilling present will stretch into a diminished future. His last name Angstrom connotes both insignificance – an angstrom is a miniscule unit of measurement – and angst in the form of existential anxiety and anger at his lot in life.

On the near margins of the American Dream, Harry is the opposite of happy: he is surly, selfish, and mean, at times even sadistic. As the novel opens, he joins a group of teens in a game of pickup basketball on his way home from work and delights in the fact that he can dominate them at the age of twenty-six. He's so proud of himself that he spontaneously quits smoking and jogs home to brag to his pregnant wife Janice only to find her half-drunk and watching a children's program on television, having shipped off their son Nelson to Harry's parents' house. This scene illustrates failed versions of all the tenets of the 1950s American Dream outlined above. Harry rents his house rather than owning it. He's an inadequate breadwinner at a low-paying, unfulfilling job and Janice is an inadequate homemaker who is equally bad at cleaning, attending to her child, and cooking, which were the three main expectations of the role as reified in the 1950s. Neither has any interests, hobbies, or meaningful connections to their community. The car they drive belongs to Janice's parents. Neither has had the benefit of higher education. Both have lost their religious faith, a major subject of the novel.

Television replaces formal religion for Harry and Janice. After Harry arrives home in the opening scene, they watch *The Mickey Mouse Club* with rapt attention as Jimmy the Mouseketeer imparts a quasi-sermon about the proverb "know thyself." The lecture smacks of the dimension of the American Dream that rewards self-improvement; Jimmy says, "'be what you are. Don't try to be Sally or Johnny or Fred next door; be yourself. God doesn't want a tree to be a waterfall or a flower to be a stone. God gives to each one of us a special talent.' Janice and Rabbit become unnaturally still; both are Christians. God's name makes them feel guilty." The lecture continues: "Learn to understand your talents, and then work to develop them. That's the way to be happy" (10). This simplistic advice is self-contradictory, both a defense of individualism and a warning that God has prescribed a fate that cannot be altered. Harry interprets it as an excuse to pursue the gratification of his own desires at the expense of others' needs.

Harry's frantic instincts – related to his nickname Rabbit – are at war with his desire to seek guidance, often from older men like this absurd figure on TV. Disgusted by Janice's slovenliness and probable alcoholism, hampered by the demands of fatherhood, and frustrated with his own debased life as a former hometown hero, he instinctively does what the title indicates: he runs away from home. The ill-fated road trip is a nightmarish parody of the cross-country journeys described in *On the Road*. Harry has a romantic fantasy to drive southward from eastern Pennsylvania to the Gulf of Mexico where he will sink his toes into the sand and make love to a rich, southern woman. He becomes hopelessly lost and asks, belatedly, for directions from a gas station attendant who troubles Harry's quest by responding, "The only way to get somewhere, you know, is to figure out where you're going before you go there" (26). He frantically drives in a zigzag pattern like a rabbit running and realizes that his instincts have betrayed him, sending him in circles when he thought he was heading southwest. The map he scrutinizes becomes "a net, all those red lines and blue lines and stars, a net he is somewhere caught in" (33). Eisenhower's highway system, rather than providing the freedom of mobility, becomes for Harry one of many traps leading him back to his unalterable fate.

Having spent a fruitless night going nowhere, Harry returns to his hometown, but not to his home. He seeks the advice of his former high school basketball coach, a doddering old man named Tothero who gives him a place to sleep as well as a dose of contradictory advice. Harry tries to impress his former coach by bragging about his abstemiousness, but Tothero baffles Harry by suggesting he could save his marriage by drinking with his wife rather than judging her for drinking too much. Tothero alternates between imparting pseudo sermons based on his coaching experience and veering off wildly into lunatic pronouncements about women. He sets Harry up with a sometime prostitute named Ruth and Harry moves in with her, desperate to get away from his miserable domestic situation but unimaginative about how to explore a true alternative to it. Rabbit tries to imagine their first night together as their wedding night by enacting a ring ceremony before they have sex, and Ruth allows this fantasy to play out since she also seems to desire a stable, monogamous relationship even though she recognizes that he is "bad news" (84). Rabbit is pulled between the two domestic worlds he's created, though, especially when Janice's family enlists a minister named Jack Eccles to try to guide him back to his legal and moral responsibilities as a husband and father.

Eccles's attempt to set Harry back on his original path is doomed for many reasons. Most pointedly, Eccles lacks the conviction needed to sway Harry to believe in God and in his own inherent goodness. More, Harry's charisma is a stronger force than Eccles's weak faith. Eccles covets Harry's freedom even as he tries to perform his expected duties, and Harry, an alpha male, responds to Eccles's mentoring by trying to beat him at everything (including his own game, golf) and by attempting to seduce his wife. Harry is motivated only by his "own worst instincts" (115) combined with his corrupted philosophy based loosely on what he heard on a children's TV program; he tells Ruth, "If you have the guts to be yourself ... other people'll pay your price" (129). Because he is committed to self-gratification above regard for others, it's clear that the novel hurtles toward tragedy, and it delivers in the most painful way imaginable. When Janice gives birth, Harry returns to her, abandoning the now-pregnant Ruth. Frustrated with his wife's lack of sexual attention after she is healing from childbirth, he fixes her drinks hoping to seduce her, then runs away from her again when she will not yield to his advances. In one of the most painful scenes in literature, Janice, despairing at having been abandoned a second time, continues her drinking binge and becomes so incoherent that she is unable to prevent her newborn daughter from drowning in the bathtub. An innocent infant has paid Harry's price.

Updike has said his novels are all debates with the reader, and the central question he identifies in *Rabbit, Run* is, "What is goodness?" (*Shore* 850). It would seem the answer lies outside the book's scope, for although Harry attempts to be "good" for a short time, atoning for his sins by trying to become a dedicated father to Nelson and by working an honest job as a gardener, he repeatedly falls into his pattern of rotten, immoral behavior. He reaches yet another low point when he refuses to accept any of the blame for his daughter's death and publicly points his finger at Janice at the funeral: "You all keep acting as if *I* did it. I wasn't anywhere near. *She's* the one" (253). We could define goodness by what it is not – Harry is clearly bad, and goodness might be to behave opposite to him – but the novel also begs the question of how we might frame Rabbit's story in order to explain him, if not forgive him.

If we use the American Dream context to analyze Harry, we can begin to see a tangible source of his misplaced anger, his dissatisfaction, and his frantic energies. Rabbit is at war with an ideal that he can't readily define but that is embedded in his unconscious mind. The premise underlying his thinking is that success builds on success, that mobility is always upward. Yet he understands that life doesn't work that way; he tells Eccles, "I once did something right. I played first-rate basketball. I really did. And after you're first-rate at something, no matter what, it kind of takes the kick out of being second-rate" (92). If the value of his life is in the past, his future does not seem worth working toward; to paraphrase the gas station attendant, he doesn't know where he's going, so he doesn't get anywhere. His tangible talent – the grace he once felt on the basketball court as a "natural" (6) – does not lead upward: it leads nowhere. Although this context does not absolve him of responsibility for his monstrous behavior, it does provide insight into his actions. Unexamined belief in the Dream is far more likely to lead to disappointment than fulfillment, and the collateral damage in Updike's novel is unspeakable.

Horatio Alger's Legacy in the Gilded Age and the Jazz Age

Harry absorbs the script of the American Dream from his entire culture, not just the childish, distorted version he sees on *The Mickey Mouse Club*. From its inception, American literature promulgated versions of the cheery commitment to work that would lead directly to prosperity. Benjamin Franklin's *Autobiography* (1791) is the foundational text here, showcasing its famous author's pluck and industry as he steadily rises from poverty to prosperity. Another foundational text, De Crevecoeur's *Letters from an American Farmer* (1782), promulgates the "land of opportunity" myth for those willing to work: "The American ought therefore to love this country much better than that wherein either he or his forefathers were born. Here the rewards of his industry follow with equal steps the progress of his labor" (7). The fictional works of the nineteenth century that are nearly synonymous with this utopian dimension of the Dream were young adult novels written by Horatio Alger, Jr. The best-known of his novels, *Ragged Dick* (1867), demonstrates without subtlety or ambiguity the lesson that hard work and honesty lead to upward mobility. "Ragged" Dick Hunter is a homeless, preadolescent orphan who earns his money shining shoes on the streets of New York. He is winning, humorous, and notably optimistic despite his challenging circumstances. True to his nickname, he wears torn, dingy clothes and, at the beginning of the novel, sleeps in a cardboard box. The narrator is quick to point out that he's not perfect: "Our ragged hero wasn't a model boy in all respects" (5). His vices include smoking, gambling, and spending his earnings on unedifying entertainment. Despite these flaws, he is poised for success, which is not just material gain, but what he repeatedly calls "'spectability." His potential is based on a strong work ethic; contrasting him with a less successful friend, the narrator summarizes, "energy and industry are rewarded, and indolence suffers" (8). At the same time, work should be deliberate and purposeful; as one mentor tells him, "you must not only work hard, but work in the right way" (36).

The novel's message is so straightforward and unwavering that it's not worth spending much time on here, but it's important to point out that even though Dick's persistent industry and cheerful attitude get him far, he's also the beneficiary of some right-place-right-time luck. For instance, he lands his first non-shoe-shining job because he happens to be on a ferry when a rich man's son falls overboard and needs rescuing. In addition to industry and optimism, other facets of his moral code are repeatedly emphasized, often in contrast to the behavior of other individuals. In a novel full of scammers and thieves, Dick is both honest in all his dealings and able to spot deceit in others. He is also supremely confident, a trait that wavers only when others praise him (reflecting another virtue – humility). He is ambitious and enterprising, as when he seizes the opportunity to show the nephew of a rich New Yorker around town which results in the new set of clothes that help him gain entry to society's higher echelons; as he puts it, "I changed my business accordin' as I had to" (33). He is generous, and when he gives his savings away to others in need – which he often does – he is ultimately repaid with interest. He realizes that hard work by itself is not enough. To move above his station, he must gain a formal education – measured by grammatical correctness, literacy, and neat penmanship – as a complement to his street smarts before he can claim his place; education is repeatedly deemed "more valuable than money" (86). The trajectory of his life is steadily upward. By the end of the novel, he has transformed from a bootblack to a smartly dressed young man with a steady income and a healthy savings account who signs his name Richard Hunter, Esq., signaling that the American Dream has delivered a shiny new identity. As his friend summarizes, he has become "A young gentleman on the way to fame and fortune" (115).

The extreme popularity of Alger's novels can be attributed to the seductiveness of the formula. Impoverished street urchins can achieve status, fame, and fortune if they stick to the plan, and they become someone new in the process. It's a transformation narrative. Between the untroubled version of the American Dream story in *Ragged Dick* and the nightmarish rendition in *Rabbit, Run* the tradition evolved and took on new dimensions, but Updike was certainly not the first to critique the myth in fiction: novels between these two poles involve scrutiny of the Alger myth as naïve and simplistic at best, a dangerous fantasy at worst. The high period of realism in the late nineteenth century and the rise of its darker companion naturalism in the early twentieth saw a great many novels at the intersection of the pursuit of advancement through work and domestic tragedy.

One representative text from the high period of realism is William Dean Howells's *The Rise of Silas Lapham* (1885). The novel opens with a newspaper reporter interviewing the titular Lapham for a puff piece about the way this self-made man rose from humble beginnings to financial success. Lapham's business is paint, which could be seen as a metaphor for the way the newspaper story of Lapham's life covers the cracks and flaws of his true identity. The journalist knows he is writing about the clichéd type of American depicted in Alger's novels; he prods his subject, "Parents poor, of course ... Any barefoot business? Early deprivations of any kind?" (12). Lapham comes across as dull-witted and vain throughout the book, but he sees through these questions and responds, "I guess if you see these things as a joke, my life won't interest you" (12). The reporter has already acknowledged that it's not exactly Lapham's life that makes him a subject for this type of piece: "you're just one million times more interesting to the public than if you hadn't had a dollar" (11). A self-made millionaire is an automatic American success story, and the reporter paints his portrait to flatter Lapham on the surface while subtly allowing his flaws to peek through.

The prototype of a successful American, Lapham is "simple, clear, bold, and straightforward in mind and action" and he is characterized by "single-minded application and unwavering perseverance" (26). A former colonel in the Civil War, he is brawny, masculine, decisive, competitive, gruff, and unsubtle. These characteristics prepare him for business success, but also prevent him from moving readily into the upper class to which his fortune would seem to grant access. Lapham's goal is not only to become rich, but to demonstrate to those who were born rich that he is superior because he earned his wealth. The newspaper article penned in the novel's opening chapter chronicles the rise of Lapham indicated in the title, but the remainder of the novel focuses on his gradual financial downfall thereafter, all the way to disgrace and bankruptcy.

The slow-motion fall of Silas Lapham is caused by three main antagonisms that constitute the novel's interwoven plot lines: (1) his business dealings with a corrupt former partner named Rogers; (2) his vain construction of a showy house in Boston's newly developing Back Bay; and (3) the courtship of his daughter Penelope by Tom Corey, a scion of the aristocratic blue-blooded Boston Lapham both resents and wants to join. His involvement with Rogers seems to be something he has moved beyond before the novel opens; Lapham silently dismisses Rogers's reemergence in his life early in the narrative, causing an argument with his wife Persis who accuses him of bilking Rogers out of his share of the company. "I never wanted a partner," he reminds her after she questions his business ethics, "It was a business chance" (47). Persis doesn't fully understand the truth of the deal that caused Rogers's departure because she has concentrated on her domestic duties in accordance with the era's gender norms. When Rogers returns and effectively swindles Lapham out of his fortune, she recognizes her avoidance of the paint factory as an error: "she forgot how much she had left herself out of his business life. That was another curse of their prosperity. Well, she was glad the prosperity was going; it had never been happiness" (293). Three of the main premises of the American Dream myth are rendered false here, namely that the Dream is for an autonomous, independent individual, that men and women play separate roles in attaining the Dream for their families, and that wealth brings happiness. In this sense, the "rise" of the title is not the assumed ascendancy from rags to riches, but rather the rise of both Laphams to a more sophisticated understanding of what's valuable in a materialistic world and the moral enlightenment that comes with such a realization.

The second plotline that challenges the American Dream mythology is about one of its cornerstones, homeownership. The couple discusses their difficulty breaking into Boston society and Persis concludes, "we're in the wrong neighborhood" (34). She seems reticent to build a new house on their lot on Beacon Street because she recognizes that she and Silas are essentially country people who will never lose their country sensibility, but he resists this sentiment: "I guess we live as well as most of 'em now, and set as good a table" (36). Building the house becomes his obsession and it escalates from a shelter into a showpiece when he hires an architect rather than a builder; he boasts, "give an architect money enough and he'll give you a nice house every time" (54). Lapham knows nothing about design and is thus vulnerable to overspending, but he sees that consequence as a tangible mark of his status rather than a problem. Money must be spent elaborately to project power; as Tom Corey's father puts it, "there's no doubt but money is to the fore now. It's the romance, the poetry, of our age. It's the thing that chiefly strikes the imagination" (62). There's no doubt that Howells is critiquing this materialistic mindset of the era Mark Twain dubbed "the Gilded Age." The conspicuous consumption represented by Lapham's house is clear evidence of his vanity, and when he accidentally burns it down a week after the insurance policy has expired, securing his bankruptcy, we are meant to see how foolish it is to focus on the display of wealth rather than one's moral self.

The third plotline involves the earnest Tom Corey who both wants to work for Lapham and to marry one of his daughters. A large part of the novel involves widespread misunderstanding about which daughter he's courting: everyone assumes it is Irene, who everyone considers the prettier but less intelligent sister. Tom gradually reveals that the object of his affection is Penelope, the less conventionally attractive sister who is better read and whose conversational style is sarcastic rather than charming. His choice might be seen as a distraction from the novel's main concerns, but it underscores the importance of valuing the substantial over the superficial. Additionally, both sets of parents in the Corey/Lapham feud must learn that their children are not playthings, but human beings whose happiness depends on love rather than money. If part of the American Dream myth involves childrearing with the aim of leaving behind an inheritance that will guarantee a smooth path for the next generation, the novel also rattles that foundation.

More fundamentally, though, the interaction between the Lapham and Corey families represents a culture clash. When Tom approaches Silas for a position in his paint company, Silas genuinely likes him and perhaps regards him as the son he never had who can eventually take over the business. On a first encounter, he declares that the lad has "a good, fair and square, honest eye" but he worries that he's been coddled by his parents' wealth: "I don't see how a fellow like that, that's had every advantage in this world, can hang 'round home and let his father support him ... I like to see a man *act* like a man. I don't like to see him taken care of like a young lady" (56–7). The two-edged sexism of this statement is directly linked to Lapham's understanding of the masculine American Dream which involves self-reliance and "manly" courageousness and industry in the cutthroat world of business. Like the vanity that went into building his house, these values are revealed to be the flaws that lead to Lapham's downfall rather than the assets that created his material success.

His resentment toward Tom's privilege is also tied to his tendency to brag about and even exaggerate his own achievements. Tom notices this tendency and reports it to his father who calls it "vulgar" behavior, but Tom disagrees: "I don't know that it was vulgar. Perhaps his successful strokes of business were the romance of his life" (64). With some self-deprecation, as he realizes his son has more ambition than he does, the elder Corey jokes, "we shall never have a real aristocracy while this plebian reluctance to live upon a parent or a wife continues the animating spirit of our youth" (65). Tom and Penelope's courtship shatters all parental expectations – for both the nouveau rich and the established wealthy – and offers promise for the future. In the present, though, the confrontation between the two antagonistic classes culminates in a dinner party that is the climax of this minimally plotted text. Prior to it, Lapham's resentment toward the Coreys is extreme: "he had long hated their name as a symbol of splendor" (85). The dinner party is a minefield of potential faux pas as the Laphams struggle to figure out how to dress, how to speak, and all the other subtle codes of etiquette that define the established upper classes. Silas feels he is comporting himself brilliantly at the party, especially once the men separate from the women after dinner for cigars and more wine, but he is unused to drinking and he ends up making a fool of himself, bragging of his business successes boorishly in a grotesque distortion of his depiction in the newspaper article.

His loutish drunken performance at the dinner party can be seen as his turning point from a confident success to a bankrupt has-been, for his lack of judgment at this important foray into the upper-class world precipitates multiple poor business decisions that leave him destitute. Yet the novel's ironic title points to a more important ascendancy than the material gain implied by the American Dream. The marriage between Tom and Penelope "brought Lapham none of the triumph in which he had once exulted at the thought of an alliance with the Coreys" (312). This newfound understanding of what actually matters is in contrast to the "social success for which people crawl and truckle and restored him, through failure and doubt and heartache, the manhood which his prosperity had so nearly stolen from him" (312–3). In contrast to Lapham's swagger, his desire to succeed at the expense of others, and his vainglorious display of status, manhood is recast as other-directedness and humility, and the male-oriented Dream is thus redefined. His moral rise depends directly on his material fall. Unlike Updike's Rabbit Angstrom who fails to advance materially and declines morally, Lapham's story avoids tragedy through its protagonist's moral progress. The burning of Lapham's house is the best thing that could have happened to him whereas the drowning of the Angstrom baby is the worst thing imaginable in Harry's life, and worse still because it effects no visible change in him.

Nearly half a century after the Gilded Age moralism of Howells's novel, F. Scott Fitzgerald published *The Great Gatsby* (1925), a prime candidate for the Great American Novel whose popularity has been sustained not only by its entrenchment in high school curricula, but by a government program that distributed the novel to G.I.s during and after World War II. There are countless ways to approach Fitzgerald's Jazz Age classic, but it is ultimately a dark tragedy (leavened by gorgeous prose and a charming narrative voice) about the dangers of single-minded romanticism and the misguided belief that the past can be redone. In terms of the American Dream myth, it continues Howells's pattern of troubling the relationship between material gain and happiness. Gatsby's house, even more than Lapham's, is the focal point.

As in *The Rise of Silas Lapham*, *The Great Gatsby* reveals a conflict between the old rich and the new, but the difference is that Jay Gatsby pretends he was born into the upper class, hiding even the basic fact of his real name – James Gatz – for fear that it might reveal his humble origins. The narrator Nick Carraway positions himself as having a foot in both the aristocratic and working worlds, but he clearly comes from wealth; even in the first paragraph, his father reminds him, "just remember that all the people in this world haven't had the advantages that you've had" (1). A Yale graduate who takes a finance job in New York City, Nick moves into a comparatively modest house on Long Island across the water from his "enormously wealthy" (6) second cousin once removed (Daisy Buchanan) and her vile husband Tom, and next door to an oversized mansion owned by Gatsby. Even before we meet the mysterious Gatsby, we see his house, which cannot be missed; Nick describes it as a "colossal affair" that imitates European style and features "a marble swimming pool, and more than forty acres of lawn and garden" (5). When Nick first meets him, Gatsby calls immediate attention to his mansion, declaring factually, "I've got a nice place here' ... he moved a broad flat hand along the front vista, including in its sweep a sunken Italian garden, a half acre of deep pungent roses, and a snub-nosed motor boat that bumped the tide offshore" (7–8).

Nick will eventually learn more about Gatsby, but initially the mystery man is nothing more than the owner of a palatial house, which is also how the many guests at his lavish parties know him. Every weekend Nick watches across his yard as caterers and musicians arrive by the truckload. In the absence of a family, Gatsby's house becomes a vehicle for entertainment, and the guests – who barely know him – are little more than decorations, "gaudy with primary colors, and hair shorn in strange new ways, and shawls beyond the dreams of Castile" (40). Nick meets one drunken guest he calls "the owl-eyed man" in Gatsby's library who is pleased to discover that Gatsby's books are "absolutely real" rather than cardboard facades (46). The observation seems to testify to Gatsby's authenticity, but it is quickly undermined when the man observes that Gatsby "didn't cut the pages" (47), evidence that he never read the books. This detail intensifies the fact that Gatsby's very identity is comprised of what Nick calls the "romantic speculation he inspired" (44): guests variously claim he inherited family money from Kaiser Wilhelm, or attended Oxford, or was a German spy, or was a bootlegger, or, most insidiously, that he once killed a man. Nick's skepticism about Gatsby's origins is on high alert; he says, "I would have accepted without question the information that Gatsby sprang from the swamps of Louisiana or from the lower East Side of New York ... But young men didn't – at least in my provincial experience I believed they didn't – drift coolly out of nowhere and buy a palace on Long Island Sound" (49). The myth insists that even if one has risen to glorious wealth, one must come from somewhere, and Gatsby's dissemblance is revealed when Nick asks him where in the Midwest he grew up and he answers, "San Francisco" (65).

His house, then, becomes a way to distract from his humble origins as well as from the apparently sinister and probably criminal way he earned his money, and although this ruse works for most of his guests, it doesn't work for Nick who claims an unnatural predilection for honesty. The bigger purpose of the house, though, is to woo Daisy, Gatsby's one-time lover who married Tom for money when Gatsby had to leave for an army tour. Tom's wealth is extraordinary – he once bought Daisy "a string of pearls valued at three hundred and fifty thousand dollars" – so Gatsby believes his only recourse to win her back is to become even wealthier, and his house, like Lapham's, is the way to display that wealth (77). Nick asks his erstwhile lover Jordan why Gatsby wants to arrange a meeting with Daisy, and her simple answer is telling: "He wants her to see his house" (80). Preparing for the meeting, Gatsby spruces it up even more, lighting it "from tower to cellar" and causing Nick to remark, "Your place looks like the World's Fair" (82). When Daisy arrives, he tours her around as though it is a museum and he clearly regards it as proof of his new selfhood; Nick observes, "He hadn't once ceased looking at Daisy, and I think he revalued everything in his house according to the measure of response it drew from her well-loved eyes" (92).

Gatsby's distorted sense of the value of homeownership is related to his childhood poverty, which produces a violent urge to reinvent himself. Like Ragged Dick, he is on his own – the offspring of "shiftless and unsuccessful" parents – and when we first encounter him, drifting around Lake Superior looking for manual labor, he is even attired like Alger's hero, "in a torn green jersey and a pair of canvas pants" (99). When he spies a wealthy man's boat, he realizes "that yacht represented all the beauty and glamor in the world" (100–1), and attaches himself to its owner, thereby inheriting the seed money for his fortune. Unlike Ragged Dick, the newly rechristened Jay Gatsby builds on that fortune through shady means.

The loathsome Tom Buchanan realizes Gatsby is either a crook or a fraud and presses Nick on this front: "I'd like to know who he is and what he does" (110). Nick deflects, insisting that Gatsby's not a bootlegger and mumbling rumored truths like "He owned some drug stores, a lot of drug stores" (110). Bent on confrontation, Tom labels Gatsby "Mr. Nobody from Nowhere" (130) and insists that he won't stand around letting "a common swindler" (134) hit on his wife; Gatsby exclaims, "She never loved you … She only married you because I was poor" (131). Although Daisy and Gatsby clearly loved one another once and still do, money is an undeniably corrupting force in this world. Daisy attaches herself to money, but even more, her identity embodies it. Gatsby says of his beloved, "Her voice is full of money" and Nick realizes the odd truth of the statement: "That was it. I'd never understood before. It was full of money – that was the inexhaustible charm that rose and fell in it, the jingle of it, the cymbals' song of it … High in a white palace the king's daughter, the golden girl" (120). Gatsby's scheme is to give "Daisy a sense of security; he let her believe that he was a person from much the same stratum as herself – that he was fully able to take care of her" (149). In other words, he silently promises to keep this golden princess protected high in the white palace he has built in her honor. Nick puts a fine point on it: "Gatsby was overwhelmingly aware of the youth and mystery that wealth imprisons and preserves, of the freshness of many clothes, and of Daisy, gleaming like silver, safe and proud above the hot struggles of the poor" (150). What he is perhaps not aware of is that the gatekeepers of the aristocracy are not going to allow the formerly poor to enter the kingdom. As we see in Howells's novel, the newly rich are studiously kept out, as Gatsby is barred from Daisy's world first by her family and later by Tom.

Gatsby's tragic end, according to Nick, indicates that he "paid a high price for living too long with a single dream" (162). In the context of this chapter, though, the Dream is not of his own design. Gatsby sees wealth as the only goal even if he imagines Daisy as the symbol of it. She has money in her voice, and she's compared to gold and silver in the above quotations. It's evident that the object of his desire is not actually Daisy but rather his right to win her through the acquisition of wealth. Even after his senseless death, his house lives on as a monument to his achievements; his father "saw the height and splendor of the hall and the great rooms opening out from it into other rooms [and] his grief began to be mixed with an awed pride" (169). This pride swells as he continues to see the grandeur of the place while ignoring his son's demise, claiming he "was bound to get ahead" (175). The sense of triumph here amplifies the irony of Nick's thudding two-word sentence describing the reality of Gatsby's funeral at the end of that same paragraph: "Nobody came" (175).

The Dream and the Consequences of Passing

The fact that Gatsby dies young and that his father still feels pride in the notion that he "got ahead" is testimony to the power of the Dream to allow material wealth to blind Americans to what is truly important. This power is both what drives characters to pursue wealth and what distorts the vision of those who envy others who have attained it. The protagonists of the next trio of novels must cope with the tension between achieving the Dream and the psychological consequences of forsaking one's racial or ethnic identity to do so. The concept of passing – a term originally applied to early twentieth-century African Americans who denied or obscured their racial identity to have a chance at succeeding in the white world but here also applied to a Jewish/Catholic couple entering the Protestant world – is a variation on Gatsby's self-transformation with a crucial twist: the costs of this practice necessitate severing ties with one's family or community. The protagonists of the remaining novels in this chapter manage to ascend from their modest beginnings into the white, upper-middle-class world, but this supposed "rise" in fortune comes with a heavy price.

Related to the word "rise" around the time of Howells's novel was the concept of racial uplift, which informs Booker T. Washington's immensely popular (if critically scrutinized) autobiography *Up from Slavery* (1901). Late nineteenth- and early twentieth-century African American fiction writers were beginning to be published and recognized, notably Charles Chesnutt, though the Harlem Renaissance of the 1920s would mark a much sharper spike in accomplishments in this field. Chesnutt was known primarily as a short story writer. The tepid reception of his novels published between 1900 and 1905 convinced him that he could no longer earn a living as a writer, and he moved on to other pursuits. Chesnutt's novels remained obscure throughout his lifetime and have only recently begun to receive the critical attention they deserve, especially *The Marrow of Tradition* (1901), ahead of its time in terms of confronting the violence of race relations around the turn of the century.

Picking up where Chesnutt left off, James Weldon Johnson's *The Autobiography of an Ex-Colored Man* (1912) focuses on the painful coming-of-age of a nameless protagonist who does not initially realize he has African heritage. The novel illustrates the principles of W.E.B. DuBois's "double-consciousness" concept advanced in his influential work *The Souls of Black Folk* (1903), a book directly alluded to and praised in this novel (129). When DuBois was a schoolchild, a young white girl's discrimination against him led to his realization that Black Americans tend to experience distorted self-perception. He identifies the inferiority and confusion that comes from regarding the self through the perspective of the racist other. Similarly, the protagonist of Johnson's novel moves with his mother from the South to New England as a child and finds himself siding with the white children in the class who verbally abuse and physically menace the Black students. The narrator is deeply affected by one such incident and reports, "[I] went home and told my mother how one of the 'niggers' had struck a boy with a slate. I shall never forget how she turned on me. 'Don't you ever use that word again,' she said, 'and don't you ever bother the colored children at school. You ought to be ashamed of yourself'" (10). He soon after learns the truth of his own mixed-race identity when the school principal asks the white scholars to stand up. When the narrator rises, the teacher gently admonishes him to sit and wait until the Black students are called. He confronts his mother who informs him that he is mixed race despite his appearance. His African American heritage comes from her side of the family and similarly is not detectable in her features.

The narrator thus questions his identity and learns to distrust everything, including his own intuition. The situation does not improve when his rich white father appears on the scene doling out enough money to make the narrator comfortable. His mother dies soon afterward, and he is left to make his way in the world alone with a profound sense of uncertainty about his place outside of his main talent as a pianist. Left on his own, he pursues the Dream as a way of defining and protecting himself. He reflects on that "fateful" day at school, fixated on "the dwarfing, warping, distorting influence which operates upon each colored man in the United States" who is "forced to take his outlook on all things, not from the viewpoint of a citizen, or a man, nor even a human being, but from the viewpoint of a *colored* man" (14, 15). A shy and private boy, he seeks answers from literature and journalism rather than from people.

He eventually stumbles across *Uncle Tom's Cabin* which he describes as "a book that cleared the whole mystery" of his troubled existence even as he acknowledges that it "has been the object of much unfavorable criticism" (30). He repeats some of this criticism – Tom is too good and Simon Legree too evil to be plausible – but maintains, "it opened my eyes as to who and what I was and what my country considered me" (31). He carries this consciousness with him on his identity quest which leads him back to the South, initially to attend college in Atlanta, and later through communing with the Black working class.

His attempt at higher education is short-lived since his life savings are stolen on his first day. This theft shatters his plans, but it turns out to be a blessing in disguise as it forces him to get a job processing tobacco, thrusting him into the Black community. His narrative reads more like an anthropological report than a life story at this point in the novel as he examines the unique qualities of the Black vernacular, describes the rituals of the dance known as the Cake Walk, and contrasts the food served in Black restaurants to what he is used to. He is disappointed to learn that his one skill – teaching piano – is not likely to earn him a living in the South as potential Black pupils cannot afford it, but he is also aware that his skin and features are white enough that he could "pass" in the white world if he so desired. At a crossroads when the cigar factory where he works closes, he feels the urgent desire – "like a fever seized me" (67) – to join his coworkers who move to New York to pursue financial gain.

The New York the narrator experiences is a prototype of what we now associate with the Harlem Renaissance that would capture the nation's imagination a decade after Johnson's novel was published. The narrator is caught up in a frenzy of energetic street life and sophisticated club culture. He joins a game of craps where he wins a large sum of money with ease, then he is drawn into a club where ragtime jazz intoxicates him, where rich white women spend lavishly on the Black men in attendance, where champagne flows, and where minstrel actors insist on reciting Shakespeare rather than yielding to requests for performances that would reinforce racial stereotypes. He quickly realizes that gambling will do him more harm than good and decides to use his gifts as a pianist by merging classical music with the ragtime that has infatuated him. This innovation earns him the attention of Black audiences as well as wealthy white patrons, one of whom hires him for private functions and eventually takes him to Europe. This "millionaire" tries to dissuade the narrator from his epiphanic plan to return to the South to become a famous Black composer with a knowledge of ragtime, but the narrator follows his intuition back into the troubled heart of America.

His travels cause him to adjust his understanding of race relations. On the boat back from Europe he engages an impressive-looking Black man on the subject and hears his theories about how African Americans must achieve the highest level they can in the professions, culture, and education, thus serving as shining examples of the race's potential, an idea clearly reflective of DuBois's "talented tenth" concept. Later, in a smoking car on a Southern train, he witnesses an ugly debate between Southerners and Northerners about "the Negro problem." It is noteworthy that he doesn't participate in the debate while passing for white, and also noteworthy that he comes away from it slightly sickened by the sentiments expressed with such raw candor, but also with "an admiration for the man who could not be swayed from what he held as his principles" (126) – that is, the Southern racist who would not deviate from his conviction that Blacks were inferior and always would be. Several contradictions swirl around the narrator's brain. On one hand, he wants to bring his talents into the deep South and, in the service of his work, "to catch the spirit of the Negro in his relatively primitive state" (132), but on the other, he complains with great distaste about the poverty he witnesses, and he longs nostalgically for his luxurious days in Europe.

As he forms and reforms his opinions on race relations in the South, he observes an event that permanently changes him: a brutal lynching. As in the smoking car on the train, he is taken for white and thus not targeted by the vicious mob, and he is again doomed to be a silent witness. He leaves the murder scene with a new conviction:

> I would neither disclaim the black race nor claim the white race; but ... I would change my name, raise a moustache, and let the world take me for what it would ... it was not necessary for me to go about with a label of inferiority pasted across my forehead ... I understood that it was not discouragement, or fear, or search for a larger field of action and opportunity that was driving me out of the Negro race. I knew that it was shame, unbearable shame. Shame at being identified with a people that could with impunity be treated worse than animals. (146)

The familiar trope in American novels of reinventing oneself here takes an insidious turn. The narrator admits his shame but buries it inside himself as a way of crassly pursuing "every possible way to make a white man's success" which he sums up in a word: "money" (148). Following the American Dream script, he goes from rags to riches and falls in love with a white woman. With trepidation, he tells her of his racial heritage, and she spends half a year processing the information but eventually returns his vow of love. They marry and have two children, both of whom are, like him, light enough to pass, but she dies giving birth to the second, leaving him alone with his children. His love for them is countered by a significant burden of self-loathing for refusing the call to improve the racial situation in his country. He labels himself "a coward" and "a deserter" (161) and looks with regret at the yellowed notes of his musical compositions as evidence of "a vanished dream, a dead ambition, a sacrificed talent" (162). The typical American achievements of financial success and marriage are nothing compared to the feelings of loss born of shame caused by a society that refused to let him define or express himself honestly.

The conclusion of this novel is undeniably tragic and fraught with conflicted feelings. It initiates a trend that continues through the Harlem Renaissance and beyond, namely that Black or mixed-race protagonists are unsure whether to embrace Black folk culture or to follow their individual desires to succeed in the America defined by white values and standards even while suffering discrimination. This dilemma is well framed by Langston Hughes's enduring essay "The Negro Artist and the Racial Mountain" (1925) which begins by scrutinizing a nameless Black poet (known to be Countee Cullen) who claims he does not want to be thought of as a Black poet. Hughes interprets this to mean that Cullen is ashamed of his culture, particularly of its folkways. Hughes's writing tends to celebrate expressions of Black vernacular culture (notably jazz) while Cullen's work reveals a good deal of anxiety about crossing the divide between the two worlds. This anxiety – a clear holdover from slavery's power to segregate and hierarchize American society – is the subject of Nella Larsen's tense Harlem Renaissance novel *Passing* (1929).

Passing seizes on the complicated emotions expressed at the conclusion of Johnson's novel and increases their intensity considerably. The novel centers on the friendship of Irene Redfield and Clare Kendry, two light-skinned mixed-race women who grew apart after childhood and who reunite in adulthood. The opening scene reveals the tension and discomfort explored throughout the novel. Irene, overheated and exhausted on a sweltering summer day in downtown Chicago, seeks cool refreshment at the rooftop restaurant of a restaurant reserved for white people. Her attention is drawn to a beautiful woman who also seems to be scrutinizing her. This woman turns out to be Clare, and the two women navigate the troubled waters of having to perform whiteness in a posh public setting as they reconnect. Though both are passing for white at the restaurant, much of Irene's life is spent in the African American community, including at home with her Black husband and children who suffer incidents of racism. Clare, by contrast, is fully passing for white and has not divulged her mixed-race identity even to her white husband, who is a virulent racist.

Unlike the narrator of *The Autobiography of an Ex-Colored Man* who identifies shame as the sole cause of his decision to pass for white,

Irene's emotions are complex. Before she identifies Clare at the Chicago restaurant, she reveals something of her mindset: "Irene felt, in turn, anger, scorn, and fear slide over her. It wasn't that she was ashamed of being a Negro, or even of having it declared. It was the idea of being ejected [from the restaurant] that disturbed her" (16). The reader doesn't know if she is being honest with herself here as the novel repeatedly reveals her difficulty identifying or expressing her true feelings. Even though she denies shame as the feeling she is experiencing, it is evident that she has repressed a great number of emotions, and shame is likely a significant one. Developing ideas gleaned in Johnson's novel, *Passing* reveals that a segregated society elicits disturbing negative emotional and psychological responses. This problem is identified, but a solution is not posited.

Irene is a prickly protagonist who is difficult to warm up to. She initially rebuffs Clare's attempts to renew their friendship, and when Clare finally breaks through, Irene remains standoffish and unsympathetic. She judges Clare for her decision to pass as white, yet she occasionally does the same thing, as she did in the restaurant. As if to press her on this hypocrisy, Clare invites Irene and Gertrude – another old friend who also occasionally passes for white – to her house. Their conversation is initially contentious: Clare and Gertrude express concerns about giving birth to children whose mixed-race heritage is clear in their features, claiming "nobody wants a dark child" (36) as though stating a universal fact rather than racist conditioning. Irene remains tight-lipped during this conversation, likely thinking of her own dark sons at home. The conversation takes a most uncomfortable turn when Clare's husband Jack Bellew enters, referring to his wife as "Nig," a nickname he has given her because, as he explains, "she's gettin' darker and darker. I tell her if she don't look out, she'll wake up one of these days and find she's turned into a nigger" (39). Irene's response to this outrageousness is to laugh so hard and for such a long time that her throat and sides hurt. There is clearly no mirth in this laughter, only anxiety. When she calms down, she coolly asks him to articulate his position on Black people. "I hate them. And so does Nig," he declares (40). Clare smiles through the encounter while Irene can barely contain her urge to blurt out the truth about the mixed-race identity of all three women in the room.

Clare's cool resolve and Irene's seething rage partly explain the rift that develops between the two friends, for both can suppress their feelings, but Clare is so good at it that Irene does not know what her true emotions are. The figurative masks these women wear while passing are not just social conventions but represent a damaging psychological condition in which the concept of a true self is evasive. Unable to know herself, Irene finds it impossible to know others, even her husband; at one point she thinks,

"It was as if he had stepped out beyond her reach into some section, strange and walled, where she could not get at him" and she describes his expression as "unfathomable" (86). Feeling ever more distant from him, she imagines that he and Clare are having an affair, or at the very least that he desires Clare. As Clare returns covertly to the African American community, Irene believes that her friend is usurping her social position while exercising her freedom and flaunting her undeniable beauty at dances and social functions. Irene feels the same inability to interpret Clare that she felt with her husband as Clare's beautiful face appears "Unaltered and undisturbed by any emotion within or without" and Irene's reaction is strong: "Rage boiled up in her" (93). She wants to be rid of Clare and believes all she has to do is to tell Bellew the truth of his wife's heritage. This realization causes a moral crisis:

> She was caught between two allegiances, different, yet the same. Herself. Her race. Race! The thing that bound and suffocated her ... Irene Redfield wished, for the first time in her life, that she had not been born a Negro. For the first time she suffered and rebelled because she was unable to disregard the burden of race. (98)

Clare, in short, has made Irene aware of the complexity of African American identity at a moment in history when Black culture was being denigrated openly on the one hand and celebrated in the service of racial pride on the other. In addition to depressing Irene – a condition described as "dull, indefinite misery" (85) – this situation demonstrates how pressure to pass in order to access the Dream menaces friendships between Black individuals and threatens to destroy notions of Black community.

Irene frequently describes Clare's passing as dangerous rather than daring or liberatory behavior, and she is correct. Clare's racist husband ultimately discovers that his wife has been socializing in Harlem society and confronts her at a party. This confrontation results in Clare's death after she plummets from a sixth-story window. The novel is deliberately ambiguous about what happens at the fateful moment: either Bellew pushes Clare, Irene pushes Clare, or Clare jumps. Irene is in shock and has no clear memory of the crucial incident, but the text implicates her. The novel's last words, spoken by an investigator on the scene, are, "Death by misadventure, I'm inclined to believe. Let's go up and have another look at that window" (112). This seemingly innocuous procedural comment recalls a moment in the text when Irene is coming to terms with the widening gulf between her and her husband: "his gaze was on her, but in it there was some quality that made her feel that at that moment she was no more to him than a pane of glass through which he stared" (88). In other words, she is a window, which the investigator believes is key to figuring out the mystery of Clare's death. Whether or not the reader accepts this interpretation as evidence of Irene's guilt does not finally matter to Clare, who dies for nothing more than attempting to explore and express her true identity after initially forsaking it to achieve the Dream. Whether or not Irene was directly responsible, she can clearly feel no triumph, catharsis, or even relief at her friend's death, only the shocking numbness of realizing the deep injustice of a society that values status over friendship. In some ways, her survival is worse than Clare's death as she descends into a psychological hell from which she can never escape.

Philip Roth's *American Pastoral* (1997) is one post-1950s example of the persistence of the narrative in which the Dream produces misery even when it appears to have been achieved. Social class is a major concern in Roth's novels throughout his long career, beginning with *Goodbye, Columbus* (1959), published around the same time as *Rabbit, Run*. That debut novel is the story of a Jewish lower-middle-class striver who is both drawn to and repelled by the wealthy Jews who have fled humble Newark for the air-conditioned comfort of the suburbs. In *American Pastoral* we see a similar dynamic half a century after the establishment of the American Dream template, yet in this case Roth peers under the surface of the life of one of those wealthy suburbanites rather than viewing him from the point of view of a contemptuous outsider.

Roth utilizes his novelistic alter-ego, the first-person narrator Nathan Zuckerman, to scrutinize the success story of Seymour "the Swede" Levov. This technique of examining the successful subject indirectly parallels the journalist who outlines Lapham's life and Nick Carraway's portrait of Gatsby. Like Rabbit Angstrom, the Swede is a hometown sports hero who is mythologized and raised to the level of "a god" (5). The Swede is so nicknamed because he is blue-eyed and fair-skinned, in contrast with the majority of Newark Jews; Nathan calls him "as close to a goy as we were going to get" (10). His athletic prowess positions him to succeed in the world of Gentiles instead of the usual path to success for this community, "advanced degrees" (3). In keeping with the pattern of the American Dream, the Swede's parents rose from poverty; his mother was "a tidy housekeeper" and his father Lou was "one of those slum-reared Jewish fathers whose rough-hewn, undereducated perspective goaded a whole generation of striving, college-educated Jewish sons" (10–11). He made the family fortune moving up from "wet, smelly, crushing work" in a leather tannery (11) to eventually owning a glove factory that struggled until a chance conversation between Lou and a major department store owner about Swede's athletic prowess caused the company to skyrocket. The Swede's sports achievements thus propelled the family business, and he goes on to become a Marine, to be recruited to a minor league baseball team, to reject that prospect in order to run the family business, and to marry an Irish Catholic beauty who won the Miss New Jersey pageant. As Nathan summarizes, referring to the attainment of the American Dream from the perspective of underprivileged, urban, Jewish kids, "He'd done it" (15).

Like Nathan, readers are conditioned to see the Swede as an unmitigated success story, but outside of Alger, American Dream novels are bent on disillusionment. In his sixties, the Swede contacts Nathan to help him write a posthumous tribute to his father, and Nathan – a prominent writer – briefly considers this unusual request, but later realizes it was a ruse. He finds out a few weeks after the meeting that the Swede had been terminally ill and concerned with his own legacy more than his father's. At the time of the encounter, though, Nathan still has his boyish visions of the triumph of "this regal Swede" (34) and cannot see beneath the surface of his flawless exterior. He realizes, "You fight your superficiality, your shallowness, so as to try to come at people without unreal expectations ... and yet you never fail to get them wrong" (35). He elaborates on this idea, the essential theme of the book which also applies to the American Dream: "The fact remains that getting people right is not what living is all about anyway. It's getting them wrong that is living, getting them wrong and wrong and wrong and then, on careful reconsideration, getting them wrong again. That's how we know we're alive: we're wrong" (35). Nathan emphasizes the Swede's innocence as an essential facet of his character, but the loss of his own innocence (when he is a nearly elderly man) is part of what the narrative is about. Anyone who believes in the American Dream is childishly naïve because they desperately crave the simplicity and optimistic triumph of the narrative. Nathan needs his hometown hero to have "done it," to have effortlessly succeeded in a Protestant world that strove to keep out the urban Jews who worked hard to achieve what had been dangled as a possibility. To have this happen, his hero cannot have suffered; in addition to being good-looking, rich, and accomplished, he must be happy: "Happy people exist too," he tells himself. "Why shouldn't they?" (30). At Nathan's forty-fifth high school class reunion, when the Swede's brother Jerry tells him how deeply miserable this success story's life had been, Nathan embarks on a quest to learn all about the Swede's life, and then to tell his true story.

The source of the Swede's misery is his daughter, Meredith (ironically called Merry) who Jerry succinctly describes as "the family monster" (68). One cornerstone of the Dream narrative is childrearing, and the Swede brags lightly about his three sons during his meeting with Nathan, but he never mentions Merry. Jerry identifies her as "the Rimrock Bomber" (68), an infamous radicalized activist who detonated a bomb in her hometown to protest American involvement in Vietnam, killing a beloved small-town doctor. Jerry attributes all the Swede's misery to Merry, arguing that his brother was a victim, a "liberal sweetheart of a father" who had a "perfect life" and who was "so in love with his own good luck" that his own daughter and her friends "hated him for it" (69). Afflicted with a severe stutter and lacking her parents' good looks, Merry overflows with resentment and anger toward her parents, and Jerry believes this is why she set out to ruin their lives. Nathan's quest is to fill in the outlines of this story through a combination of research and narrative license.

Merry's stutter seems to be a root cause of her misery, but the Swede believes the stutter must have been caused by something else, yet he struggles to pinpoint it. She was wretched even as a newborn, screaming constantly for years, long after it could be explained by colic. A psychiatrist suggests that Merry's affliction arose when she realized she was not born with the same grace, charm, or good looks as her parents, that her feelings of rejection or inferiority created an unconscious barrier that the stutter represented. The Swede can't accept this explanation, or any other that would implicate him. He identifies other incidents that might have led to his daughter's radicalization, such as the time when she was eleven and asked him to kiss her like he kissed his wife. Shocked in the moment, he scolds her and unconsciously imitates her stutter. Realizing with horror what he has done, he impulsively succumbs to her request, adding trauma in an attempt to assuage it. Other incidents accumulate as possible explanations for Merry's anger. When a Buddhist monk self-immolates on television to protest the war in Vietnam, Merry is deeply unsettled and attaches her spiritual life to the incident. Nathan reflects, "The fate of those monks back in 1963 appeared to have nothing whatsoever to do with what galvanized into expression, in 1968, a newly hatched vehemence against capitalist America's imperialist involvement in a peasant war of national liberation ... and yet her father spent days and nights trying to convince himself that no other explanation existed, that nothing else sufficiently awful had ever happened to her" (157). The Swede, a prosperous, well-meaning father and husband, did not realize that he could be perceived as an oppressor. His loss of innocence is thus connected to his country's loss of innocence in the Sixties when the victory culture narrative was questioned and disintegrated. Nathan realizes this connection and observes of the Swede, "He is our Kennedy" (83).

As with Kennedy's assassination, the search for possible explanations is endless. The Swede's life is undeniably ruined by his daughter's actions, but who's to blame? Who or what caused Merry to murder an innocent bystander in a misguided attempt to protest the war? There are no easy answers, and yet the strain on the Swede and his family is enormous. He tries to continue on his path: "nothing to be done but respectably carry on the huge pretense of living as himself, with all the shame of masquerading as the ideal man" (174). Meanwhile, his wife Dawn becomes hospitalized for suicidal depression, and he has the added burden of trying to make her whole again. She blames him for setting her up for a fall; she tells him, "You had to make me into a *princess*!" (178), but just as it's not the Swede's fault for excelling at a capitalist game he did not invent, we also learn that the culture as a whole created in Dawn an unrealistic set of expectations about her worth by allowing competitive beauty contests to be a viable path to success. Money, attractiveness, athletic prowess – all the superficial measures by which Americans judge one another – are false gods that are supposed to lead to happiness, the elusive goal that cannot be achieved through a panacea.

Following her depression after the tragic crime that destroys her family, Dawn continues to chase beauty and eternal youth vis-à-vis a facelift and follows it up by cultivating the standard cornerstone of the Dream: building a new house (while declaring her hatred of their old stone house). Swede can't believe she rejected the stone house as he had associated it with happiness from a young age: "At school he'd find himself thinking about which girl in each of his classes to marry and take to live with him in that house" (190). For a time, before Merry's birth, the pursuit of happiness is achieved through the most conventional means. Though Dawn feels they are outsiders to waspy Protestant New Jersey exurbs, the Swede sees no barriers to his success; he declares, "We don't *have* to live like everybody else – we can live any way we want to now. We did it. Nobody stopped us" (308). He reiterates and deepens his sentiment which is strong after buying his dream house: "Why shouldn't I be where I want to be? Why shouldn't I be with *who* I want to be? Isn't that what this country's all about? ... We own a piece of America, Dawn. I couldn't be happier if I tried" (315). As with Gatsby or Lapham, the love of a house almost supersedes the love of anyone to share it with. He compares Dawn's hatred of it to "an infidelity – all these years she had been unfaithful to the house" (193). Both he and Dawn later engage in actual infidelity, and his ex-lover Sheila utters an aphorism that haunts him: "We all have homes. That's where everything always goes wrong" (378). The Swede's attention to surfaces and to material things is largely what sets him up for a fall.

His brother Jerry puts a finer point on it when critiquing his relationship to Merry: "As a thing – you loved her as a fucking thing. The way you love your wife" (274). This critique comes at a vulnerable moment after the Swede reconnects with Merry years after the bombing and finds her profoundly altered. She has become a Jain – a member of a

Hindu sect committed to nonviolence to an extreme degree – and she has lost considerable weight, is missing a tooth, and has overcome her stutter. She lives in an abandoned building in now-blighted Newark and confesses to the Swede that she killed three additional people in bombings during her revolutionary phase. She also confesses that she was sexually assaulted after she left home, and Swede's sense of his inadequacy as a father is triggered: "All of that protection and he could not prevent her from getting raped" (267). He turns to Jerry for comfort, but his brother instead excoriates him, not differently from the way Merry had during their unpleasant reunion. "How strongly you still crave the idea," she tells him, "of your innocent offspring" (248). Jerry piles on: "You have a false image of *everything*" (276). Unable to take anymore, the Swede breaks down and cries, "Everything is horrible!" to which his brother triumphantly declares, "*Now* you're getting it. Right! My brother is developing the beginning of a point of view. A point of view of his own instead of everybody else's point of view" (278). Because of the Swede's innocence, his belief in the essential goodness of his country, and of his own right to move up through its ranks, he must be brought low after achieving the Dream, or so the narrative indicates. The violent ruptures in the nation represented by Kennedy's assassination, violent protests over the Vietnam War, and race riots (notably the 1967 riot that decimated Newark, the city in which the Levov family fortune was built) are paralleled by Merry's persistent attacks on her family, her attacks on her government that result in the deaths of anonymous bystanders, and the attacks on Merry by faceless rapists. Swede had always believed strongly in America: "he lived in America the way he lived inside his own skin. All the pleasures of his younger years were American pleasures, all that success and happiness had been American" (213). After the relentless, decade-long violence stretching from Kennedy's assassination to his daughter's revolution-inspired murder, he must confront the truth of what his brother boldly declares: "This country is *frightening*" (276). The "pastoral" of the title refers to an American Eden that exists only in its mythology; the three sections of the novel are "Paradise Remembered," "The Fall," and "Paradise Lost." Like the biblical story, the Fall is from innocence into experience and also from ignorance into understanding. The forces of chaos in America are too strong to be contained, managed, or ignored, contrary to what the Dream promises. The revelation of this message is threefold: Nathan must be disillusioned about his imagined version of the Swede's perfect life, the Swede must lose his belief in the Dream to the point that he declares "everything is *horrible*," and the reader must reckon with what Jerry deems the "real American crazy shit" (277) explored in a novel that misleads us in its title into expecting a pastoral tale.

Save *Ragged Dick*, novels that showcase those who achieve the Dream run from bleak to *relentlessly* bleak. It is as if American novelists want to impress upon readers how dangerous the Dream actually is. In ancient Greece, tragedy was precipitated by a hero's fatal flaw, which often amounted to a refusal to accept reality. In the American novel tradition, the fatal flaw is built into the culture at large. Individuals follow the Dream unconsciously, and the results in the above novels are tragic, almost always resulting in death or destroyed lives (and only in the mildest version a destroyed house and ruined business). In ways that are unsubtle or even graphic and brutal, American novelists over time have had one thing to say to their readers about the Dream: *wake up*.

Further Reading

Chabon, Michael. *The Amazing Adventures of Kavalier and Clay* (2000)
Cheever, John. *Oh What a Paradise It Seems* (1982)
Dreiser, Theodore. *An American Tragedy* (1923)
Dubus, Andre (III). *House of Sand and Fog* (1999)
Franzen, Jonathan. *The Corrections* (2001)
Lewis, Sinclair. *Babbitt* (1922)
Mailer, Norman. *An American Dream* (1965)
Oates, Joyce Carol. *We Were the Mulvaneys* (1996)
Thompson, Hunter S. *Fear and Loathing in Las Vegas* (1972)

3 Domestic Discontentment
The Marriage Plot Anti-Dream

Chapter 2 reveals the American Dream to be destructive to the upwardly mobile middle class and Chapter 5 exposes it as a fantasy unavailable to the working class. The majority of American Dream narratives analyzed in those chapters focus especially on male protagonists. Throughout much of the history of the American novel, women's roles were strictly prescribed. The novel tradition first reflected and later pushed hard against the tripartite domestic role American women were expected to fulfill: wife, mother, and homemaker. The institution of marriage has long been considered the bedrock of a stable American society, yet it doesn't take much scrutiny to realize that the opportunities for freedom and prosperity posited by the American Dream have traditionally been available to men with women playing a supporting role. This stabilizing force from the point of view of society can be interpreted as a severely limiting force when viewed through the historical experiences of women.

As the American novel tradition was gaining its footing in the mid-nineteenth century, one of its most celebrated authors, Nathaniel Hawthorne, lamented the rise of his female contemporaries in a letter to a friend: "America is now wholly given over to a damned mob of scribbling women" (75). This infamous statement set the stage for a long, unfortunate history of vitriol or neglect as male American critics and novelists denigrated or ignored the achievements of their female colleagues as an extension of the broad dismissal of the efforts and accomplishments of women within the domestic sphere. In the early decades of the tradition, the male critical establishment assumed that female-authored novels were meant to entertain, lightly divert, but mostly validate the position of women in the domestic sphere as the moral center of the primary unit of social stability, the family. The waves of feminism that reshaped the shoreline of American history and culture starting in the late nineteenth century also eroded the assumptions about how women's lives were reflected in American novels.

DOI: 10.4324/9781003252863-4

As the twentieth century ushered in new ways of thinking, marriage came under scrutiny as a potentially oppressive institution. The late nineteenth century briefly entertained "the marriage question," or the possibility that women weren't compelled to marry despite enormous societal pressures to do so. It wasn't until the late twentieth century, well after American women gained the right to vote, that true alternatives to marriage – through professional opportunities, sexual liberation, and the overt expression of queer identities – became viable. An important through-line in the history of American novels by and about women involves the way protagonists have responded to the pressures of marriage. In many of these novels, female protagonists are either deprived of female community and suffer as a result or achieve that community and flourish despite the oppressive expectations of traditional domesticity.

Origins: Marriage as Necessary, Evil

From the beginning of the tradition, the mob of scribbling women Hawthorne identified were concerned with the imbalanced power structure embedded in marriage. Susanna Rowson's *Charlotte Temple* (1794) is foundational in this regard. Until *Uncle Tom's Cabin* was published in 1852, *Charlotte Temple* was the bestselling novel in America, spanning over two hundred editions. Students of the British novel's origins will find familiar motifs and tropes in *Charlotte Temple*. Though much shorter than the novels of Samuel Richardson, it strongly echoes his emphasis on a young woman whose virtue is tested by a persistent extramarital seducer. Richardson's *Pamela* (1740) is subtitled "Virtue Rewarded." *Charlotte Temple* could have easily been subtitled "Vice Punished," not only for Charlotte's failure to reject the advances of her seducer Montrafort, but for the evil machinations of her devious acquaintance Mademoiselle La Rue who facilitates the seduction and who later refuses to comfort Charlotte. Indeed, La Rue gets her just deserts in the end and is the subject of the novel's final, unambiguous sentence which constitutes its moral: "vice, however prosperous in the beginning, in the end leads only to misery and shame" (120). What is noteworthy for the purposes of this chapter is that La Rue essentially destroys Charlotte by preventing her from connecting with her family and with female friends. Our unfortunate heroine is carried away from England to America, and it is there that she is isolated and, in the parlance of her times, ruined. The novel argues that family and female companionship are essential to the growth and health of young women, and in their absence, all the opportunities and promises of the New World mean nothing.

In eighteenth-century terms, Mademoiselle La Rue represents the worst qualities a young woman could possess: she is selfish, vain, greedy, and deceitful. Charlotte, though essentially good and well-meaning, is merely weak, and she gradually yields to Montrafort's advances while La Rue orchestrates the affair. It is not only Charlotte's loss of innocence that is meant to trouble the reader, but also her neglect of her family in favor of a love affair; as the narrator says, "Oh my dear girls – for to such only am I writing – listen not to the voice of love, unless sanctioned by paternal approbation: be assured, it is now past the days of romance ... pray for fortitude to resist the impulse of inclination when it runs counter to the precepts of religion and virtue" (29). Such narrative interruptions are consistent enough throughout the novel that it occasionally reads like a conduct manual. Yet it is important to point out that the narrator positions herself as a wise, female mentor to the "girls" who are the explicit audience of the tale. Charlotte did not have such a mentor, and her downfall is due not only to the grim determination of her male seducers (Montrafort and his even more insidious sidekick Balcour) but to the fact that their behavior separates her socially from other women.

It is noteworthy that Montrafort is a British officer during the American Revolution. He carries Charlotte off to America, impregnates her, and abandons her, inviting the reader to consider Charlotte in the context of imperial conquest. The political and historical dimensions of the text are muted, though, compared to the novel's concerns with the threat to the virtue of young women and the need for strong family guidance. After Montrafort leaves her for another woman, Charlotte is less concerned with her societal reputation, her loss of an annual income, or even her child's future than she is with the harm she has done to her parents by running away from home. When Charlotte first yields to Montrafort's seduction, La Rue encourages her to read a letter he has sent, and Charlotte responds, "I am afraid I ought not ... my mother has often told me, I should never read a letter given me by a young man, without first giving it to her" (31). This could be considered maternal protectiveness raised to the level of excessive control, but it demonstrates the importance of the older generation of women guiding the younger generation. As the narrator often directly addresses young women, she also speaks to older ones to remind them of their vital role: "Now, my dear sober matron, (if a sober matron should deign to turn over these pages, before she trusts them to the eye of a darling daughter,) ... I mean no more by what I have here advanced, than to ridicule these romantic girls" (28). Charlotte's sorrowful tale is meant to be cautionary to young women, but also to reinforce the necessity for older women (including mothers) to remain active mentors. The novel intends to remind young women of their *future* role; the narrator also says, "my dear young readers, I would have you read this scene with attention, and reflect that you may yourselves one day be mothers" (54). Fathers also play a part, but a much less direct one. As for young men, they will sin and either repent or move on. "I am a villain," Montrafort realizes, and he feebly attempts to atone, but it is Charlotte who pays a price (69).

Charlotte, locked up in the New World like a fairy-tale princess, realizes too late what might save her; she tells the evil Belcour, "how can I be happy, deserted and forsaken as I am, without a friend of my own sex to whom I can unburthen my full heart" (95). She tries to appeal to Mademoiselle La Rue (now Mrs. Crayton) to fill this role, but this is the wrong path as La Rue's values remain staunchly opposed to the virtues held up by the novel, namely charity, forgiveness, and generosity. In some ways, the intended readers of the novel are envisioned as the type of female friends that Charlotte lacks. The narrator addresses her "young, volatile reader," whom she also calls "dear, cheerful, innocent girl" and begs her to read the tale through to the end as it temporarily seems like Charlotte is being punished while La Rue graduates into wealthy, married contentment: "innocent girl, I must request your patience: I am writing a tale of truth ... my young friends, the tear of compassion shall fall for the fate of Charlotte, while the name of La Rue shall be detested and despised" (98-9). Although Charlotte does not manage to find a supportive female community in the narrative, Rowson posits that a community of female readers has formed in its place. These moments of authorial direct address create a space in which the world of the novel and the world of the reader blend.

Charlotte's principal shortcoming from the novel's ethical perspective is disobedience toward her parents, but it is significant that she also disobeys society, specifically flouting its most stable convention: marriage. Charlotte is "ruined" for having premarital sex, and what might be considered rebellious behavior is, in the context of eighteenth-century mores, a sin, even one punishable by death in terms of narrative outcomes. As Cathy Davidson points out in her introduction to the novel, "female sexual pleasure is simply not at issue in the text" (xvii). It would be a long time after 1794 before women novelists could begin to explore sex as a liberatory act. Rowson, consciously or not, had identified an enduring topic in the female American novel tradition, namely that the institution of marriage itself is antagonistic. Indeed, at the very conclusion of her historical novel *Hope Leslie* (1827) whose main concerns involve the intersection of Native American and Puritan cultures in New England, Catharine Maria Sedgwick includes a direct admonition to her readers about marriage:

> [Hope's] hand was often and eagerly sought, but she appears never to have felt a second engrossing attachment ... She illustrated a truth, which, if more generally received by her sex, might save a vast deal of misery: that marriage is not *essential* to the contentment, the dignity, or the happiness of woman. Indeed, those who saw on how wide a sphere her kindness shone, how many were made better and happier by her disinterested devotion, might have rejoiced that she did not 'Give to a party what was meant for mankind.' (350)

This message is reiterated in other nineteenth-century texts consistently enough to constitute an ongoing debate for a readership conditioned by early American society to believe just the opposite, i.e. that marriage is a condition that is natural, normal, expected, and necessary for a stable society. Sedgwick's message encourages the female reader to consider alternatives. Even defending one's right to say no to a marriage proposal as Jo March originally does in Louisa May Alcott's *Little Women* (1868) is potentially empowering (even though Jo eventually marries) because it gives the protagonist agency and some degree of control over her destiny.

The Early Twentieth Century: Awakenings

By the turn of the twentieth century, when the related temperance and suffragist movements were gaining steam, American women novelists illustrated resistance to the conventions of marriage in starker terms. The enduring, lengthy short story "The Yellow Wallpaper" (1892) by Charlotte Perkins Gilman demonstrates how fiction could be used to critique the institution, depicting the naïve narrator as a victim of her husband's extreme control as he commits her to an asylum-like room and isolates her rather than allowing her to exercise her creativity or to connect with a community of women. One enduring novel that illustrates a sustained critique of marriage and also begins to address the topic of female sexual desire and pleasure is Kate Chopin's *The Awakening* (1899). Its protagonist, Edna Pontellier, is a discontented socialite in wealthy *fin-de-siecle* New Orleans. She has adopted the familiar roles of wife and mother, but neither gives her any satisfaction. Her rebellion takes the form of an internal struggle that makes her seem moody or possibly mentally ill on the surface, but Edna's real transformations and changes take place beneath the surface, in difficult to articulate passions and transformations of mind.

Her husband Léonce is a dull, controlling man, much like Edna's father. He is more passionate about making money and keeping up societal appearances than he is about Edna. When he notices that she has a mild sunburn, he declares, "'You are burnt beyond recognition,' he added, looking at his wife as one looks at a valuable piece of personal property which has suffered some damage" (31). They have little in common and virtually all their conversations involve his scolding her for her inadequacies as mother and housekeeper. The narrator concurs with this assessment but doesn't regard it as a flaw: "In short, Mrs. Pontellier was not a mother-woman" (37). This character trait puts her decidedly at odds with the other women in Grand Isle. Due to the social mores of her milieu, Edna can't initially identify the cause of her spiritual malaise: "An indescribable oppression, which seemed to generate in some unfamiliar part of her consciousness, filled her whole being with a vague anguish" (35). The "awakening" of the title is a gradual realization of what this anguish is, but she is never able to express it adequately. She initially comes at it through similes: "It was like a shadow, like a mist passing across her soul's summer day" (35).

Seeking freedom, she pursues two outlets: sexual freedom with a would-be lover Robert LeBrun and artistic freedom through sketching. Robert is flirtatious with married women, and at first, Edna considers him a friend, but her passion for him grows, swelling into something like an obsession that causes her to lose control over her behavior. She understands this change, especially since she's experienced it before: "she recognized anew the symptoms of infatuation which she had felt incipiently as a child, as a girl in her earliest teens, and later as a young woman" (75). The repetition of this behavior pattern would seem to indicate a failure to grow up, but Edna's plight is much more complex, psychologically. Something lodges in her unconscious that presents as a radically private self: "She had all her life long been accustomed to harbor thoughts and emotions which never voiced themselves. They had never taken the form of struggles. They belonged to her and were her own, and she entertained the conviction that she had a right to them and that they concerned no one but herself" (77). This would be a fair assessment if it were fully true, but there is struggle throughout Edna's narrative, and these unvoiced thoughts and emotions are most likely caused by repression. The voices in her head torment her one night and we witness her tear apart a handkerchief, stomp her wedding ring into the carpet, and smash a vase.

Despite the symbolism of her attempt to destroy her wedding ring, her malaise can only partially be attributed to a passionless marriage. She thinks she might be better off if she didn't experience either "anguish" or "the taste of life's delirium" (86). She is prone to highs and lows, in other words, and following certain moments of extreme passion she shuts down and goes through her motions mechanically. Léonce is so troubled by her mental state that he consults a doctor who studies her but does not see cause for concern. The reader is given access to her more morose thoughts, though: "There were days when she was unhappy, she did not know why, – when it did not seem worth while to be glad or sorry, to be alive or dead; when life appeared to her like a grotesque pandemonium and humanity like worms struggling blindly toward inevitable annihilation" (88). Her mental state is related to her stifling marriage and conformist society, but there is something personal and existential about it, too. Her art does not relieve her as much as a sympathetic reader might hope, partly because it is not valued by others and partly because she cannot produce it when her mood is low. Her confidante Mademoiselle Reisz, who plays piano passionately enough to move Edna to tears, tells her what is holding her back: "the artist must possess the courageous soul" (94).

Her transformation in this regard happens one night when she insists on swimming after dinner, further out than others wish she would: "She wanted to swim far out, where no woman had swum before" (57). Her soul is invoked in this crucial passage as it had been in her conversation with Mademoiselle Reisz, but courage is replaced by two words with slightly different connotations: "She grew daring and reckless" (57). What could be courage shades into desperation: "As she swam she seemed to be reaching out for the unlimited in which to lose herself ... A quick vision of death smote her soul, and for a second of time appalled and enfeebled her senses" (57). The imagery-rich scene encapsulates Edna's plight. She strives for independence and unique experiences, but she also feels untethered and confused when she has them. Perhaps this is what her friend means by courage.

When Robert suddenly leaves on an impulsive journey to Mexico, her obsession for him grows stronger, even more so after he fails to communicate with her. She succumbs slightly to the advances of a known rogue named Alcée Arobin and even yields to a mild attraction for Robert's brother Victor, but it is Robert for whom she truly longs. When he returns, they finally confess their love for one another, but only after Edna makes the first move. Robert admits that he never expressed his passion because she was already married and she scoffs, "I am no longer one of Mr. Pontellier's possessions to dispose of or not. I give myself where I choose. If he were to say, 'Here, Robert, take her and be happy: she is yours,' I should laugh at you both" (139). This confident expression of autonomy, which follows her decision to move out of Léonce's house, would seem a triumph if her fate were happier. When Robert says goodbye forever because he does not want to be a "cur"

(139) for falling in love with a married woman, she gives in to the seductive power of the sea which provided her with a brief feeling of independence as well as a vision of death that "smote her soul." Her final journey into the ocean is more surrender than journey. What is awakened in Edna is a frustrating desire, a yearning for a self that cannot be because it isn't allowed. Léonce, Robert, and Alcee all have freedom – the freedom of mobility, the freedom to live adventurous, independent lives without being judged, the freedom not to be regarded as anyone else's possession. If the only way Edna can achieve this freedom is through suicide, the novel indicates a social condition that is unsustainable. It would seem better never to have been awakened at all, but that interpretation strongly suggests that American women (who still did not even have the right to vote in political elections in Chopin's time, amongst many other deprivations) cannot achieve full humanity without a social revolution.

Edith Wharton's *The Age of Innocence* (1920), the first novel by an American woman to win the Pulitzer Prize in fiction, also critiques the institution of marriage among the monied classes. Wharton's novel is more satirical than Chopin's, and the authors' styles reveal their different aims while highlighting the development of modernist thinking and artistic techniques. *The Awakening* is largely about Edna's complex psychology, indicated by halting, incomplete thoughts and abbreviated chapters that suggest important gaps. Wharton's novel achieves its satirical effect by remaining distant from its characters, training its gaze on its subject much the same way its characters scrutinize each other through opera glasses in the masterful opening scene for the purpose of commenting on how the subtleties of their milieu's behavior deviate from expectations. Wharton further achieves her effect by setting the narrative back in time: though published in 1920, she is skewering New York's upper crust as it existed in the late nineteenth century, with the novel's title ironically commenting on this era.

Yet another remove that allows Wharton to satirize the way marriage affects American women is by seemingly placing a man – the cleverly named Newland Archer – at the center of the narrative. Archer is presented as a foolish romantic as he observes the opera box initially occupied by his betrothed May Welland who sits clad all in white with white flowers all around her, "with eyes ecstatically fixed on the stage lovers" as the opera reaches its crescendo (5). He translates this scene grotesquely to amplify his vanity – "he contemplated her absorbed young face with a thrill of possessorship in which pride in his own masculine initiation was mingled with a tender reverence of her abysmal purity" – and fantasizes about reading *Faust* to her on their honeymoon, "confusing the scene ... with the masterpieces of literature which it would be his manly privilege to reveal to his bride" (6). Chopin clearly wants the reader to dismiss Léonce Pontellier as a materialistic boor not deserving of our attention, but Wharton tricks us into sympathizing with Archer by making him the focal character while still revealing in passages like this one that he is essentially cut from similar cloth as Léonce.

Newland is caught in a familiar conundrum: he is passionately in love with one woman but fated to wed another. Wharton renders nineteenth-century New York society as a place that lives by strict, unspoken codes, and Newland is trapped by the need to keep up social appearances while burying what needs to be expressed. When May's cousin, Countess Ellen Olenska, returns from Europe after a failed marriage, Newland is initially smitten and eventually obsessed with her. While Newland sees May as the picture of cherubic innocence, Ellen exudes Old World sophistication and experience. She is a bohemian outsider to provincial New York whose sense of decorum takes a back seat to her passion for art and meaningful conversation. At first, Newland is intimidated by this "bold, brown" (27) alternative to his blonde, virginal bride-to-be and he retreats from her flirtation: "he thanked heaven that he was a New Yorker and about to ally himself with one of his own kind" (28). This feeling doesn't last, though, as he increasingly finds May dull and superficial and is drawn to Ellen's deeper currents. He has internalized the pressures of "his own kind," including his mother:

> There was no better match in New York than May Welland, look at the question from whatever point you chose. Of course such a marriage was only what Newland was entitled to; but young men are so foolish and incalculable – and some women so ensnaring and unscrupulous – that it was nothing short of a miracle to see one's only son safe past the Siren Isle and in the haven of a blameless domesticity. (32)

The word "blameless" is important: once one has been safely ensconced in marriage, it is thought, one can no longer be blamed for whatever is eroding society.

The problem with Newland's attraction to Ellen is not only that he is betrothed, but that she is still married to Count Olenski. Even if she were to obtain the divorce she seeks, she's still viewed by New York society as a taboo match for Newland and as a free radical who will throw off the equilibrium of the public sphere. There are two evident sins one can commit in this book: financial ruin or a failed marriage. Ellen is tainted by both as it seems her divorce – which Newland tries to help facilitate in his capacity as a lawyer – is being held up by the Count's unwillingness to leave money to Ellen, though there are inevitable rumors that she had an affair. As her own mother puts it, "her life is finished" (133). Newland passionately defends her: "I'm sick of the hypocrisy that would bury alive a woman of her age if her husband prefers to live with harlots ... Women ought to be free – as free as we are" (36). It is here that the novel's critique becomes most pointed, for Newland knows he's expressing an impossible dream rather than upholding the American Dream.

Newland's vision is distorted because of his romantic sensibility, and he fails to see both May and Ellen in realistic terms. He projects onto May an ideal of naïve innocence. He reflects on his outburst about equality: "'Nice' women, however wronged, would never claim the kind of freedom he meant, and generous-minded men like himself were therefore – in the heat of the argument – the more chivalrously ready to concede it to them" (38). His belief in chivalry has him both publicly defending Ellen and submitting to an unfulfilling marriage with May, which is his duty: "with a shiver of foreboding he saw his marriage becoming what most of the other marriages about him were: a dull association of material and social interests held together by ignorance on the one side and hypocrisy on the other" (38). This shiver of foreboding is enough to send him recklessly into pursuing his dream of a life with Ellen. One problem is that the whole society is watching and will eventually do whatever it can to send Ellen away and to keep Newland and May together, which is eventually what happens.

The other problem, though, is that Newland underestimates May. Rather than the superficial, pretty ornament he imagines her to be, she is a shrewd observer who is well aware of the fact that the men of her society like Newland don't believe her capable of fulfilling her own needs. While it is true that she doesn't have the freedom that a man has, she does have much more agency than he realizes, and she uses it to squelch Newland's individual desires in favor of the will of the tribe to which they belong. As Newland and Ellen make their feelings for one another clear, May *seems* ignorant of the situation, but she is carefully calculating how to keep Newland so that she doesn't end up ostracized like Ellen. Immediately after their wedding, Archer observes, "May was still, in look and tone, the simple girl of yesterday" (163), but the careful reader will notice that Newland (whose first name connotes an innocent America) is the simple one. His last name is Archer, and yet May is called "Dianalike" (167) and she wins an archery contest that enables her to wear a silver pin depicting an arrow. His belief in chivalry coupled with male freedom prevents him from understanding her complexities and her needs, but she consistently hits her mark, controlling his extramarital lust and quietly demolishing his utopian visions for a life in which he could live with Ellen without simultaneously being shunned.

He surrenders by degrees: "Archer had reverted to all his old inherited ideas about marriage. It was less trouble to conform with the tradition and treat May exactly as all his friends treated their wives than to try to put into practice the theories with which his untrammelled bachelorhood had dallied. There was no use in trying to emancipate a wife who had not the dimmest notion that she was not free" (169). Archer believes that he has come to this conclusion on his own, but May has exercised the full range of her power while keeping Newland innocent, or rather ignorant.

It dawns on Archer that there is more to May than he has previously understood in a fascinating passage in which May's eyes communicate to him a lengthy "mute message" (232) expressing that she knows exactly what he is up to, and that she is silently giving him permission to visit Ellen. This message contradicts his belief that he is exercising his vaunted male freedom. From this moment on Archer becomes more desperate in his romantic plans with Ellen, flailing as he continuously tries to convince her that they belong together despite the impossible circumstances. Ellen insists to him, "We'll look, not at visions, but at realities" (251), and yet he persists until the moment when he can no longer keep up the illusion: "There were certain things that had to be done – and if done at all, done handsomely and thoroughly – and one of these, in the old New York code, was the tribal rally around a kinswoman about to be eliminated from the tribe ... the separation between himself and the partner of his guilt had been achieved, and that now the whole tribe had rallied about his wife on the tacit assumption that nobody knew anything, or had ever imagined anything" (289). Newland was never free after all, and the last time we see May "her blue eyes [are] wet with victory" (297). This is the first time Newland sees her clearly. We are witnessing a world in which marriage continues to deprive women of their freedom, and yet May exercises invisible power despite this structure while Ellen apparently lives a full, rich life in Paris even though she resisted Newland's vision of their sharing a life together. The painful final scene in which he refuses to go see her in Paris after many years of separation clearly indicates his own deep sorrow but obscures the fact that Ellen has been just fine without him, despite the fact that her mother declared her life "over" after her first marriage failed.

Multiple Marriages: The Twentieth Century and Beyond

American women novelists in the twentieth and twenty-first centuries have obviously explored alternatives to marriage. Looking only at a concentrated period in the early 1970s as second-wave feminism took root, we see a proliferation of enduring novels that focused on careers (Joan Didion's 1970 *Play It as It Lays*), same-sex relationships (Rita Mae Brown's 1973 *Rubyfruit Jungle*), or sexual liberation (Erica Jong's 1973 *Fear of Flying*), to name a few. But while the second wave of feminism in the 1960s caused a widespread questioning of marriage's limitations for women, it did not eradicate its importance as a context for novel plots. (Even in the preceding examples, Jong's and Didion's protagonists are married, if not happily). One way to scrutinize the institution of marriage is to examine unhappy ones and to either posit alternatives or to consider what might lead to fulfillment rather than to the despairing ending of Chopin's *The Awakening*.

One significant work in this regard is Mary McCarthy's *The Group* (1963) which, as the title implies, features a collective protagonist in contrast to the nineteenth-century novels whose titles named the protagonist such as Sedgwick's *Hope Leslie*, Fanny Fern's *Ruth Hall*, or Frances Ellen Watkins Harper's *Iola Leroy*. *The Group* identifies eight recent graduates from Vassar, young women making their way into adulthood during the Great Depression and yet preserved from its most brutal effects by varying degrees of class privilege. Though it takes place during the mid-1930s into the early 1940s, the novel reflects the simmering questions of changing women's roles during the early 1960s when it was published, coinciding with Betty Friedan's influential 1963 study *The Feminine Mystique* about the lack of fulfillment afforded by the traditional housewife role. Although it is initially dizzying to keep track of the eight members of "the group" and their various personalities and interests, a pattern emerges over the course of the narrative: these highly educated and talented college graduates have limited workplace opportunities and are expected to marry. This idea surfaces bluntly in Polly's narrative: "There was only one point on which all Polly's acquaintances, odd or not, agreed, and that was that she ought to be married. 'You pretty girl. Why you no marry?' said the iceman, adding his voice to the chorus" (258). She replies that she is waiting for the right man, and in a separate discussion with an acquaintance she describes that man as akin to "the least obvious suspect" in a murder mystery, the one no one would guess. The acquaintance retorts, "You mean ... you will fall in love with a married man. All the other suspects are obvious" (258). This is, in fact, what happens. The prospect of being either an "other woman" or a wife is at odds with the group's mythology which elevates Vassar girls "of perfectly good background who were going into business, anthropology, medicine, not because they had to, but because they knew they had something to contribute to our emerging America" (11). This belief is largely contradicted by what transpires in the novel.

The Group, daring for its time, is rife with detailed descriptions of premarital and extramarital sex, and yet it opens with a wedding as though to establish the norm. Although there is no central protagonist who emerges from the group, Kay's story constitutes a through-line around which the other storylines unfold, and a model of the unhappy marriage to be avoided. The novel opens with Kay's wedding and ends with her funeral, a path from traditional comedy to tragedy. Although the group goes through the motions of celebrating Kay's marriage, it is subtly clear that they disapprove of it partly because they sense that Harald is not good for her. Their sense was correct. Over the course of the novel he has multiple affairs, makes drunken scenes at parties, is fired from his position in a theater under suspect circumstances, forces Kay to work a menial job so he can pursue an artistic career that never materializes, is publicly arrested, and (worst of all) physically abuses Kay, then commits her to an insane asylum. While the surviving members of the group are grieving and trying to figure out whether Kay's fall from a twentieth-story window was an accident or suicide, Harald continues to denigrate her while highlighting his own debased qualities. He's convinced her death was suicide because of "Sheer competitiveness ... For years I've been trying to kill myself, ever since I've known her ... She decided to show me how to do it. *She* could do it better" (374). During this embittered rant he reveals his contempt not only for Kay but for the group, and indeed for all women. It is hard to imagine a more reprehensible character in American literature, but it is noteworthy that the only true power he has derives from the institution of marriage. From the moment they take their vows, Kay is essentially his possession, one that he consumes and discards.

Each member of the group pursues happiness either by accommodating the housewife role or by resisting it. One member, Dottie, chooses the path of extramarital sex with a rogue named Dick Brown whom she meets at Harald and Kay's wedding. She is a virgin when they meet, and he is vastly experienced. The encounter is almost clinical as Dick describes to her the anatomical reasons why she is feeling what she feels, which reminds her of trips to the doctor. After sex, he tosses her a pair of pajamas and says, "Tonight's lesson is concluded" (39). Even though Dick is drunk and obnoxious, Dottie discovers she enjoys sex after the initial pain and manages to achieve orgasm twice. Dick is quite clear about the terms of the affair: he orders her to get birth control and says, "you must promise me you won't fall in love with me" (48). She obediently agrees to both directives because they align with her new-found philosophy: "Sex, Dottie opined, was just a matter of following the man, as in dancing" (46). Despite the sexual pleasure she experiences, she remains tied to convention. She is fearful and anxious as she obtains birth control, wondering about the stigma of requesting it without a wedding ring on her finger. Despite Dick's demand, she does fall in love with him and, realizing he has forbidden it, flees New York and accepts the prospect of a passionless marriage with a different man.

The parameters drawn by Kay's and Dottie's stories – the first two in the book – suggest that the choices available to the group don't allow for both good sex and a good marriage, to say nothing of a fulfilling career. A Vassar woman who is not part of the group, Norine, has an ongoing affair with Harald and confesses the details of it to Helena after Helena discovers them kissing at a party. Norine suggests that her husband cannot have sex with her because they are married and thus he considers her "good." Helena, appalled, tells her to "enlighten him. Tell him what you do with Harald ... That ought to get his pecker up" (139). Helena goes on to harangue Norine about her unwillingness to adhere to her conventional role in other ways, castigating her for not cleaning up their apartment and for naming their dog Nietzsche instead of Rover. Norine, who remains a destroyer of convention and a foil to the group throughout the novel, laughs at this advice and continues to indulge in extramarital sex and domestic disorder.

By 1936, three years after Kay and Harald's wedding, half the group are married. One of the unmarried members of the group, Libby, is eager to elevate her secretarial role to a professional career in publishing. There is obvious attraction between her and her boss, Gus LeRoy, who gives her assignments that she approaches with gusto, but he tells her, "you're not cut out for straight publishing ... let's say you're not hard-boiled enough. You're essentially a sympathizer" (198). It's easy to see the gender bias in this statement, but he puts a finer point on it: "Publishing's a man's business, unless you marry into it. Marry a publisher, Miss MacAusland, and be his hostess" (199). She leaves the company amicably and without acting on their attraction: "She and Gus LeRoy were the best of friends; he was married after all" (201). Libby pivots to another publishing-related job working for a literary agent, but her marriage aspirations end in one of the darkest scenes in the book. She expects her lover Nils to propose one night, but instead he attempts to rape her before dinner. She manages to fend him off and when he learns she's a virgin he declares, "What a bore you are, Elizabeth ... It would not even be amusing to rape you" (222). Libby wonders if Nils might have guessed that she occasionally masturbates and elects to bury that secret along with the painful memory of that night rather than share either detail with the group. Psychoanalysis is a repeated touchstone in the novel as characters tend to analyze themselves and each other in Freudian terms, attempting to sort out confusion and understanding as they trace a continuum between repression and expression.

In addition to the once-taboo subject of sex both inside and outside marriage, *The Group* also takes on discontentment with childbearing and childrearing. Priss is the main character illustrating this topic, particularly her breastfeeding, a practice that was eschewed by the previous generation. Priss's husband is a pediatrician and she frequently senses that he is using her as a case study rather than understanding her needs. He certainly has her on display: even while she is in labor, she is ordered to put on makeup because both her husband and his colleague "thought it was important for a maternity patient to keep herself up to the mark" (224). Breastfeeding is not her decision, and she finds the experience stressful, especially when the nurses criticize her for her initial failings and suggest, to her husband's chagrin, that she switch to bottle feeding. In response to his outrage, "Priss nodded meekly. She seemed to have no mind of her own" (242). He admits that she is an "experiment," and when she asks him to explain the word he replies, "To prove that any woman can nurse" (243). She acquiesces but continues to distrust her intuition and to feel anxiety around other parenting worries such as toilet training. She debates her discontentment with the free-thinking Norine who criticizes the wisdom of the current medical establishment as part of "the age of measurement" (342). This type of thinking resonates with Priss who continues to feel unfulfilled in her role but does not see a way out of it. Norine states, "Our Vassar education made it tough for me to accept my womanly role" which is "to dress well and set a good table" (344). "The trouble is my brains," she concludes, and Priss's silence confirms that it's trouble for her, too, and likely for all of the group.

The only one who escapes the pattern is Lakey who comes out as gay after returning from an extended trip to Europe. The group greets her as she steps off the boat with her lover Maria and she is elegant, prosperous, and younger-looking than the rest of them who arrive with their multiple children and who "think awkwardly of schedules, formula, laundry, diapers" while Lakey unpacks luxurious gifts (369). The group has largely given into convention, and they feel ambivalent about accepting Lakey's sexual orientation; on one hand, "It was astonishing, but within a month some of the girls found themselves talking of 'having Lakey and Maria to dinner,' just as they might speak of a normal couple" (372). Still, their acceptance doesn't come easily: "the group felt, with one accord, that what had happened to Lakey was a tragedy. They tried not to think of what she and Maria did in bed together" (372). This is clearly the cost of their societal repression. When they first realize the nature of the relationship, they say of

Maria, "This woman was her man" (370). They insist on trying to figure out the relationship in heterosexual terms: "Obviously, Maria, in her pajamas and bathrobe, was the man, and Lakey, in her silk-and-lace peignors was the woman, and yet these could be disguises – masquerade costumes" (373). It bothers the group that Lakey's lesbian relationship is inscrutable, but she couldn't care less. She even uses her sexuality to torment the odious Harald by suggesting that Kay might have been a lesbian, too, and he reacts violently, telling her, "You ought to have stayed in Europe, where the lights are going out ... You have no part of America!" (377–8). Here is where the upshot of McCarthy's novel becomes clear: with regard to women's roles, America had become conventional and retrograde by the mid-twentieth century, a further erosion of what Wharton had depicted in *The Age of Innocence*. Someone like Lakey who removes herself from the group (and groupthink) by living abroad can achieve a level of acceptance and satisfaction unavailable to the others.

Marriage's oppressive power is far from the only topic of novels by American women, but it has proven an enduring stumbling block to a full realization of female selfhood. Varying responses might be to escape it, to suffer through it, or to resist it. Zora Neale Hurston's *Their Eyes Were Watching God* (1937) presents an original critique of marriage by having its protagonist Janie marry three times, all for slightly different reasons, and to learn from experience rather than simply accepting common wisdom. The novel's publication history is legendary: harshly reviewed in her lifetime by such male tastemakers of the African American canon as Sterling Brown, Alain Locke, and Richard Wright, Hurston died in obscurity and was rediscovered in the early 1970s thanks in large part to the efforts of Alice Walker. By the 1980s Hurston's novel was not only back in print but was the subject of a wealth of critical attention, and it claimed a lofty place in the canon. Many contexts can be used to frame its concerns as it is a novel that touches on Black identity in the era of segregation, the judicial system, class struggle, and environmental devastation in the form of a hurricane, but in the context of this chapter, it is a valuable text in terms of female agency and empowerment. Janie's stamina and strength indicate that the bad marriages she endures ultimately make her stronger.

In the opening pages, Janie is judged by her community based on her looks: the men desire her, and the women are jealous of her. She is subject to the gossip of her peers no less than Ellen Olenska is in Wharton's novel. The difference is that she realizes what they're saying and doesn't seem to care. Rather than take her cues from society, her adolescent eyes look to nature to understand relationships: "She saw a dust-bearing bee sink into the sanctum of a bloom; the thousand sistercalyxes arch to meet the love embrace and the ecstatic shiver of the tree from root to tiniest branch creaming in every blossom and frothing with delight. So this was a marriage!" (11). The sheer bodily ecstasy of this early revelation will haunt her adult life as she weighs her passionless marriages against this scene.

Her grandmother ("Nanny"), who is both her guide and her parental figure, encourages her to marry Logan Killicks out of "protection" (15) against premarital pregnancy after she sees Janie kissing a boy. Nanny admits that her perspective originates in her tainted past: "Ah was born back due in slavery so it wasn't for me to fulfill my dreams of whut a woman outghta be and to do" (16). Her motives are noble – she wants Janie "to school out and pick from a higher bush and a sweeter berry" (13) – but she is imposing her dream on her granddaughter, a dream that doesn't account for Janie's basic desires. Janie initially believes love will develop after marriage because "Nanny and the old folks had said it, so it must be so" (21). The ethos of this novel is quite different from *Charlotte Temple*, though, in which the protagonist is punished for not obeying the wishes of her elders. Janie realizes that Nanny's advice is misguided, but she is initially trapped: "She knew now that marriage did not make love. Janie's first dream was dead, so she became a woman" (25). There is irony in this final phrase linking womanhood to shattered dreams, but Janie is a strong enough protagonist to overcome it. Logan realizes she's "powerful independent" (30), which is not the quality he was hoping for in a wife. She throws her apron down, picks a bouquet of flowers, and sets off in search of a love-filled marriage with her second suitor, Joe Starks.

If Logan's flaw was indifference to Janie's needs and desires, Joe's flaw is personal ambition achieved by exploiting Janie. An entrepreneur and politician, Joe at first seems to have married Janie so that they can build a prosperous future together, but it becomes clear that he views her as a tool to create his personal success. Once the community has declared him mayor and her "Mrs. Mayor Starks," they ask her to speak, but Joe intervenes: "mah wife don't know nothin' 'bout no speech-makin'. Ah never married her for nothin' lak dat. She's uh woman and her place is in de home" (43). Speech is power in this novel, ranging from gossip to courtroom testimony, so to deprive Janie of her voice is to relegate her to subservience.

Joe initially seems a better match than Logan because he pays attention to Janie, but this attention amounts to excessive control. The men sit around the store that Janie runs telling humorous stories about a mule, but although "Janie loved the conversation ... Joe had forbidden her to indulge" (53). He makes her wear a head-rag because he is jealous of the way other men regard her hair. The marriage becomes antagonistic as Joe repeatedly tells her that women can't think for themselves; she realizes, "He wanted her submission and he'd keep on fighting until he felt he had it" (71). His abuse escalates from verbal to physical, and Janie's response is to withdraw into herself: "She had an inside and an outside now and suddenly she knew how not to mix them" (72). Her resolve does not hold, though: she lectures a group of men who are holding forth about how to oppress their spouses. Joe tells her, "You getting' too moufy, Janie" (75). She gets even more vocal, though, after he insults her looks and her age; she retorts, "Ah reckon Ah looks mah age too. But Ah'm uh woman every inch of me, and Ah know it" (79). She goes on to publicly insult his deteriorating looks and senses a double standard when he reacts sullenly: "Why must Joe be so mad with her for making him look small when he did it to her all the time?" (81). After his health deteriorates rapidly, he dies bitter that he could not fully bend Janie to her will. She, on the other hand, shakes off his years of abuse; looking in a mirror immediately after Joe dies, she thinks, "The young girl was gone, but a handsome woman had taken her place" (87). Since the beginning of the novel, though, a woman's attractiveness makes her a commodity: "She had found a jewel down inside herself and she had wanted to walk where people could see her and gleam it around. But she had been set in the market-place to sell" (90). Believing in her self-worth more than in society's judgment of her worth, she rejects the notion that she needs to remarry after Joe's death.

Her final relationship is the unlikeliest one because she is not expecting it, and because it comes in the person of Tea Cake, a much younger man whom the townspeople consider shiftless and immature. However, it is the most successful one because it is based on her own desires and not on society's expectations. It is not a fairy-tale romance by any means: it includes a healthy dose of mutual jealousy and mistrust as it develops, born partly of Janie's skittishness after her two unfulfilling marriages. Yet Janie and Tea Cake persevere despite societal disapproval because they are working toward a common goal, and because there is an undeniable attraction between them that does not render Janie a commodity. She articulates this idea to her friend Phoeby: "Dis ain't no business proposition, and no race after property and titles. Dis is uh love game. Ah done lived Grandma's way, now Ah means tuh live mine" (114). Her relationship is spiritual as well as pragmatic: watching Tea Cake fall asleep, "Janie looked down on him and felt a self-crushing love. So her soul crawled out from its hiding place" (128). The uniting of her soul with her self gives her the strength to endure Tea Cake's death, and to accept her own mortality. She has to euthanize Tea Cake after he contracts rabies, and she is put on trial for murder. Awaiting the verdict, "It was not death she feared. It was misunderstanding. If they made a verdict that she didn't want Tea Cake and wanted him dead, then that was a real sin and a shame" (188). Much of the Black community turns against her during the trial, but significantly she bonds with the white women who hear the verdict being read: "the white women cried and stood around her like a protecting wall and the Negroes, with heads hung down, shuffled out and away" (188). Though the Black community later makes amends, it is important that women, regardless of race, understand her plight and do not misunderstand her act of killing Tea Cake. The novel's message regarding the complex realities of what constitutes a successful relationship between men and women is a hopeful one, and Janie emerges as a rare figure in the canon of American novels by women: someone who succeeds at "the love game" despite the strict rules designed and enforced by her society. It is also significant that the novel is framed as a story Janie tells her best friend Pheoby: female companionship is essential, and it serves to comfort Janie after Tea Cake dies.

Alice Walker's *The Color Purple* (1982) is strongly influenced by *Their Eyes Were Watching God* and it extends many of Hurston's concerns. Its protagonist and narrator, Celie, is also forced into a loveless marriage – basically sold into it – by her stepfather who also repeatedly raped her when she was a young teen, and her sister Nettie flees home to avoid the same fate. Her husband Albert is an abusive tyrant who clearly will never love Celie, mostly because he pines for his former lover, a hard-living blues singer named Shug Avery. One major departure from Hurston's novel is that Celie does not want to move on to a better marriage with a different man: rather, she wants a relationship with Shug. The development of the possibilities of homoerotic love, glimpsed in McCarthy's *The Group*, is more fully explored here. A good marriage is not what will satisfy Celie. The alternatives presented in the book are lesbian sex, an artistic outlet, a fulfilling vocation, and a supportive female community.

Sex is generally painful or traumatic for Celie because her stepfather repeatedly raped her, resulting in two pregnancies. Albert treats sex as nothing more than a wife's duty; according to Celie, he "clam on top of me, do his business, in ten minutes us both sleep. Only time I feel something stirring down there is when I think bout Shug" (69). The introduction of Shug into the narrative changes Celie's trajectory. Shug enjoys sex with a wide variety of partners, and after she explains to Celie how to achieve sexual pleasure, they also become lovers temporarily. Celie is heartbroken when she realizes the relationship is not permanent, but one of the many lessons the novel frames is the understanding that love cannot involve control or possession. After Shug runs away with a younger man, Celie matures enough to conclude, "Just cause I love her don't take away none of her rights ... Who am I to tell her who to love? My job just to love her good and true myself" (276). Shug's brand of love is not lifelong commitment. Albert and Celie struggle to characterize Shug and Albert's pugnacious daughter-in-law Sofia: "Sofia and Shug not like men, he say, but they not like women either" (276). Because Shug cannot easily be classified by traditional understandings of gender, she unlocks new notions of masculinity and femininity in both Celie and Albert, who end up close friends despite their tumultuous marriage.

The range of acceptable female behavior is tested throughout the book. Sofia is much larger than her husband Harpo, and his attempts to control her physically generally end with her soundly beating him up. Sofia's defiance is something Celie has never witnessed. She approaches her marriage with a meek attitude: "I don't fight, I stay where I'm told. But I'm alive" (22). As the narrative evolves and she sees strong, defiant women like Sofia, Shug, and Harpo's second wife Squeak (who overcomes her diminishing nickname and insists on being called by her real name), she also stands up to Albert. In a climactic scene in which Celie is filled with a strength she's never felt before, she curses him and hurls his insults back at him: "I'm pore, I'm black, I may be ugly and can't cook ... But I'm here" (214). This powerful declaration forges Celie's self, but it also helps transform Albert into someone who ultimately respects and admires her, and he even participates in the traditionally feminine activity of sewing right alongside Celie.

Sewing is the outlet she discovers to fulfill her creative side. What started as a diversion becomes an obsession: "Since us started making pants down home, I ain't been able to stop ... I make so many pants Shug tease me" (218). This is parallel to the way Squeak can't stop singing once she starts, emulating the confident, successful Shug. Celie starts a company that makes pants for men and women alike, deepening the novel's interests in androgyny. "Men and women not suppose to wear the same thing," Albert declares, "Men spose to wear the pants" (278), ironically alluding to a cliché about male marital control. Celie takes this opportunity to teach him about clothing choices in Africa, which she has learned about in letters from Nettie, who has discovered her vocation as a missionary (and who is happily married). Celie's own art – which also becomes a successful business – is another way out of the trap of gender binary thinking.

The narrative develops the theme of support among women, radiating out from Celie's deep relationship with Shug, her mentor and guide as well as her sometime lover. The subplots of Sofia, Squeak, and Nettie contribute to Celie's ultimate comfort in her mature self, and they are all stories of overcoming various obstacles. Nettie and Celie reunite after years apart, and their long separation does not diminish the bond between them, the essential support that women offer one another even when absent. The novel is epistolary: the letters Nettie writes to Celie are intercepted by Albert and the letters Celie writes to Nettie are returned as undeliverable as Nettie traverses the globe, but they continue to write to one another nonetheless, relying on the spirit of female support to get them through the traumas they face.

Despite the prevalence of heterosexual marriage as a troublesome topic in novels by American women over time, there are many branches of the tradition that do not deal with it at all. Coming-of-age novels like Harper Lee's *To Kill a Mockingbird* (1960), Toni Morrison's *The Bluest Eye* (1970), or Brown's *Rubyfruit Jungle* are substantial contributions to the tradition that focus on various dimensions of girlhood that do not indicate a trajectory into marriage. The tradition of lesbian novels including Gertrude Stein's genre-bending *The Autobiography of Alice B. Toklas* (1933), Patricia Highsmith's *The Price of Salt* (1952), or Leslie Feinberg's *Stone Butch Blues* (1993) explores various dimensions of lesbian or nonbinary experience not typically reflected in the mainstream of literary fiction by American women. A focus in women's novels on work or even just survival can be traced through novelists like Willa Cather and Ann Petry. Novels that emphasize family relationships or female friendship are evident in works by Gloria Naylor or Amy Tan, to give just a couple of examples. Space constraints prevent a deep consideration of any of these important traditions here, and many others have also evolved and developed in such a way to continue to challenge the centrality of the marriage plot. My intent is not to suggest that all American novels by women are concerned with marriage. Over more than two centuries of the tradition, though, the topics of marriage and motherhood have been an enduring corrective to the male-oriented Dream script.

One dimension of female experience that has less frequently been explored in novels until recently is aging. The novel at the beginning of the tradition, *Charlotte Temple*, set a precedent for stories about the perils faced by young women and was intended as a lesson for that demographic. Recent works like *Olive Kitteridge* (2008) by Elizabeth Strout (as well as its sequel *Olive, Again* [2019]) consider the way old age presents a new set of concerns and narrative possibilities. In the context of this chapter, the twice-widowed Olive is a study in how to find meaning when marriages end and when motherhood fails to fulfill.

Olive Kitteridge, which won the Pulitzer Prize for fiction, is structured as a series of interrelated short stories like the novels by Julia Alvarez and Jennifer Egan discussed in Chapters 6 and 7, respectively. This structure enables the freedom to concentrate on essential episodes that determine plot and character development in a nonlinear way. The titular Olive might be the protagonist of one chapter, the antagonist of another, and sometimes she just passes through the narrative in a kind of cameo. She is a memorably arch character, a no-nonsense Yankee schoolteacher from Maine who was never afraid to tell anyone what she thought of their behavior. Her tough exterior is her protection from the world, but it is consistent, so much so that when her husband Henry hears her expressing "dismay" in a phone conversation with a woman whose husband was just killed in a hunting accident, he is surprised that "all her outer Olive-ness seemed stripped away" (18). Most of what constitutes "Olive-ness" is a gruff, judgmental, pragmatic personality that would seem to make her unlovable, and in fact we see Henry longing for another woman early in their marriage and her son Christopher wanting to get as far from her as possible. Marriage and motherhood are not fulfilling for her, either, as much of the time Olive seems joyless and possibly depressed.

Indeed, after her own son's wedding Olive steals away to a room to be by herself and reflects on the day, including when the bride's mother had asked if she cried at weddings and Olive replied, "I don't see any reason to cry" (67). This toughness masks her true feelings, though, both in terms of the loss of her son's presence – "they'd gotten pretty used to him" (66) – and the occasional lack of fulfillment in her marriage. She thinks about the newlyweds: "Of course, right now their sex life is probably very exciting, and they undoubtedly think that will last, the way new couples do. They think they're finished with loneliness, too" (68). She gives the impression through various tense interactions with Christopher and Henry that she dislikes them, but the truth is that she buries any tender emotions largely because she was close to her father who died by suicide when she was younger. In an unguarded moment on Christopher's wedding day, she thinks, "deep down there is a thing inside me, and sometimes it swells up like the head of a squid and shoots blackness through me. I haven't wanted to be this way, but so help me, I have loved my son" (71). She can't figure out whether this thing inside her is her heart or her soul, but she knows no one else can see it.

Despite her tribulations with Henry and the fact that their relationship seems to lack passion, they develop a bond over their many decades together that illustrates that marriage can be a salve. Looking at a picture of her husband when he was a child, she says to the image, "You will marry a beast and love her" (161). Her low self-opinion here is coupled with the fact that she knows love is possible, even if it is not always joyful. Their marriage involves mutual support and a depth of understanding that would likely not be available in a less formal relationship. Her relationship with her son is another story. Christopher apparently hates her and makes no secret of his feelings when she visits him in New York City. Olive blames this behavior on Christopher's wife and on the fact that the couple is in therapy; she tells Henry on the phone, "In therapy they go straight after the mother. You come out smelling like a rose, I'm sure" (223). Christopher calls her "paranoid" and "furious" and declares, "It's tiring, very wearing for those around you" (229). She leaves abruptly, hurt and confused by Christopher's treatment of her. Concluding that he and his wife are "cruel" (232), and she essentially becomes estranged from them.

Spurned by her son and touched by several deaths or wayward lives in her hometown, she turns to Henry as her only support, but he dies suddenly after a massive stroke. Olive, on her own, creates rituals involving her dog as her only companion, including a lengthy walk by the ocean, but the depth of her despair is evident: "Her one concern was that such daily exercise might make her live longer. *Let it be quick*, she thought now, meaning her death – a thought she had several times a day" (253). On one of these walks, she encounters a man her age named Jack Kennison who has collapsed. Her opening words to him are typically brusque: "'Are you dead?' she asked loudly" (253). He tells her he doesn't care if he dies but qualifies it by pleading with her to stay with him, claiming, "I don't want to die alone." She responds, "Hell. We're always alone. Born alone. Die alone." Jack tells her that his wife died recently, and Olive acknowledges how that must feel: "Then you're in hell" (255). They become a couple and eventually marry. Post-widowhood marriage is recast for these two as a way to avoid the hell of being alone, and perhaps that's enough. The expectations are low. Like Olive, Jack is a highly flawed character, and a successful marriage involves an understanding that to be human is to be flawed. Romance is kind of a joke to Olive and Jack. Before they marry, he reflects that she is "a strange woman," and even though he "liked her quite a bit," he still pines for his deceased first wife, claiming that kissing Olive is like "kissing a barnacle-covered whale" (*Again* 9). When she stays over in Jack's guest room for the first time, she experiences a whirlwind of conflicting emotions when she hears the roar of his laughter: "The terror, the thrill of his laughter – it was nightmarish, but also as though a huge can she had been stuffed into had just opened" (*Again* 41). Late in life she and Jack attempt, through marriage, to stave off loneliness and alienation, and when he predeceases her, she feels an even deeper loss: "Oh, the loneliness! It blistered Olive" (*Again* 260).

Marriage, in Olive's case, is not a social trap or a means of gender-based oppression as was the case in many of the novels discussed earlier. Like the relationship between Janie and Tea Cake in *Their Eyes Were Watching God*, Strout's novels argue that marriage has benefits as long as the partners enter into it from a position of equal power, with a clear-eyed understanding of both how it will benefit them and what they must sacrifice. It helps that Olive is not romantic. Since she doesn't believe that marriage will either save her or provide the sole meaning to her life, she is able to use it for comfort and also to feel its loss when it is over. After grieving both husbands and accepting that her son seems "to have come around" a little to rebuild their connection, she reflects, "she had been loved by two men, and that had been a lucky thing" (*Again* 288). Yet the final chapters in her story involve her developing friendships with other women in similar positions to hers, as though the benefit of marriage was to prepare her for the first time in her life to join a community of women. The protagonists of novels discussed in this chapter for whom marriage is a social arrangement supporting the American Dream narrative experience marriage as oppressive to both the individual and community spirit. Protagonists like Janie and Olive provide a refreshing counternarrative.

Further Reading

Alcott, Louisa May. *Little Women* (1868).
Brown, Rita Mae. *Rubyfruit Jungle* (1973).
Didion, Joan. *Play It as It Lays* (1970).
Feinberg, Leslie. *Stone Butch Blues* (1993).
Fern, Fanny. *Ruth Hall* (1854).
Highsmith, Patricia. *The Price of Salt* (1952)
Jong, Erica. *Fear of Flying* (1973)
Lee, Harper. *To Kill a Mockingbird* (1960)
McMillan, Terry. *Waiting to Exhale* (1992)
Metalious, Grace. *Peyton Place* (1956)
Naylor, Gloria. *The Women of Brewster Place* (1982)
Plath, Sylvia. *The Bell Jar* (1963)
Stein, Gertrude. *The Autobiography of Alice B. Toklas* (1933)
Tyler, Anne. *Breathing Lessons* (1988)

4 "Not a Story to Pass On"
Slavery and the American Novel

The first original American literary genre is not the novel, but rather the slave narrative. Roughly one hundred of these vitally important texts were published in the leadup to the Civil War, and as James Olney has pointed out, they follow a surprisingly consistent structural pattern, with nearly all of them beginning with the phrase "I was born" to signal not only origin, but authenticity (50). Despite their foundational importance, because of their adherence to convention in the service of the abolitionist cause, slave narratives limited the creative freedom of their writers. The development of the novel about slavery, deferred until the slave narrative had performed its essential duty, provided a range of artistic liberation unavailable in the original prose genre. The explicit purpose of slave narratives was to convince readers that slavery was an abhorrent, immoral, and anti-Christian practice that should be abolished at all costs. The purpose of novels written after 1865 that deal with the experience of slavery is multifaceted. Toni Morrison's goal, for instance, in writing *Beloved* (1987) was obviously not to abolish slavery but to peer deeper into the horrors of the experience and to show how it can never truly be forgotten, individually or collectively. The novel concludes, "This is not a story to pass on" (324), that is, it is a story that does not die, a ghost story that continues to haunt the minds of all thinking Americans long after abolition.

With a heavy debt to slave narratives, the legacy of slavery in the United States novel tradition is long-lasting. Even twenty-first-century writers explore dimensions and nuances not only of slavery itself, but of its enduring historical, psychological, and sociological repercussions. The system of slavery and its aftereffects – including but not limited to segregation, racial hierarchy, inequality, persistent discrimination, alienation, and psychological trauma – is an unwavering sickness in America that has no clear remedy, and it has caused unspeakable damage that cannot be repaired. The American Dream script which is a recurrent touchstone in the tradition may not seem to obtain within this category, and indeed it is true that novels primarily attuned to slavery do not have the luxury to consider the possibility of material prosperity when basic freedom is the goal. Still, there are invisible lines between the Dream script and novels about slavery. The American Dream deliberately conceals its dependence on the historical system of slavery, pretending that freedom and prosperity do not come at a high price.

Slave Narratives and the Nineteenth-Century Novel

The best-known slave narratives remain essential reading. Works such as *The Confessions of Nat Turner* (1831), *The Narrative of the Life of Frederick Douglass, American Slave* (1845), and Harriet Jacobs's *Incidents in the Life of a Slave Girl* (1861) continue to engage students of American literary history. This last work moves in the direction of fiction as its author adopts a pseudonym and titles her chapters after plot points in the tradition of the nineteenth-century novel. There is a confluence between it and the bestselling novel of the nineteenth century, Harriet Beecher Stowe's *Uncle Tom's Cabin* (1852), which Abraham Lincoln supposedly credited as a main catalyst for the Civil War. Virtually all slave narratives were framed by testimonies by white abolitionists attesting to the good character of the author and legitimacy of the text, a publishing convention that can be seen to compromise Black voices by placing them within a framework dictated by the white literary establishment. The infamous story of Jacobs's resolve to tell her own tale her own way after Stowe refused to mentor her is a clear indication of the troubled relationship between Black and white novelistic renditions of the slave experience beginning in the nineteenth century and continuing through the controversy around William Styron's *Confessions of Nat Turner* (1967) which prompted a group of prominent Black writers and scholars to denounce the white novelist's presumptuousness for appropriating Turner's life story. As the novel developed from Stowe's time to the present, the subject of slavery opened up limitless possibilities for artistic expression as Black authors sought not only to reclaim their history, but to consider new perspectives that add to our understanding of it.

Uncle Tom's Cabin derives its authenticity from research and the author's imagination rather than from her direct experience. Unlike slave narratives which are relatively short, and which coalesce around an individual's experience, Stowe's novel is a sprawling "loose baggy monster" (to quote Henry James) in the Victorian tradition with multiple interwoven plot lines. Jacobs's slave narrative is keenly aware of novelistic conventions that would have been familiar to white readers at the time who were conditioned to respond emotionally as well as intellectually to the plight of fictional characters. This is an important context for understanding *Uncle Tom's Cabin* whose sentimentality and Christian framework are evident features that have not helped the novel age well. Its legacy has been checkered, to put it mildly. It has been critiqued for participating in a tradition of Black stereotyping that tainted American culture throughout the Jim Crow era and beyond. The phrase "Uncle Tom" continues to be a derogatory term for a subservient African American whose loyalties and devotions do more to preserve racial hierarchy than to seek equality. Black writers have been especially critical of the novel's legacy. Richard Wright titled his fiery story collection *Uncle Tom's Children* (1938) as a deliberate clapback to the Christian meekness of Stowe's titular character. James Baldwin launched his career with a 1945 essay called "Everybody's Protest Novel" that attacked *Uncle Tom's Cabin*, calling it summarily "a very bad novel" for its "self-righteous, virtuous sentimentality" which is "the mark of dishonesty, the inability to feel" (14). George C. Wolfe's satirical play *The Colored Museum* (1985) ridicules Stowe's character Topsy as a particularly offensive stereotype. Regardless, *Uncle Tom's Cabin* cannot be sidestepped in this context given its enormous popularity in its time and its influence thereafter. As discussed in Chapter 1, multiple critics considered it the closest thing to the Great American Novel when that term was first being explored.

Stowe clearly profited from her bestselling novel even if her motivation for writing it was purely the cause of abolition rather than financial gain. Aside from the ethical quandary this circumstance presents, the author's position relative to the slave experience is related to a marked distance between the narrative voice and its subjects, a distance that can prove troublesome. Even Stowe's preface is likely to make twenty-first-century readers wince despite the author's good intentions. The "hard and dominant Anglo-Saxon race" and the "exotic race" from Africa are "essentially unlike," according to this framework, but the author trusts that the Christian spirit will conquer the "misunderstanding and contempt" that have made slavery possible; she concludes, "it has been seen how far nobler it is in nations to protect the feeble than to oppress them" (10). Though hopeful, the preface's tone is condescending, and the gulf between the narrator and the novel's characters is evident from the outset. Enslaved people are referred to in the first chapter as not only "feeble," but "helpless and unprotected" (19), a premise that underscores this distance. This tendency permeates the novel; for example, the narrator says, the "instinctive affections of that race are peculiarly strong ... . They are not naturally daring and enterprising, but home-loving and affectionate" (118). The titular Tom who is the exemplar of all these qualities "had the soft, impressible nature of his kindly race, ever yearning toward the simple and childlike" (176). This patronizing perspective is not limited to the narrator's voice; Emily Shelby, a white character who is sympathetic despite her participation in the slave trade, refers to enslaved people as "poor, simple, dependent creatures" (47). The depiction of Topsy, an incorrigible enslaved girl who describes herself as "the wickedest critter in the world" (292), is perhaps the most problematic in the novel even though we're supposed to be fond of her; the narrator says of Topsy, "The creature was as lithe as a cat, and as active as a monkey" (289) and her master, the well-meaning iconoclast Augustine St. Clare, uses the same racially offensive term when addressing her (329). Even though the overall aim of the novel is to abolish slavery and to diminish racial hierarchy, any inherent biases of Stowe's readers aren't likely to be challenged by such characterization.

The novel opens with a deal between a slaveholder named Shelby who is in financial trouble and a trader named Haley. The genteel-seeming Shelby condemns Haley and his practice, yet he is equally abhorrent as he encourages a young, enslaved boy named Harry (whom he refers to as "Jim Crow") to dance and playact as he throws him pieces of fruit. The type of slavery practiced in Kentucky, where the scene takes place, might seem less harsh than that practiced in the deep South, but the narrator cautions against believing in the "oft-fabled poetic legend of a patriarchal institution" (19). As long as slavery is legal, the narrator says, there is no way to regard any version of it as acceptable. This sentiment is slightly at odds with the depiction of Emily Shelby, though, who claims to want no part in her husband's dealings with Haley, and who is thus considered "a Christian and an angel" (52) by the enslaved Eliza. Haley later calls out this hypocrisy when the Shelbys' son George berates him for his immoral practice of trading enslaved people; he says, "So long as your grand folks wants to buy men and women, I'm as good as they is" (125). Although he is right (though the word "bad" might be more appropriate than "good"), the novel depicts slaveholders along a continuum of cruelty, with Tom's third owner Simon Legree the nadir and the novel's most obvious villain. Moreover, it does not offer a coherent solution for individuals who want to alter the system from within. Even supposedly benevolent slaveholders like St. Clare express frustration that they cannot do anything to reduce slavery's effects given the system's far reach.

The legality of slavery is a recurrent touchstone in the novel. The enslaved couple Eliza and George are married, for instance, but George's master Harris forces him to marry a different woman, and George reminds Eliza (and the reader) that the law prevents enslaved people from marrying of their own free will. Harris moves George from factory work to farm labor after learning that he has invented a labor-saving machine. When a manufacturer questions the decision, Harris snarls, "Is n't the man *mine*?" (23), a question that Simon Legree reiterates regarding Tom (415, 476).

The novel is filled with incidents of enslavers flouting their power, sometimes merely to reinforce their legal right to do so, and enslaved people are made keenly aware of their lack of rights. George complains bitterly of his plight: "who made him my master? ... what right has he to me?" (27). Eliza begs him to be patient and trust in God, but George, who does not share her religious conviction, is determined to escape instead of putting faith in divine providence. En route to Canada he snaps at a character who tells him he is disobeying the laws of his country: "what country have *I*, or any one like me, born of slave mothers? What laws are there for us? We don't make them –, we don't consent to them" (135). George's solution is not just to escape from Kentucky to a free northern state, but to continue on to Canada where slavery is illegal.

Once Eliza learns that Shelby has sold both Tom and her son Harry into an uncertain and likely harsh future "down the river," i.e. in a hellish plantation state in the deep South, she also decides to flee. The novel's tension heightens when Tom, described as "the hero of our story" (34), decides not to escape with her, sacrificing his individual desires for the good of the Shelby enterprise; he says, "It 's better for me alone to go, than to break up the place and sell all. Mas'r an't to blame" (55). Tom's self-sacrifice and reluctance to judge – Christian virtues modeled after Jesus's willingness to be martyred for humanity's sins – are keys to understanding both why the novel was so popular in its time and why its star has dimmed since then. The desire of a nineteenth-century readership to see the Christian values upheld in a character like Uncle Tom was strong, but readers in subsequent centuries are more likely to regard George and Eliza as the novel's heroes since they do what is necessary to escape slavery. When George becomes involved in an armed standoff with vigilantes trying to capture him for profit, the narrator brings up heroism again: "as [George] was a youth of African descent, defending the retreat of fugitives through America into Canada, of course we are too well instructed and patriotic to see any heroism in it; and if any of our readers do, they must do it on their own private responsibility" (232). Stowe stops short of condoning violence as a way of changing hearts, minds, and especially laws in the United States. Even the defiant George feels remorse after battling the vigilantes and he and his Quaker comrades nurse a wounded one back to health.

Christianity is clearly under some scrutiny in the novel, though, just as it was in Douglass's *Narrative* which draws a sharp distinction between true Christianity and the corrupt version of it used to uphold slavery. The Quakers who help George and Eliza in their path to freedom are exemplars of the former model. When a public debate breaks out about God's will, one character asserts, "It pleased Providence, for some inscrutable reason, to doom the race to bondage" (151). Other characters at the scene weigh in on the issue, some resisting interpretations of scripture that justify slavery. Although the novel pushes the reader firmly toward abolitionism, supporters of slavery aren't silenced: "there's a great deal to be said on both sides of the subject," as one woman concludes (150). This scene ends with the narrator directly addressing the reader (as "sir") and calling on the politicians of the land to solve the issue rather than blaming the scurrilous traders. There will be a Judgment Day for all Americans who did not work to end the slave trade, and that, rather than civil war, is the future projected by the novel.

Augustine St. Clare puts a fine point on the novel's Christian context when he sarcastically speaks out against religion: "When I look for a religion, I must look for something above me, and not something beneath" (217). The heaven he seeks is embodied rather heavy-handedly in his daughter Eva whose premature death is foreshadowed from the moment she appears. Uncle Tom may be the hero, but Eva gets at least as much space in the story, and the two of them share a role as self-sacrificial figures modeled after Jesus. Eva is the only one able to change the ways of the "wicked" Topsy, for instance, simply by telling her that she is loved. Eva's heartrending death ushers in a renewed hope for the future. On death's doorstep she rapturously declares that she sees "love, – joy, – peace!" (346). Before her passing, she envisions a world in which slavery doesn't exist and her dying wish is for Tom to be reunited with his family. Tom takes up her evangelistic role after she dies, trying feverishly to convert both Augustine and an enslaved woman named Cassy who cannot believe in God after all the misery she has suffered.

Tom's spirit of Christian forgiveness and acceptance is so strong that he even chides his wife Aunt Chloe and some of the children for wishing ill of the demonic Haley; he says, "Pray for them that 'spitefully use you, the good book says" (73). Later in the novel he does the same for the villain Simon Legree when George calls him "satan": "he's a poor mis'able critter! It 's awful to think on' t!" (487). Tom earnestly professes his obedience and loyalty to Shelby, and both Shelby and Haley are chagrined for imagining Tom would run off as Eliza has. Tom is a paragon of Christian virtue throughout the novel. He is repeatedly tested and triumphs over the despair that some other enslaved people express. Tom's most challenging test comes at the hands of the atheistic Legree who tries to force him into cruel acts such as whipping his comrades, but Tom triumphs over a "soul-crisis," seeing himself not as a suffering martyr but as a triumphant citizen of God's heavenly kingdom (456). Once Tom realizes that Legree, like all men, can harm his body but not his soul, he achieves a holy status. His fellow sufferer Cassy tries to convince him to murder Legree, but Tom adheres to Christ's message that violence is not the path to justice. This "turn the other cheek" mentality is, again, one that is not likely to resonate with readers who do not share Stowe's religious convictions. Even though it might have changed hearts and minds, despite the legend of Lincoln's pronouncement, *Uncle Tom's Cabin* is a highly unlikely novel to have inspired the Civil War as it condemns violence and posits the solution to the slavery conundrum outside of the U.S., either in the form of escape to Canada or repatriation to Liberia, a free state for liberated enslaved people in Africa.

Uncle Tom's Cabin was not the only novel about slavery written prior to the Civil War, and three Black novelists are worth mentioning here. William Wells Brown's 1853 novel *Clotel, or The President's Daughter* is the first novel by an African American author. It is undeniably important and compelling, and unlike Stowe's novel, it was written by an author who experienced slavery directly. As it fictionalizes the stories of Thomas Jefferson's enslaved mistress and her progeny, *Clotel* is a bold foray into topics that challenged the status quo of American cultural mythology. As a novel, it mixes the pleasures of a well-plotted narrative with the inclusion of other genres, some previously published. Given its experimental nature as a generic miscellany, it figures into this study in Chapter 7. Like Stowe's novel, it also includes fictional debates about the nature of slavery that are too stagey to be plausible, but that are intended to advance the rhetoric of abolition more than to advance the plot of the novel. In its time and since, *Clotel* has not enjoyed the widespread readership of *Uncle Tom's Cabin* due largely to its unusual approach to fiction as opposed to Stowe's skill at writing novels that elicit a strong emotional response. *The Bondwoman's Narrative* (believed to be written in the 1850s) by the enslaved author Hannah Crafts has not had the same impact as Stowe's or Brown's novels because it was unpublished until the prominent scholar Henry Louis Gates, Jr. discovered it and published it for the first time in 2002. Because of its publication history, it enters the conversation more as a kind of time capsule than a widely circulated text. Though *The Bondwoman's Narrative* is a novel, it is perhaps better studied in the context of slave narratives, especially given its first-hand account of the experience of slavery, rendered into fiction that has many of the features of a slave narrative. Harriet Wilson's *Our Nig* (1859) was published and circulated in its time, but also fell into obscurity and was also brought back to light by Gates in 1983. *Our Nig*, not well received by its contemporary readers and critics, was written during the era of slavery but was about a free Black woman living in the North. It is an early study of the devastating psychological and sociological aftereffects of slavery in the form of persistent discrimination and the preservation of social hierarchy.

Mark Twain published *The Adventures of Huckleberry Finn* (1885) two decades after the end of the Civil War. His motivation in setting his most enduring book during the era of slavery is not entirely straightforward, but its many American themes and motifs cannot be divorced from the history of slavery. *Huck Finn* can be read as a work of humor, satire, adventure, the loss of innocence, individualism, and so forth, but the very heart of it and the reason it remains relevant is because of its nuanced treatment of Jim's plight and Huck's decision to "go to hell" (235) rather than to support the system of slavery by turning his friend over to the authorities. Stowe's characters make choices that result in the freedom of formerly enslaved people, such as the Quakers who harbor George and Eliza in their attempt to escape, or George Shelby who severs his family's ties to slavery after Tom's death. The difference is that Huck, without family, money, or a full understanding of the system of slavery, seems utterly powerless, and yet his decision is truly liberatory in that it frees Jim physically as well as Huck mentally, at least for a time. The controversial final chapters in which Tom Sawyer returns to lead Huck into sadistic practices that preserve racial hierarchy and facilitate slavery demonstrate the need for ongoing vigilance regarding the return of history. In other words, slavery isn't over when Huck decides to go to hell rather than support it, and it isn't over at the end of the narrative. Twain suggests that it might not be truly over when the novel was published in 1885, either.

There's ample self-awareness in the novel's opening pages to support such a reading. The front matter states "persons attempting to find a moral in [this narrative] will be banished," satirically suggesting that the novel is amoral when in fact it is just the opposite. In terms of banishment, that fate is what Huck chooses when he decides hell is preferable to a nation that condones slavery; when he earlier expresses a desire for hell over heaven to his would-be educator Miss Watson, he claims "all I wanted was a change; I wasn't particular" (2). Hell is change; heaven is the status quo, or in Huck's analysis, "all a body would have to do [in heaven] was to go around all day long with a harp and sing, forever and ever. So I didn't think much of it" (3). The status quo in the 1840s when the novel takes place involves an acceptance of the system of slavery. Going to hell is the only way to change it. Huck's choice of damnation is a sin in the eyes of society – certainly damnation would not have been condoned in Stowe's novel – but the idea he forms and eventually blurts out indicates that his conscience is the seat of morality, and to liberate it he must be willing to articulate its opposition to the supposedly "sivilized" society into which he was born.

Many elements of *Huck Finn* can't be covered here in the interest of space and focus. In the context of this chapter, the novel's throughline involving Huck's gradual understanding of Jim's lived experience in contrast with his own and his moral decision to side with Jim over society is of primary interest. Revealing the depth of his conditioning and the poisoned state of his country's racism, Huck almost never uses the word "slave" to refer to Jim. He is at first "Miss Watson's big nigger, named Jim" (5) and later, when he encounters Jim on the island, he is "Miss Watson's Jim" (46). (The novel's liberal use of the n-word has produced a host of problems throughout its history, reaching a peak in 2010 when Alan Gribben reprinted a widely criticized and even ridiculed edition in which that word was converted to "slave" throughout the text, eradicating Twain's satirical intent in a naïve attempt to avoid the troubling history of a supercharged word). The word "slavery" is almost deliberately sidestepped throughout Twain's novel; when Huck asks Jim how he came to be on the island, rather than identifying his action as an escape from the system of slavery Jim says hesitantly, "*I run off*" (48). The lengthy staged debates over the ethics and legality of slavery in *Uncle Tom's Cabin* are nowhere to be found in Huck's story, except that he swears to keep Jim's secret even though, he says, "People would call me a low down Ablitionist [sic] and despise me for keeping mum – but that don't make no difference" (48). Jim's status as an enslaved person and Huck's contrasting identity as a free white boy are societal distinctions that have little bearing on their relationship as they hide from their tormentors in the wilderness. Jim is Huck's teacher, his confidante, and his fellow survivor. Huck's ignorance of slavery means he is poised to be educated, not unlike the reader: we share Huck's approach to Jim as an individual man with specific needs rather than as a symbolic victim of society's sickness. The breakthrough of *Huck Finn* in this regard is that it does not ignore slavery, but rather comes at it indirectly, through realistic human interaction rather than through implausible debates meant to enlighten the reader.

This is not to say that Huck is enlightened just because he is ignorant of the broad outlines or specific vocabulary of slavery. Huck has been conditioned to be a racist though not a slaveholder. Long before Tom Sawyer returns to torment Jim in the novel's final chapters, Huck's capacity for cruelty is revealed, and he follows Tom instinctively. Tom's first impulse is "to tie Jim to the tree for fun" (6). Although Huck refuses, less for his concern for Jim than for his own safety, he demonstrates similar behavior when he and Jim are alone together in exile. At first, he puts a dead rattlesnake on Jim's sleeping roll to frighten him, and the result is that the snake's mate arrives and bites Jim, nearly killing him. Huck feels remorse for his actions but does not confess to Jim what he did. Later he gaslights Jim after their raft and canoe become separated, convincing him that the frightful experience that separated them was only a dream. When Jim learns the truth, he expresses his wounded feelings with great honesty: "when I wake up en fine you back again', all safe en soun', de tears come en I could a got down on my knees en kiss' yo' foot I's so thankful. En all you wuz thinkin 'bout wuz how you could make a fool uv ole Jim wid a lie" (95). Huck feels ashamed, as Jim indicates he should, but he says, "It was fifteen minutes before I could work myself up to go and humble myself to a nigger" (95). Despite this weak apology, his guilt festers and he pulls away from Jim and feels like he might be better off if they separated for good, suggesting he trusts his conditioned underlying belief that racial segregation is natural and expected. These moral setbacks are evidence that Huck has absorbed at least some of the poisoned ethics of his society, and it also heightens the intensity of his moral decision to side with Jim against that society and to go to hell instead. Twain renders the relationship between the two in a complex way, replacing the sentimentality that characterizes the relationship between Eva St. Clare and Uncle Tom in Stowe's novel with a nuanced, troublesome interaction that reveals some of the psychological trauma of slavery – suffered by both races involved – that cannot be easily understood through sociological inquiry.

The text becomes more complex after Huck wrestles with his conscience and decides not to turn Jim in. This moment of moral triumph does not appear to have produced in Huck a long-term commitment to the cause of supporting Jim and enslaved people like him; just the opposite, in fact, as he is aghast that Tom wants to help him "steal [Jim] out of slavery" (248). Huck believes himself to be a craven criminal for his desire to free Jim, but he can't believe Tom would sink as low as he is. Worse, in the name of making the plot to free Jim more complicated so that it matches the derring-do of the pirate books Tom favors, they end up tormenting Jim, intensifying some of the same cruel behavior Huck displayed when he was alone with him. Skeptical of these plans, Jim "couldn't see no sense in the most of it, but he allowed we was white folks and knowed better than him" (273). The irony here is thick as we later learn Jim has been legally free all along, but that irony doesn't change the fact that the childish pranks of Tom and Huck are made possible through the hierarchical system that persists despite the supposedly heroic triumph of Huck's conscience. Sensitive readers do not find the ending happy or the final chapters funny but are aware of Twain's satirical purpose not only condemning slavery, but warning against ignorance about its persistence. When Huck lights out for the territory in the novel's conclusion, he is enacting a version of the American Dream that reveals his privilege when we consider what Jim has had to endure.

Beloved and New Narratives of Slavery

The critical term "neo-slave narrative," alternatively called "new narratives of slavery," most generally refers to recent narratives that utilize the setting of antebellum America and the experience of slavery. These novels frequently build on an implicit critique of slavery to scrutinize other features of inequality in American cultural history, including bias in literary history. Toni Morrison's *Beloved* marks a highwater mark of a trend in novels about slavery that take historical figures and incidents and reshape them as fiction for various artistic and rhetorical purposes. Alex Haley's *Roots* (1976) – which was converted into a major television series that succeeded in bringing the overlooked story of slavery into American living rooms – was based on carefully researched genealogy. Subtitled "A Family Saga," *Roots* built on archival research as well as crucial oral histories and was marked by its sweeping narrative arc, giving it an epic quality. The same could be said of Ernest J. Gaines's 1971 novel *The Autobiography of Miss Jane Pittman*, narrated by a character whose long life yielded insights into history that spanned generations. Both novels were narrated with such historical accuracy that readers wondered whether to label them fiction or nonfiction. The impulse to firmly anchor new narratives of slavery in history evident in the novels by Gaines, Haley, and Morrison is a feature of many others from the late twentieth century including David Bradley's *The Chaneysville Incident* (1981) and Charles Johnson's *Middle Passage* (1990).

Although all these works are worthy of attention, it goes without saying that *Beloved* is the most prominent novel in the category of new narratives of slavery. One of the most studied and widely read American novels of the past fifty years – indeed, of all time – it is undoubtedly Morrison's crowning achievement and the pinnacle of a career that made her the first and only African American author to receive the Nobel Prize in Literature. Published more than a century after the end of the Civil War, Morrison's novel teaches us that Americans are only beginning to understand the widespread, enduring devastation of slavery.

Beloved is based on the true story of Margaret Garner, a mother who escaped slavery and murdered her infant daughter rather than allow her to be captured and returned under the Fugitive Slave Law. The novel's protagonist Sethe is modeled after Garner, but the story involves many characters, especially Sethe's lover Paul D, her surviving daughter Denver, her mother-in-law Baby Suggs, and the titular Beloved, who most readers interpret as a reincarnation of the murdered infant. Beloved is a ghost who haunts Sethe's house before she becomes an actual character who emerges from the river in a symbolic rebirth only to torment Sethe, befriend the isolated Denver, seduce Paul D, and divide the fragile African American community. Beloved's return indicates that slavery's effects run even deeper than previously understood, and that late twentieth-century American culture had not fully confronted them. Morrison's novel is thus timely and timeless.

It is also a novel of astounding stylistic sophistication that demands a great deal of work on the reader's part. *Uncle Tom's Cabin*, the novel that gave an unprecedented number of contemporary readers a glimpse into the experience of slavery, does not obscure its intent: its plot-driven forward motion, its reliance on Christian typology, and its frequently heavy-handed editorializing make its meaning loud and clear. Morrison, who famously wrote her master's thesis on Virginia Woolf and William Faulkner, uses a variety of unconventional narrative techniques to keep the reader active, including multiple narrative voices, a non-chronological timeline, stream of consciousness, and many more. *Beloved*, like all of Morrison's novels, demands careful reading and rereading, refusing to yield easy conclusions and continuing to haunt the reader just as Beloved haunts her beleaguered mother.

One of the novel's chief concerns is to scrutinize the human tendency to judge individuals. When someone commits infanticide, judgment is universal, and justification or sympathy are nearly impossible reactions to imagine. Sethe's act is so horrifying to comprehend that the community collectively buries it. Paul D, who was raised on the same plantation as Sethe, does not know about her desperate act when he initially reenters her life, and Sethe is not keen to confess it. In fact, she has largely repressed the memory of her daughter's demise, and a portion of the novel involves "rememory," or the process of bringing the past back to life and reanimating it. Paul D's reintroduction into her post-slavery life is what "stirred her rememory" (222). Burying memories is no more effective than burying her infant daughter, though; nothing stays dead, and as Amy Denver – a white woman who helps Sethe escape – says, "Anything dead coming back to life hurts" (42). She's referring to the scar tissue on Sethe's back from multiple whippings, but the pronouncement also pertains to Sethe's memories and to the ghost of Beloved.

Sethe's community doesn't want to come to terms with her act partly because they interpret it as a collective mark of shame. The community is equally reluctant to blame Sethe or to exonerate her. She is lightly ostracized, and after Beloved rejoins the household, she is downright shunned. The community who had escaped slavery in search of a better life had made tremendous efforts to heal under the leadership of Sethe's mother-in-law Baby Suggs, who took on the role of a spiritual leader in a public site called The Clearing. Before her death, Baby Suggs emerged as a leader who can bring everyone together: "Uncalled, unrobed, unanointed, she let her great heart beat in their presence" (102). Hers is an alternative religion that deliberately leads her followers away from judgment and from the hatred of white slaveowners and toward collective self-love. After Sethe kills Beloved, Baby Suggs's faith and hope wither and die: "Baby Suggs, holy, believed she had lied. There was no grace – imaginary or real, – and no sunlit dance in a Clearing could change that. Her faith, her love, her imagination and her great big old heart began to collapse" (105). Without her optimism and her spiritual guidance, the fragile community disintegrates, and Sethe enters a dark psychological hell.

Paul D's return is meant to heal her. When he sees the tree-like scar on her back he wants only to protect her, which he attempts to do by driving the ghost out of her house. She initially has a hard time convincing him about how the specific circumstances of the trauma she experienced on the plantation were different from his. Her abuses included the actions of a cruel overseer called Schoolteacher who studied and documented the ways he believed she was more animal than human and his two nephews who pinned her down and stole her breast milk after she gave birth to Beloved. Paul D and Sethe attempt to maintain a loving relationship, but ghost-Beloved's presence drives them apart. When Paul D learns what Sethe did, he judges her by telling her "What you did was wrong" and takes it a step further by reigniting the comparison between her and an animal that Schoolteacher initiated: "You got two feet, Sethe, not four" (194). What isolates her from her community in general also cuts her off from her lover, and the fact that her horrific act is decades in her past does not matter: her guilt over Beloved's death, like the physical and psychological scars of slavery, has not healed.

Even Denver, who was a newborn when Beloved died, carries the trauma of her mother's act. She is an awkward girl with no friends, and when Beloved joins her and her mother to form a tight family unit cut off from the rest of the community, she is initially grateful for the companionship. The relationships within the house sour, though, as the love Sethe, Denver, and Beloved show for each other becomes possessive. Denver's life was tainted from early on as she was present during the infanticide and spent time with her mother in jail thereafter; she admits in a monologue, "Beloved is my sister. I swallowed her blood right along with my mother's milk," which literally happened as Sethe tried to nurse her younger daughter before cleaning the blood from her breasts (242). Denver competes with her mother for the returned Beloved's attention, but it becomes clear that Sethe and Beloved's love for one another has swollen and become greedy, so much so that there is no place for Denver. Frustrated, she leaves the house and enters the wider world, paving a path for her healing.

The reintroduction of Beloved into this wounded world is necessary so that Sethe and others can confront the horrors of the past, but the catharsis comes with a great deal of pain. Paul D finds himself alone, drunk, and despairing after leaving Sethe's house. Denver withdraws from her mother. Sethe becomes paranoid and tries to attack a benevolent white man who comes into her yard as she believes he is Schoolteacher returning to steal her child again. The community has to intervene in an act of mob violence that finally drives the reincarnated ghost off Sethe's property. It is only in the novel's final pages that growth and healing begin to take place, after the ghost-Beloved has been sent away with no guarantees that she won't return. Paul D and Sethe reunite, gently, and he is now willing to understand that what she needs is not protection as much as permission to love herself. He says hopefully, "we got more yesterday than anybody. We need some kind of tomorrow," and the path to this future involves her learning to forgive herself and to recognize that she has worth: "You your own best thing, Sethe" (322). The post-slavery challenge framed in *Beloved* is to remember and confront the horrors of the past even though "Remembering seemed unwise" (324) and to do whatever it takes to promote self-love and community harmony in the aftermath of slavery. These twinned acts may seem antithetical, but such is the complexity of Morrison's vision: loving the self involves a deep acknowledgment of the past's power. The antidote is neither repression nor the paralysis that comes with dwelling on the past.

Taking Liberties With/From History

The two nineteenth-century novels about slavery discussed earlier in this chapter were written by white authors, and in the early twentieth century, white authors as Willa Cather, William Faulkner, and Margaret Mitchell continued to address the subject in fiction. As the twentieth century continued, African American authors insisted that the story of slavery be retold from a Black perspective. Margaret Walker's *Jubilee* (1966) was a groundbreaking publication in this trend. Just a year later, during the heart of the Black Arts Movement, William Styron published the controversial Pulitzer Prize-winning novel *The Confessions of Nat Turner* which retold the story of the infamous leader of a slave rebellion that was an early harbinger of the Civil War. Many Black writers and intellectuals in the turbulent late 1960s and early 1970s were incensed that a white author like Styron would appropriate Turner's story and they were troubled by depictions of both Turner and some of the white characters in the novel. Some Black writers including James Baldwin and Ralph Ellison defended Styron, but the voices attacking him were louder and more numerous.

Part of the impulse for Black novelists to produce new narratives of slavery was to get history right, but another part was to expose the way the historical record is best regarded as a catalyst for creativity and further analysis, not the final version of the story by any means. As a subject for novels within an ongoing tradition, slavery provides opportunities to create new contexts for understanding beyond the familiar renditions of it as an evil to be eradicated or, later, a historical trauma to be overcome. This impulse allows contemporary novelists to use slavery to examine and critique other dimensions of American culture. In contrast to Morrison, Gaines, Haley, and Johnson, other late twentieth-century writers treat history's framing of slavery with far less reverence, including Ishmael Reed in *Flight to Canada*, a satire featuring Abraham Lincoln as a character that also targets the legacy of *Uncle Tom's Cabin*. In Reed's postmodern dismantling, slave owners are dimwitted and obsessive, so much so that they are unable to prevent the escape of the novel's protagonist Raven Quickskill (a poet), and unwilling to see that a character named Uncle Robin (who, like Uncle Tom, stays on the plantation rather than escaping) might be capable of theft or manipulation. The target of Reed's satire is widespread, but his willingness to reimagine interracial dynamics in the antebellum era destabilizes history itself and opens up more imaginative possibilities for novelists. Satire is not the most common literary mode in novelistic treatments of slavery, but Twain's project was not unique. *Flight to Canada* satirizes not only the stupidity of slaveholders but misconceptions about slavery based on historical myths and misunderstandings. The historical distance between Reed's novel and the era of slavery coupled with his explicitly defined aesthetic does not leave room for the errors of misreading that have occasionally been attached to Twain's novel.

Satire is only one path to convert historical facts into original fiction. Octavia Butler's *Kindred* (1979), published three years after *Flight to Canada*, uses paranormal experiences to create a bridge between contemporary America and the era of slavery. The protagonist, Dana, is repeatedly and mysteriously transported to and from a plantation in the antebellum South. Butler's novel is groundbreaking in its use of time travel to dig deeper into the experience of slavery and connect it to post-slavery psychology. Dana is summoned by a white boy named Rufus who repeatedly needs her to save his life. The first time she encounters him he is a child, drowning, and they don't meaningfully interact, but the second time he is a surly pre-teen preparing to burn down his family's house. This time they speak and begin to navigate the differences between their worlds, such as when Rufus questions the fact that Dana is wearing pants or when Dana repeatedly tells Rufus to use the word "black" to describe her and others like her as opposed to the offensive racial epithet that flows too easily from his mouth.

Dana is mystified about why she is being teleported to the past, and her white husband Kevin is understandably troubled whenever she vanishes and returns seconds later, physically and psychically altered by her journeys across time and space. She learns on her second trip back in time that she and Rufus are likely blood-related as she reflects on the names that populate the genealogy recorded in her family Bible. She searches for an enslaved girl named Alice whom Rufus has identified as a friend, and who Dana recognizes as an ancestor. On Dana's journey, she encounters a band of vigilante patrollers who seize Alice's parents from their home and whip them brutally. Dana witnesses this act and her reaction might explain why she has been transported here from the 1970s: "I had seen people beaten on television and in the movies. I had seen the too-red blood substitute streaked across their backs and heard their well-rehearsed screams. But I hadn't lain nearby and smelled their sweat or heard them pleading and praying, shamed before their families and themselves" (36). According to the novel's logic, the mediated late-twentieth century cannot adequately depict the horrors of slavery, not even given the high-budget televised rendition of *Roots*. Dana must become an eyewitness to make slavery real to her, and the reader is similarly drawn into the past from the vantage point of a contemporary world that is markedly different, yet perhaps more connected than anyone would like to admit.

The novel showcases Dana's shock regarding the contrast between her 1970s life and the era of slavery. She registers every difference, from food to clothing to language, yet she also must learn to fit in when she is back in time. Because she is Black and in the antebellum South, she is assumed to be enslaved and she must adopt certain behaviors; for instance, someone in her position would not be able to look a white man like Rufus's father in the eye, so she averts her glance. The enslaved people she meets are suspicious of her, not only because of her strange clothes (like pants and shirts made of polyester) but because she talks "more like white folks than some white folks" (74) – essentially, that she has assimilated. This resentment the other Black characters express intensifies as the novel continues; one says, "You always try to act white. White nigger, turning against your own people!" (165). In modifying her behavior to avoid the violent treatment she receives – including whippings and beatings that leave her with permanent scars and missing teeth – she also begins to understand that she cannot take for granted the relative privilege she enjoys in the late twentieth century. Her marriage to a white man is somewhat novel in the 1970s, less than a decade after the Loving court decision that upheld segregated marriage in Virginia, but although it is not common in her world, it is unimaginable in Maryland in the 1810s.

Kevin is concerned for her well-being after she returns from one excursion physically harmed, and he manages to join her on the next trip back in time, a dynamic that complicates her personal journey into the horrors of her ancestral past. As they playact the roles expected of them based on race and gender, they must live separately in the slave quarters and the plantation home, and Dana worries that she will be transported to the present without him. Moreover, she is concerned that the customs and values of this world will "rub off on him" or "mark him somehow" (77). As their initial journey into the past together lengthens into weeks and months, she is bothered that they become "accepted, accepting" of the perverse world they have entered: "how easily we seemed to acclimatize" (97). She elaborates on this theme later when she begins to lose her rebellious spirit: "Slavery was a long slow process of dulling" (182). She is horrified when Kevin expresses childish excitement about being in this world, eager to "go West and watch the building of the country" (97) without acknowledging that the country was already being built, with a heavy reliance on slavery. Dana embarks on a mission to improve this world by trying to educate Rufus and the other children, but she becomes frustrated and declares the place "diseased" (99) and wants to return to the present. When Kevin suggests the era of slavery isn't as brutal as he had imagined, she highlights his privilege, pointing out that he has seen a very different version of this world from the perspective of a white man. In their present-day marriage, they've never had to confront racial differences in any contentious way, but those differences have clearly been simmering. The historical fact of slavery is an obstacle that stands between them, and perhaps always did. Dana's journey into the past can be read as a confrontation with that troublesome idea.

The couple becomes separated when Dana returns to the present and Kevin, stranded in the nineteenth century, heads to the North. Dana's next return to the past becomes a quest to reunite with him. Rufus grows into her somewhat trusted ally, yet she is concerned that he is becoming a copy of his cruel father. When he declares a history book she has brought back from the present "abolitionist trash," Dana replies, "That's history. It happened whether it offends you or not. Quite a bit of it offends me, but there's nothing I can do about it" (140). She wonders whether she has the power to do something about it, to alter history through her unique ability to bring knowledge from the future into this debased world. Rufus betrays her in her quest to find Kevin by hiding letters she has written to let Kevin know she has returned. When the couple reunites and returns to the present, something has changed. Each separately concludes that their present-day home is no longer home and that they are doomed to exist in the early nineteenth century. Dana deliberately returns to the past without Kevin and stays there long enough to question the foundation of her identity; she realizes, "I had worried I was keeping too much distance between myself and this alien time. Now, there was no distance at all" (220). Setting aside the paranormal time travel, this statement showcases an African American character who had once removed herself from the historical horrors of slavery and has now become so immersed in them that she cannot escape. Even after she has decisively broken with the past and ended her bizarre relationship with Rufus, whose character development features equal measures of progress and decline, she finds she is still drawn to the past which has indelibly scarred her, physically and psychically. After she returns permanently to the present, she still finds herself investigating the historical record to locate traces of Rufus and thus her ancestral past. If we view the novel as a quest narrative, the object is the quest itself: Dana finally understands that she has always had questions to which there are no answers, but her purpose becomes a lifelong mission to pursue them anyway. History is something to be challenged in contrast with her assertion to Rufus that she can't do anything about it.

The impulse to pursue historical truths informs Sherley Anne Williams's 1986 novel *Dessa Rose* which consciously responds to the legacy of Styron's novel: in a preface, the author states her attitude toward it as "outraged" (5). Like *Beloved*, published just a year later, *Dessa Rose* is based on historical figures, also discussed (yet not named) in the author's preface: an enslaved woman whose 1829 execution following her involvement in a slave revolt was delayed because she was pregnant and a white woman who took in escapees in 1830. Turning history into a counterfactual narrative, the author imagines a scenario in which the two meet in the year 1847, allowing for allusions to Nat Turner's 1831 rebellion as well as for an uplifting ending in which the enslaved woman avoids execution. The novel combines some of the satirical impulses of *Flight to Canada* (minus much of the humor) with the imaginative possibilities seen in *Kindred* to produce an original work that complements the profound gravity of *Beloved*.

The first section of *Dessa Rose*, "The Darky," takes aim at the circumstances of the publication of Nat Turner's slave narrative in which Turner dictated his story to a white lawyer named Thomas Ruffin Gray. Its other target is Styron's "critically acclaimed novel" that "travestied the as-told-to memoir of slave revolt leader Nat Turner" (5). Both critiques implicitly question the ethics of the way stories of slavery can lead to profit and fame for white people just as slave labor did. In this section a writer named Adam Nehemiah interviews Dessa as the basis for the follow-up book to his bestselling *The Masters' Complete Guide to Dealing with Slaves and Other Dependents*, a book that had brought him "widespread recognition" (24) despite his lack of expertise in the subject. He is writing this second book at the urging of his publisher and plans to call it *The Roots of Rebellion in the Slave Population and Some Means of Eradicating Them* (23). Williams satirizes the white appropriation represented by Styron's project while paying homage to Alex Haley's acclaimed novel by having Nehemiah shorten the title to *Roots* (32). Williams also takes a dig at Stowe by including a tale of a "courageous darky Thomas," referred to as "Uncle Tom," who sells out his enslaved colleagues who are planning an insurrection (27) and thus causes their deaths. In short, Williams's target is not just Styron, but the whole white publishing establishment leading all the way back through Stowe to Gray's appropriation of Turner's oral narrative.

Dessa Rose's first section contains multiple modes of narration, including Nehemiah's journal, Dessa's oral rendition of events, an objective third-person narrator who describes the process of Dessa narrating and Nehemiah transposing, and finally a third-person narrator who inhabits Dessa's consciousness. These multiple modes implicitly question the gaps in any version of a white author's rendition of the experience of slavery; for instance, in the section narrated by a third-person narrator inhabiting Dessa's consciousness, the reader learns what she refuses to tell Nehemiah. He is fixated on the question of who gave her a file to cut through the chains to aid in her escape: "'Who had the file?' he would ask, and how could she answer that? There had been no file … . having no answers, she gave none" (56). Nehemiah resents her silence and believes her to be dull-witted, but her rhetoric is strategic: she thinks "better to be smart than sassy" (56) and her goal is not to ask "anything of the white man that did not turn his own questions back upon themselves" (60). Nehemiah considers this behavior proof of her inferiority: "she answers questions in a random manner, a loquacious, roundabout fashion – if, indeed, she can be brought to answer them at all. This, to one of my habits, is exasperating to the point of fury. I must constantly remind myself that she is but a darky and a female at that" (22). The intersection of racism and sexism, glaringly evident in this statement, is a persistent concern in the novel.

The truths of Dessa's story remain her own. Nehemiah knows nothing about her; he completely forgets her name at one point (45) and at others refers to her as "Odessa" which she forcefully claims toward the novel's conclusion is not her name: "Ain't no O in it" (232). She asks him why he is writing down her words; he responds, "I write what I do in the hope of helping others to be happy in the life that has been sent them to live" (45). After narrating some of the more painful episodes of her story, she throws his words back at him: "'You think,' she asked looking up at the white man, 'you think what I say now going help peoples be happy in the life they sent? If that be true,' she said as he opened his mouth to speak, 'why I not be happy when I live it?'" (50). In this moment her interruption prevents him from speaking, indicating that she is fully in control of the story not only in terms of what she says and does not say and the emphasis she places on certain details, but also in the interpretation of the events.

What she emphasizes in her story is her lost love with Kaine, the father of her child who was murdered by their master. The incident was precipitated when the master smashed Kaine's banjo, which represented the only freedom he had in the world, and Kaine hit him in frustrated retribution. Nehemiah can't understand the significance of the banjo incident, but the event causes Kaine and by extension Dessa to understand the power relationship they are caught in, and to do something about it. Telling the story, Dessa muses, "wasn't there no place where a nigga could just be? He – Kaine – say, he ask hisself, 'That free? How that going to be free? It still be two lists, one say, 'White Man Can,' other say, 'Nigga Can't,' and white man still be the onliest one can write on 'em.' So he don't run no more" (50). Dessa grimly realizes, "White men existed because they did; Master had smashed the banjo because that was the way he was, able to do what he felt like doing" (58). Once they understand the power dynamic of slavery with such clarity, she and Kaine gain power, though their options are severely limited. Realizing this in the aftermath of Kaine's death, Dessa is bent on escaping for the sake of their unborn child. She plants a false clue in her story that has Nehemiah lead a party to locate a rumored encampment of escaped "maroons" nearby, and while the party is off looking, Dessa again escapes; Nehemiah ruefully notes, "we did not even know that she was gone" (68). She is skilled at concealing the truth while giving him what he thinks he wants, and he is ignorant to the realities of the lives of the enslaved, which are expressed in oral traditions he can't follow and music he can't interpret.

Part two of the novel, "The Wench," introduces the white woman alluded to in the novel's preface who allows escaped slaves to live and work on her plantation, Rufel (a portmanteau nickname for Ruth Elizabeth given to her by her Black caretaker Dorcas). These chapters are told from Rufel's perspective, and she is initially a character that does not invite the reader's sympathy due to her verbal mistreatment of Black characters. Disoriented from her escape and childbirth, Dessa wakes up to find Rufel nursing her newborn son and reacts violently to this highly unusual circumstance. The two women display an immediate antipathy to each other, but the community of African Americans living on Rufel's property convinces Dessa that she cannot feed the infant until she has recovered enough to produce milk, and Rufel is the only other capable woman on the property since she is still nursing her own daughter. Rufel nurses Dessa's baby "almost without thought … . But then it had seemed to her as natural as tuneless crooning or baby talk. The sight of him so tiny and bloodied had pained her with an almost physical hurt" (101). At the same time, "she had felt some mortification at becoming wet nurse for a darky" (102). Her relationship to the Black people she has known reveals the depth of these complex feelings. The empathy she feels for the newborn is compromised when she snaps at the teenaged Annabelle for her supposed impudence: "'Nigger,' she started forward, 'you come back here ... . You know you don't just walk away a white person without a by-your-leave'" (99). When the girl impishly questions Rufel using familiar names to address her, she becomes furious: "Annabelle had put Rufel almost on the same level as herself by its use now, making Rufel appear a child, Young Missy in tantrum, rather than Mistress of the House. Shaking, Rufel screamed, 'My name is 'Mistress' to you!'" (100). Naming, misnaming, nicknaming, and renaming are significant motifs; when Rufel behaves like this to the Black characters, they privately refer to her as "Miz Ruint."

She is considered ruined because her husband Bertie has been gone on a business trip for far too long, and it is widely assumed that he's never coming back, and most likely dead. Her punishing anger, seen in the scene with Annabelle, is born of or intensified by her abandonment, including by the death of her caretaker Dorcas, whom she called Mammy. Mammy was a mother figure to Rufel, but also a teacher and a spiritual guide: "She made Rufel stand up straight, rinsed her baby-fine hair in malt water and lemon, and arranged it becomingly about her childishly thin face. And loved her. It was Rufel Mammy had loved, Rufel whose heart she had stolen from the moment she smiled" (123). The fact that Mammy named Rufel underscores how important she had been to her very identity: "Whatever Rufel had not taken to [Mammy's] pillowy bosom seemed insignificant to her now; and she had been taken to that cushiony bosom, been named there 'Fel, Rufel. To hear the names on Mammy's lips was to hear, to know herself loved" (124). Her sorrow at Mammy's abrupt death is still fresh when Dessa arrives on the scene, and Dessa's lack of knowledge of that relationship turns into one of the many flashpoints between them. When Rufel talks about Mammy in an unguarded moment, Dessa explodes, "Wasn't no 'mammy' to it ... . You don't even know mammy" (118). They are clearly talking about two different women known as "mammy" to each of them, but Dessa cannot accept that Rufel has any claim to a Black woman called Mammy; she lashes out, "'Mammy' ain't nobody name, not they real one" (119). When Dessa challenges Rufel to come up with Dorcas's name, Rufel blanks, and also realizes she doesn't know if Dorcas had children of her own. Dessa sees this as proof that white women are not to be believed, trusted, respected, or even mildly liked, and Rufel is ashamed to realize that she did not know enough about the woman she claimed to love so much. The rift between them grows.

The arrangement between Rufel and the Black characters on the Sutton farm is not straightforward. Dessa tries to figure it out and is told, "Neither Ada nor her daughter [Annabelle] belonged to the white woman; none of them did" (115). When Dessa asks incredulously if they are free, Ada responds, "I wouldn't zactly call it free .... We runned away .... She let us stay here; she need the he'p. Man gone; slaves run off .... White folks think we hers but didn't none of us never belong to this place" (116). They are essentially sharecroppers, but Rufel gets to define the financial terms in her husband's absence. When Bertie and Rufel had enslaved people, Bertie was a cruel master and Rufel's solution to her ethical dilemma was to ignore his harsh treatment of them. As she tries to understand her relationship with the Black community residents on her farm who are technically enslaved, she wonders, "What else had she refused to see?" (153). The Black characters have told her they don't want to be around when Bertie returns, and she realizes, "She would have no more rights than they when Bertie came back" (150). Her relationship with Black characters is understandably complex given her deep bond to Mammy, and her nursing Dessa's baby is only one manifestation of her need to connect with them; notably, she becomes sexually involved with a Black man named Nathan. At the end of the second section Dessa accidentally walks in on the couple making love and cries out the derogatory name "Miz Ruint," and the rest of the community chides her for uttering it since it commits the sin of "calling someone out their name," like adding an "O" to hers.

The third and final section of the novel involves a reconciliation between Dessa and Rufel. Nathan convinces Rufel to join them in a plan that will provide her with more than enough money to survive without her husband and that will allow the rest of them to escape to the West. (It is suggested among the Black community that Nathan had seduced Rufel to put this confidence scheme into place, but the reader is given access to their intimate moments, and their relationship appears to be based on genuine attraction, even love). The scheme involves Rufel and another character named Ned – who can pass for white – selling the other enslaved characters in a small town and meeting them at the next designated spot after a quick escape before repeating the whole scam. Dessa makes clear her reservations about the plan: "I just knowed there had to be some way for us to get away without having a white person in it at all" (181). The others, especially Dessa's new lover Harker, break down her resistance through patient arguments; Harker says, "We *been* trusting her all along, just like *she* been trusting us." Dessa's response: "I muttered something about her trusting in her whiteness and not our blackness" (189). This absolute refusal to cooperate with a white character has Dessa spinning her tires, and it explains her horror at seeing Rufel nursing her baby, having sex with a Black man, or implying a familial relationship with Black people, and not only when she calls Dorcas "Mammy"; Dessa bitterly remarks, "She called Ada 'Auntie' like they was some kin" (175).

Dessa and Rufel must grow to trust and respect one another if their story is to avoid a tragic outcome. While they are on the road enacting their scam – which initially works better than expected – they develop a bond, especially one night when Rufel is raped by a drunken white man and Dessa has an epiphany: "The white woman was subject to the same ravishment as me; this the thought that kept me awake. I hadn't knowed white men could use a white woman like that" (201). Although it is not immediate or absolute, the bond between them forms at this minute, and Dessa softens her understandable visceral opposition to white women while Rufel works to become even more aware of how her conditioned sense of racial hierarchy can be fully eradicated. She even goes so far as to express a desire to join her escaped friends in the West; she says, "I don't want to live round slavery no more; I don't think I could without speaking up" (218). This plan is too much for Dessa to accept, especially because Rufel considers them "friends." That friendship proves important, though, when Rufel is the only one who can help Dessa after Nehemiah returns and tries to drag Dessa back into slavery.

The growth and development of these two women indicates a willingness to address the wounds of slavery in a positive way without pretending they don't continue to exist, even in the late twentieth century when the book was written. Dessa develops an increasingly sophisticated understanding of the power of slavery; referring to her ignorance about basic facts of nature, she says, "This is what I hold against slavery. May come a time when I for*give* – cause I don't think I'm set up to for*get* – the beatings, the selling, the killings, but I don't think I ever forgive the ignorance they kept us in" (207–8). Earlier she had clung to the idea that all white people had been responsible for her suffering, and she claimed, "I made up my mind not to put my freedom in no white woman's hand" (172) when the plot to escape to the West is revealed to her. Nathan points out how her behavior might prevent freedom altogether when he says, "You a grudgeful little old something, ain't you?" (205). Although the novel more than justifies her willingness to hold a grudge, it also indicates that the ability to move away from slavery and the long-term social ills it caused has to be cooperative, not just something undertaken by the perpetrators or the victims alone. By the novel's conclusion, Dessa has not only accepted Rufel but elevated her to the status of a friend: "*I have met some good white men ... . But none the equal of Ruth*" (236, italics original). The process of reimagining history has led Williams to overcome her outrage at the fact that "there was no place in the American past I could go and be free" and to reconceive her understanding of history: "I now know that slavery eliminated neither heroism nor love" (5–6).

Colson Whitehead's Pulitzer Prize-winning novel *The Underground Railroad* (2016) takes yet another approach to the relationship between history and new narratives of slavery. The novel employs elements of magical realism and historical fantasy to convert the famed secret system of transporting enslaved people to freedom into a physical railroad that actually runs underground. This invention – as well as anachronisms such as the presence of skyscrapers with elevators in the mid-nineteenth century – opens up storytelling possibilities unavailable in straight realism. The novel is no less history-minded than any of the new narratives of slavery discussed above: it reveals the same level of research as the novels by Morrison, Butler, and Williams. Nor do Whitehead's flights of fancy cause him to avert the brutality of slavery. Novelists who try to find new ways to approach this era are not interested in tempering the torture, degradation, or dehumanization enslaved people endured. Readers of *The Underground Railroad* are subjected to many stomach-turning descriptions including a particularly gruesome scene in which a captured escapee known as Big Anthony is revoltingly tortured over a three-day period before being immolated, sometimes in front of white guests who crassly dine and take notes. The protagonist Cora had been unsure whether to risk escape despite her suffering: her master savagely beat her for trying to protect a child and she was raped by enslaved men after she tried to claim the tiny plot of land her grandmother had once used to grow vegetables. Big Anthony's murder and its immediate aftermath are the last straw: when the plantation's master gropes her, she understands, "She had not been his and now she was his. Or she had always been his and just now knew it" (48). Despite the agonizing spectacle of Big Anthony's death, she assents to a plan by her colleague Caesar and steals off through the same swamp where her mother had escaped and from there to the underground railroad, accessed through trap doors and secret passageways. Among other things, this more than metaphorical railroad represents the fruits of Black labor that benefit the Black community instead of making white people rich: "The tunnel, the tracks, the desperate souls who found salvation in the coordination of its stations and timetables – this was a marvel to be proud of" (68).

During their escape, they fight off slavecatchers, and Cora is certain she has murdered a white boy who laid hands on her, a crime that makes her even more dangerous to those who harbor her. She and Caesar are transported from Georgia to South Carolina where they are given new identities and happily adjust to their new condition in this state that supposedly has progressive attitudes toward slavery: Cora "walked down the sidewalk as a free woman. No one chased her or abused her" (87). She is taught skills like literacy and good posture that will help her overcome her years of abuse on the plantation and allow her to enter civilized society, and Caesar is trained in factory work which, though monotonous, is "unexpectedly fulfilling" (103) because he is able to see the finished product he and his fellow laborers produced, in contrast with plantation work. They are allowed to use a special scrip for Black people in local stores, and Cora likes this freedom to engage in commerce even as she realizes that "things in their local establishment cost two or three times as much as those in the white stores" (101). They're so enchanted by their new lives that they choose not to board the next few trains that come through town and debate whether they actually want to continue along the railroad, which runs at random times and to random places, but eventually in the direction of the free North.

Yet during Cora's time in South Carolina, she is initially blinded by the fact that her status has not really changed, but only taken different forms. Her new role is to work in display cases within something called the Museum of Natural Wonders which contains three rooms designed to "educate the public" (109), namely "Scenes from Darkest Africa," "Life on the Slave Ship," and "Typical Day on the Plantation" (109–110). She and two other Black women alternate between these rooms all day, performing menial tasks while ignoring children who "banged on the glass and pointed at [them] in a disrespectful fashion" (111). Turning Black subjects into a display for the mockery, amusement, and supposed education of white people forecasts a history of mistreatment not only during the era of slavery but after its end. The rest of Cora's time in South Carolina echoes historical events that plagued the years of Reconstruction and the early twentieth century, namely the deaths of more than a hundred men in the Tuskegee Syphilis Study, eugenics, the forced sterilization of African American women, lynching, race riots, and segregation. Cora gradually learns about the hidden horrors of the supposedly civilized life she is leading in this new state. After she is subjected to a medical examination in which her blood is extracted and the doctor suggests "birth control" after ascertaining that she is not a virgin, she witnesses a female colleague having a mental breakdown, screaming "They're taking away my babies!" Cora eventually understands the meaning of the surgeries the doctors are performing in the name of "population control": "The woman wasn't lamenting an old plantation injustice but a crime perpetrated here in South Carolina. The doctors were stealing her babies from her, not her former masters" (113, 123). She flees back to the underground railroad as a race riot erupts overhead.

From South Carolina she flees to North Carolina and later Indiana, all the while being pursued by a notorious slave catcher named Ridgefield. In North Carolina she is hidden away in a tiny attic space reminiscent of Harriet Jacobs's slave narrative, and through a peephole she witnesses weekly minstrel shows and ritualized lynchings on the village green. Here again Whitehead hints at the horrors of history, not only leading up to the 1850s when the novel takes place, but in the centuries afterward. We witness a group called the "night riders" who are clearly the genesis of the Ku Klux Klan, and we see the role of the patrollers, "white, crooked, and merciless" vigilantes who are the historical origin of the contemporary police whose racist interactions with the Black community have led to the civil resistance of the Black Lives Matter movement. Like the practice of racial profiling enacted by contemporary traffic enforcement officers, in Whitehead's novel, "The patroller required no reason to stop a person apart from color" (162). Through it all, Cora must negotiate her relationship with white people, some of whom are her allies who help her navigate the underground railroad and many of whom are her enemies who profit from dragging her back to slavery. Just as we see the Black community divided in the early chapters when Cora uses a hatchet to defend her measly plot of land, so we see the white community divided as when an Irish immigrant maid rats on the white family who is harboring Cora in their attic, leading to their public execution. Cora's conclusion is that the power dynamic that has structured her country is to blame: "Whether in the fields or underground or in an attic room, America remained her warden" (172). Another historical reverberation in the word "warden" indicates our current era of mass incarceration.

The very concept of America as warden, in this sense, justifies the logic of slavery, and according to the slave catcher Ridgefield, America created slavery in the name of prosperity, and called it Manifest Destiny. He tells Cora,

> My father liked his Indian talk about the Great Spirit … . I prefer the American spirit, the one that called us from the Old World to the New, to conquer and build and civilize. And destroy that what needs to be destroyed. To lift up the lesser races. If not lift up, subjugate. And if not subjugate, exterminate. Our destiny by divine prescription – the American imperative. (222)

This chapter has suggested that American novels about slavery resist the American Dream script that anchors the tradition, but this quotation reveals an insidious relationship that Whitehead arrives at through ripping apart and reassembling American history. If we substitute "Dream" for "imperative" in Ridgefield's sick-if-brutally-honest philosophical manifesto above, the relationship is clear. Slavery existed to propagate the Dream. Our favorite myth's meaning shifts considerably when we consider the perspectives of those who have been historically subjugated – yet not exterminated – over the course of its history.

Further Reading

Banks, Russell. *Cloudsplitter* (1998)
Bradley, David. *The Chaneysville Incident* (1981)
Cather, Willa. *Sapphira and the Slave Girl* (1940)
Faulkner, William. *Absalom, Absalom!* (1936)
Gaines, Ernest J. *The Autobiography of Miss Jane Pittman* (1971)
Haley, Alex. *Roots* (1976)
Johnson, Charles H. *Middle Passage* (1990)
Jones, Edward P. *The Known World* (2003)
Mitchell, Margaret. *Gone With the Wind* (1936)
Reed, Ishmael. *Flight to Canada* (1976)
Stowe, Harriet Beecher. *Dred: A Tale of the Great Dismal Swamp* (1856)
Styron, William. *The Confessions of Nat Turner* (1967)
Wideman, John Edgar. *The Lynchers* (1973)
Walker, Margaret. *Jubilee* (1966)

5 Class, Race, and the Anti-Dream Narrative

The American Dream myth is a middle-class fantasy. Ragged Dick in Horatio Alger's novel rises from poverty to the middle class, but the protagonists of the other novels discussed in Chapter 2 are not truly poor: they begin in the middle class (even if on the low end of it), and their hope is to rise somewhat higher. American novels about those who are truly impoverished or discriminated against because of racism indicate that their strivings and yearnings do not matter: they will never manage steady progress to a higher station the way Ragged Dick does. As David Minter writes, "despite the varied dreams and the many experiences of success that mark the culture of the United States, the burden of its history teaches us that its citizens should not speak of that success unless they are prepared to confront its costs by seeing it as its victims do – those excluded from it or, more drastically, sacrificed for it" (Alger 6). This chapter considers novels that might be called anti-Dream narratives because the Dream is not available. The high period of naturalism from the late nineteenth century through the early twentieth emphasized how poverty (among other social factors) was a stronger force than individual will. Contemporary novelists also tend to be sensitive to class-based limitations. The persistence of racism in America following the abolition of slavery is equally responsible for denying the Dream to Americans of African descent.

Poverty, Naturalism, and the Anti-Dream

A foundational novelistic example of the way poverty denies the Dream is Stephen Crane's *Maggie: A Girl of the Streets* (1893), a bleak tale that relentlessly argues, as its author put it, "that environment is a tremendous thing in the world and frequently shapes lives" (3). Before we meet Maggie, we see her brother in a brutal street fight. Such skirmishes happen in *Ragged Dick* as well, but in a cartoonish way; in Crane's novel, "A stone had smashed into Jimmie's mouth. Blood was bubbling over his chin and down upon his ragged shirt" (37). The depiction of violence, filth, and brutality in the novel is overwhelming. The pugnacious Jimmie is the only member of Maggie's family who cares about her fate, but even when she is a newborn, Jimmie reacts violently to her wailing: "Shut up er I'll smack yer mout'. See?" (40). Their parents are vicious drunks, and after their father dies, Jimmie is forced into the working world. He has "a belligerent attitude toward all well-dressed men" but realizes that he has few choices: "When he had a dollar in his pocket his satisfaction with existence was the greatest thing in the world. So, eventually, he felt obliged to work" (47). His job as a truck driver removes him from the house, leaving Maggie to deal with her abusive mother on her own.

As the narrator puts it, Maggie "blossomed in a mud puddle" (49). Her beauty is emphasized and is a potential liability in this world because of the predatory nature of the young men of the neighborhood. Jimmie tells her, "'Yeh've edder got teh go teh hell or go teh work!' Whereupon she went to work, having the feminine aversion of going to hell" (49). The irony here is that the only work available to her – manual labor in a cuff and collar factory – is a kind of hell: "She received a stool and a machine in a room where sat twenty girls of various shades of discontent" (50). She later reflects on her workspace as "a dreary place of endless grinding" and there is no respite in "the dark, dust-stained walls, and the scant furniture of her home" (53). Enter Pete, a handsome acquaintance of Jimmie's, who strolls into her house with imperious confidence, causing Maggie to regard him as an "aristocratic person;" the narrator comments, "Under the trees of her dream-gardens there had always walked a lover" (52).

The only fairy tale element of this bleak narrative is the protagonist's romantic longing, though. She's temporarily able to forget about the factory when she and Pete are out on dates, but only temporarily. They attend gaudy melodramas "in which the poor and virtuous eventually surmounted the wealthy and wicked" and these performances fuel her fantasies: "She wondered if the culture and refinement she had seen imitated, perhaps grotesquely, by the heroine on the stage, could be acquired by a girl who lived in a tenement house and worked in a shirt factory" (62). Reality always returns with a thump: "She wondered as she regarded some of the grizzled women in the room, mere mechanical contrivances sewing seams and grinding out, with heads bended over their work, tales of imagined or real girl-hood happiness, past drunks, the baby at home, and unpaid wages. She speculated how long her youth would endure" (59). From their first date, it's clear that Pete's desire for Maggie is merely sexual, and when she finally succumbs to his advances, she is instantly shunned by her family and residents of their tenement. Abandoned and without even the mild protections of a husband or home, she turns to sex work in a desperate attempt to survive, but her life and the novel end quickly after her "fall." Her story is summarily pathetic; she never had the opportunity to convert her dream into reality, and the choice between working and going to hell was a false one.

Naturalism persistently corrects the American Dream myth by revealing how it is inaccessible to the truly poor. Novels by Frank Norris (*McTeague* [1899] and *The Octopus* [1901]), Theodore Dreiser (*Jennie Gerhardt* [1911] and *An American Tragedy* [1925]), Jack London (*Martin Eden* [1909]) and other naturalists from this period consistently reveal the struggles and often tragic results of attempts to rise from the lower class. If upward mobility is the myth, downward mobility or tragedy are often the true outcomes of the quest. A key difference between these works and works of high realism such as *The Rise of Silas Lapham* (discussed in Chapter Two) is the relative influence of fate or free will. Lapham makes decisions that alter his trajectory, and although he is punished by the loss of his fortune, he is rewarded with moral enlightenment. Plus, he doesn't become completely destitute, and his daughter marries a rich man. Naturalist novels tend to eschew such cheery solutions; protagonists often end up dead, disillusioned, or alienated. Although the Naturalist movement flourished in the early decades of the twentieth century, the Great Depression renewed its urgency as the poverty that had long plagued the lower class became more widespread and perhaps more real to the typically middle-class novel reader. John Steinbeck's *The Grapes of Wrath* (1939) and Richard Wright's *Native Son* (1940) illustrate how naturalism's popularity and its willingness to correct the American Dream myth reached a high point in the years just before World War II.

Steinbeck's novel won the Pulitzer Prize and Wright's was the first by an African American author selected for the influential Book of the Month Club, indicating a large middle-class readership. Both Steinbeck and Wright were keen to rattle the complacency of their bourgeois readers who might not have been fully aware of the plight of the poor. Steinbeck said of his book, "I've done my damndest to rip a reader's nerves to rags" (xviii) and Wright, after realizing that his first book (*Uncle Tom's Children* [1937]) was one "which even bankers' daughters could read and weep over," vowed, "if I ever wrote another book, no one would weep over it; that it would be so hard and deep that they would have to face it without the consolation of tears" (454). Both novels are too substantial to cover in detail here, but a brief consideration of each as anti-Dream narratives illustrates how they extend Crane's premises.

The Grapes of Wrath is a mock epic in which a desperate family joins a swarm of migrants leaving drought-stricken Oklahoma for the promises of prosperous California. The narrative employs the full omniscience of a narrator who zooms in on the lives of Tom Joad and his family and pans out so far at times that humans are nowhere in sight, but the activities of the animal world are considered as parallels. As with *Maggie*, poverty is a condition that can possibly be endured, but not transcended. Early in the novel a random truck driver puts ten cents into a slot machine, loses, and declares, "They fix 'em so you can't win nothing" (7). This is essentially the theme of the book. Even though the Joads call on their strength and survival instinct to pursue a better life, the game is fixed from the beginning: the rich get richer, and the poor barely get by. The series of disasters to which the Joads are subjected is relentless, originating even before the novel begins with Tom Joad's incarceration for manslaughter and mounting thereafter to include eviction from their home, exile from their land, the deaths of both grandparents, abandonment by multiple members of the family, hunger, violence amongst the downtrodden migrant workers, a stillborn baby, and a flood. Reminiscent of the Old Testament, the challenge seems to be merely to withstand the punishments of a wrathful God (as the title alludes to) while preserving some semblance of human decency, if not traditional faith in the divine. Ma Joad states simply her family's code of generosity: "I never heard tell of no Joads … ever refusin' food an' shelter or a lift on the road to anybody that asked" (102). The code is upheld throughout the novel, even in its concluding pages: after all the trials have worn down and scattered the family, Ma encourages her daughter Rose of Sharon, whose child was stillborn, to share her breast milk with a starving stranger.

There is no glimmer of prosperity in the narrative for the Joad family, though there are repeated reminders that the greed of the wealthy compromises the Joad family's spirit of generosity. The caravan of migrants passes by big houses and fancy cars as well as other tantalizing symbols of wealth and expresses a longing for them, but from a vast distance. Ma Joad summarizes their plight: "What we got lef' in the worl'? Nothin' but us. Nothin' but the folks" (169). This realization is at odds with even the simplest formula for getting by; Tom laments, "I wisht they was some way to make [a living] 'thout takin' her away from somebody else" (187). The family and their fellow travelers understand that capitalism breeds resentment and fear: as "Okies" they are discriminated against and criminalized. At the same time, they realize that the fortunate few aren't content with what they have. Preacher Casy observes, "If [a man] needs a million acres to make him feel rich, seems to me he needs it 'cause he feels awful poor inside hisself, and if he's poor in hisself, there ain't no million acres gonna make him feel rich, an' maybe he's disappointed that nothin' he can do'll make him feel rich" (207). Thus, the vicious cycle continues: the greedy use their wealth to separate themselves from the impoverished, virtuous strivers caught in a system that oppresses them. Those who manage to survive are destined to fail if they try to rise above their station.

In *The Grapes of Wrath*, the Joads are homeless and carry their belongings on their back like the turtle that plods through the novel's early chapters, battered by forces larger than itself. In *Native Son* the Thomases are renters who live in squalor as illustrated in the opening scene in which the antihero Bigger Thomas kills a rat that has invaded their apartment. Although the novel is frequently studied in terms of race, which is certainly its most prominent concern, the related context of poverty also obtains. From the opening scene, Bigger and his mother and siblings are crowded into a single room. Despite their shared circumstance, it's evident right away that there is no equivalent of the tribal bond that helps the Joads to persevere. Bigger is a bully. After killing the rat, he sadistically dangles it in the face of his terrified sister, "enjoying [her] fear" (7) until she faints. Frustrated with what is clearly a pattern of bad behavior, his mother labels him "just plain dumb black crazy" and tells him, "We wouldn't have to live in this garbage dump if you had any manhood in you" (8). She blames him for his lifestyle, branding his friend group a "gang" (9), but they both know the reality is more complex: Bigger was born into a world of limited opportunities. The narrator reveals this premise in clear terms: "He hated his family because he knew that they were suffering and that he was powerless to help them … . He knew that the moment he allowed what his life meant to enter fully into his consciousness, he would either kill himself or someone else" (10). This realization can be seen as a self-fulfilling prophecy or as a realistic acceptance of the way his environment has dictated his fate.

The few opportunities he has are limited by his class and race. Referring to a job prospect to be a chauffeur to a wealthy family, he thinks, "Yes, he could take the job at Dalton's and be miserable, or he could refuse it and starve. It maddened him to think that he did not have a wider choice of action" (12). He tells his friends his dream is to fly a plane; his friend Gus wryly responds, "If you wasn't black and if you had some money and if they'd let you go to that aviation school, you *could* fly a plane" (17). Bigger initially laughs to stave off the pain of this truth, but he can't sustain this pose; he cries, "Goddammit, look! We live here and they live there. We black and they white. They got things and we ain't. They do things and we can't. It's just like living in jail" (20). When Bigger is not bullying his friends or his sister, he is forced to bury his murderous rage, but it is too intense to stay buried.

His subservient job at the Daltons intensifies his suppressed anger. He has already glimpsed their socialite daughter Mary Dalton who appears onscreen on a gossipy newsreel at the movie theater, but his in-person encounter with her forces him to confront reality; he "considered in amazement how different the girl had seemed in the movie. On the screen she was not dangerous and his mind could do with her as it liked. But here in her home she walked over everything" (55). Although the movies functioned as an escape for impoverished Depression-era Americans (similar to the theater in Crane's *Maggie*), the images of glamor and splendor on the silver screen often served to heighten the dejection of viewers rather than to distract from them. The movies provide Bigger and his friends with a false alternative to their world. The poolhall – a site of frequent violence – is their only other recreational outlet.

Far from the depiction of her in the newsreel, Mary and her boyfriend Jan are Communists who reject the values held by her capitalist father. On Bigger's first night driving them around, they violate the terms of class and race segregation he has always known, insisting that Bigger stop calling Jan "sir" and encouraging him to eat with them at a restaurant in the African American part of town. In a devastating series of disastrous events, Bigger returns a very drunken Mary to her room. Afraid that her mumblings will cause the family to discover he is in there with her, he inadvertently smothers her and disposes of her body in the furnace. The heinous act was not premeditated, but his damaged psychology had already led him to understand that he carried a rage that could only result in homicide or suicide. Reflecting on his crime, he arrives at a dark realization: "The knowledge that he had killed a white girl they loved and regarded as their symbol of beauty made him feel the equal of them, like a man who had been somehow cheated, but had now evened the score" (164). Like someone sinking in quicksand, his flailing leads to another series of catastrophic decisions as he tries to extort kidnaping money from the Daltons, attempts to incriminate Jan knowing how hated Communists are, goes on the lam when he realizes he is cornered, and kills his girlfriend, Bessie.

The fact that Bigger views murder as a way to "even the score" or to gain power in a world that has denied him opportunities is one of the harshest novelistic critiques of the American Dream in literary history. Like *The Grapes of Wrath*, *Native Son* demonizes capitalism and champions Communism as a viable alternative, but neither text demonstrates the achievement of equality or individual prosperity. The socialist ideas that Jan and Mary share with Bigger are so antithetical to his way of thinking that they could be seen as a primary catalyst for his murderous rage. Once Bigger is caught, Jan forgives him with boundless empathy; he says, "maybe in a certain sense, I'm the one who's really guilty" (287). He even pays for Bigger's lawyer, a Communist ideologue named Max. In the third part of the novel, dominated by Bigger's trial, Max concludes his argument by trying to enlighten the court about the lives of the poor:

"I plead with you to see a mode of *life* in our midst, a mode of life stunted and distorted, but possessing its own laws and claims, an existence of men growing out of the soil prepared by the collective but blind will of a hundred million people ... . I ask you to recognize the laws and processes flowing from such a condition, understand them, seek to change them" (388). Predictably, Max is not able to influence hearts and minds in the courtroom, and Bigger is sentenced to death. The only hope is that the reader of this "hard and deep" tale will bring about the social revolution that was not available within its pages. Max listens in "terror" as Bigger struggles to make sense of his fate by blurting, "What I killed for must have been good!" (429). This confusing conclusion only makes sense if we consider the "good" to apply not to the lost lives of Mary, Bessie, or Bigger, but to hope that the novel will enlighten readers about the consequences of inequality.

Poverty in America did not begin or end during the Great Depression, of course, and novels about the limited opportunities for the impoverished continue to be published. Noting a preponderance of fiction published in the 1980s about the lives of the working or lower middle classes, critics struggled to label them, coming up with the inadequate and condescending terms "dirty realism" and "K-Mart realism." Writers in these categories included a broad range of authors such as Frederick Barthelme, Raymond Carver, Richard Ford, and Bobbie Ann Mason. In this same vein, Dorothy Allison's *Bastard Out of Carolina* (1992), published a century after Crane's *Maggie*, illustrates the persistent relevance of these anti-Dream novels, but with an important difference: Allison's protagonist Ruth Anne Boatwright – known as Bone – is allowed to tell her own story, unlike the subjects of the novels by Crane, Steinbeck, and Wright. As a girl whose childhood is violently stolen from her, Bone is barely even introduced to the Dream, much less given the chance to believe in it.

Bone's story begins even before she was born. She is the "bastard" of the title, and her mother (known as Mama) was merely sixteen when she gave birth to Bone. The birth coincides with a car accident caused by her Uncle Travis's drunkenness. In fact, the whole family except Bone's mother were drunk during the delivery, and because of this circumstance (which is common in this family), the baby's first name was spelled three different ways on her birth certificate. When two family members give different answers about the absent father's last name, the clerk types "illegitimate" in red at the bottom of the certificate: "and there I was – certified a bastard by the state of South Carolina" (3). Mama views the mark as an indelible class identifier: "Mama hated to be called trash, hated the memory of every day she'd ever spent bent over people's peanuts and strawberry plants while they stood and looked at her like she was a rock on the ground. The stamp on that birth certificate burned her like the stamp she knew they'd tried to put on her" (3). Every year she returns to the clerk to have the birth certificate reissued, and every year she fails.

Mama marries Lyle Parsons both to avoid the stigma of a child labeled illegitimate and as a source of income; Bone says, "Totally serious about providing well for his family and proving himself a man, [Lyle] got Mama pregnant almost immediately and didn't want her to go out to work at all. But pumping gas and changing tires in his cousin's Texaco station, he made barely enough to pay the rent" (6). Mama quits her waitressing job and Lyle dies soon thereafter in a freak accident, leaving her jobless and with another mouth to feed, Bone's sister Reese. Mama's search for work reveals that she, like Maggie, the Joads, or Bigger Thomas, has limited opportunities: "A year in the mill was all Mama could take after they buried Lyle; the dust in the air got to her too fast. After that there was no choice but to find work in a diner. The tips made all the difference, though she knew she could make more money at the honky-tonks or managing a slot as a cocktail waitress. There was always more money serving people beer and wine, more still in hard liquor, but she'd have had to go outside Greenville County to do that" (8). The jobs available in her locale are either hazardous to her health or low-paying, and she can't move because she relies on her sisters to help raise her two daughters. She arrives at the only conclusion available, a desperate rendition of the Dream: "I need a husband .... and a car and a home and a hundred thousand dollars" (13). The husband alone will have to do. She marries Glen Waddell despite family members' warnings that there's "something wrong" with him (37).

It seems initially that what's wrong with Glen is that he is possessive and controlling of Mama, but his behavior quickly becomes much worse. On the night Mama gives birth to their son, Glen sexually molests Bone in the car outside the hospital; she is roughly six years old at the time. When her infant brother dies in childbirth, Glen goes into a psychological tailspin. He moves Mama, Bone, and Reese away from their extended family, claiming, "We don't need nobody else" (50). From this point he has the girls refer to him as Daddy Glen. His relationship with Mama and the girls is the textbook definition of abusive. He controls the finances, even when a little money arrives for Reese as a settlement after her birth father's death. He cannot keep his job as a truck driver for a soda company because of a combination of a bad temper and general incompetence and the family becomes nomadic: "We moved and then moved again. We lived in no one house more than eight months. Rented houses; houses leased with an option to buy; shared houses on the city limits" (64). Their poverty leads to hunger; there are stories of how the only meal Mama could cobble together was soda crackers and ketchup. Frustrated with Glen's laziness and general inability to provide, Mama storms out of the house with the girls, drops them at her brother's house, and evidently resorts to sex work to put food on the table. This desperate act only exacerbates Glen's hair-trigger temper.

The damage of their endless cycle of poverty is psychological as well as physical and emotional. Glen lamely blames others for his lot in life, especially his brothers who are relatively well off: "Nobody wants me to have nothing nice," he declares. Mama tries to instill in the girls some shred of self-esteem; she says, "We're not bad people. And we pay our way. We just can't always pay when people want," but Bone and Reese are not convinced: "We knew what the neighbors called us, what Mama wanted to protect us from. We knew who we were" (82). Such a resignation to one's lowly class position is clear evidence that Bone does not believe in anything like the Dream. The stigma Mama had tried to avoid in obtaining a birth certificate without a scarlet "illegitimate" stamp clearly permeates social opinions and the obstinacy of this stigma makes class mobility all but impossible. Deepening her low self-esteem, Bone experiences shame after shoplifting and identifies a different kind of hunger, "a hunger in the back of the throat, not the belly, an echoing emptiness that ached for the release of screaming" (98). She directs her resentment toward anyone who has more money than she does, including Daddy Glen's siblings, and this is a trait that causes both of them to act out, but in different ways.

Glen's physical and sexual abuse of Bone is renewed in her early adolescent years and she and Mama walk on eggshells around him. The novel features many of the tropes of the coming-of-age genre – making and losing a best friend, the discovery of autoerotic stimulation, a flirtation with religion as a saving force, the aforementioned shoplifting – but these rites are intensely charged because of the framework of eternal poverty. Bone desperately wants to be loved, but both her harried mother and her abusive stepfather destroy her sense of self-worth. She relies on her aunts and uncles to fill in this necessary gap in her life, and her uncles finally protect her from Glen when they discover he has been beating her to the point of broken bones and permanently scarred legs. She becomes at the age of twelve "a bowl of hatred" (252) and vacillates between fantasies of self-harm and of destruction of her community, which she partly enacts by breaking into a local department store. At one point she lashes out at her Aunt Raylene, the independent one who has mentored her: "I'm just another ignorant Boatwright," she yells, "Another piece of trash barely knows enough to wipe her ass or spit away from the wind. Just like you and Mama and Alma and everybody" (258). Raylene puts her in her place: "You better think hard ... about what you want and who you're mad at"

(263). This advice hits home and causes her to fantasize for the first time about the Dream, even identified as such: "I imagined Mama getting a job where she could sit down all she wanted, where the money was good and she never got any burns or had to pull her hair back so tight off her face that she got headaches … . I fell asleep there dreaming, loving the dream" (263).

A book that showcases as much misery as this one – and it is one of the bleakest imaginable – seems to dangle the Dream of a more comfortable life only to dash it violently. Just after Bone's pleasant indulgence in this fantasy, her Aunt Alma has a psychotic break that causes her to destroy her home and to harm herself. Following that trauma, Daddy Glen returns and brutally rapes Bone. Mama arrives in the immediate aftermath of the gruesome act and, although she drives Bone to the hospital, she seems to forgive Glen and she vanishes, leaving Raylene to take care of Bone. Mama returns one final time to hand Bone an envelope containing a clean birth certificate with no "illegitimate" stamped on the bottom, but the damage she and Glen have done is irreparable. There is no foreseeable end to the cycle of misery Bone was born into.

Race and the Anti-Dream

Another category of novels holds out hope on one level that the Dream is attainable and demonstrates its impossibility on another. The first example is a heavyweight contender for the mythical Great American Novel discussed in Chapter 1. Ralph Ellison's *Invisible Man* (1952) is a marvel of creative energy and literary wizardry that takes the sociological and psychological quagmires of Nella Larsen's and James Weldon Johnson's novels discussed in Chapter 2 to new phantasmagoric heights. It is at once sprawling and impressively structured, framed by a prologue and an epilogue that highlight the frustrating futility of the journey in between. Ellison's narrator is nameless and is often referred to in criticism as Invisible Man, a convention adopted here. The premise of the prologue and the epilogue, narrated in the present, is that Invisible Man is living alone in an underground "hole" as he describes it, lit by lightbulbs powered by energy stolen from the light and power company. As the plot eventually makes clear, he has dropped out of society literally and figuratively and is currently in a state of hibernation as he figures out how and when to reenter it, though the outlines of his plan are unclear both to him and to the reader.

The novel is a quest narrative with the object being a full understanding of the narrator's complex and self-contradictory identity as a Black man in Depression-era America. Invisible Man doesn't realize his objective until the journey is over, though. Through much of the narrative, his goal is simply success as defined by the stereotypical American Dream script: upward class mobility and personal financial gain. The first step on this journey is typically higher education. The most renowned scene in the novel opens the action, the infamous "Battle Royal" in which the adolescent narrator is blindfolded and shoved into a boxing ring with a couple dozen of his Black classmates to compete for monetary prizes and the chance for a college scholarship. The scene, laden with nightmarish surreal imagery and symbolism, is a revolting display of racist cruelty. The drunken wealthy white men of the narrator's southern town host this annual ritual which begins by parading a naked white woman in front of the scantily clad Black teens in order to arouse and confuse them, for her sexual allure is considered absolutely taboo in this segregated world. Upon seeing her, Invisible Man feels "a wave of irrational guilt and fear" and describes his confusion: "I wanted at one and the same time to run from the room, to sink through the floor, or go to her and cover her from my eyes and the eyes of the others with my body; to feel the soft thighs, to caress her and destroy her, to love her and murder her, to hide from her, and yet to stroke where below the small American flag tattooed upon her belly her thighs formed a capital V" (19). The tattoo indicates that she symbolizes the American Dream which is being displayed just out of the boys' reach. She is also the first of multiple white women in the novel who tantalize Invisible Man as a way of controlling his behavior. The effect of her presence on the narrator and his comrades is to whip them into a frenzy so that they might produce a chaotic spectacle for the sick pleasure of the white men who control this world.

Part of the narrator's wild response to the naked white woman involves vision: he wants to "cover her from my eyes and the eyes of the others." This motif of obscuring vision, coupled with the invisibility announced in the title, recurs throughout the novel literally and metaphorically. The next part of the Battle Royal scene involves blindfolding the boys before they enter the ring. The act is designed to manipulate and endanger them. When the narrator tries to loosen his blindfold, one white voice shouts, "Oh, no you don't, black bastard! Leave that alone" (22). The narrator describes the chaos: "Everyone fought hysterically. It was complete anarchy. Everyone fought everybody else. No group fought together for long" (23). The meaning of the scene can again be read symbolically: throughout the book the Black community is divided against itself by forces from the white world they cannot see, and the narrator is torn between his impulse to succeed individually and to cooperate with those in the same precarious, powerless position as he is. He squints to loosen the blindfold enough so he can see, enabling him to take advantage of his comrades who remain blind.

The cruelty deepens when the organizers remove the blindfolds and encourage the boys to scramble for money strewn around the boxing ring, but some of the coins are electrodes that shock the boys upon contact. The narrator feels greed and competition take over even as he watches his colleagues writhe in pain from electric shock. Panicked, he grabs one of the drunken white men: "I held on, surprising myself for a moment by trying to topple *him* onto the ring. It was such an enormous idea that I found myself actually carrying it out" (28). This is a significant moment because Invisible Man's unconscious intuition rather than his rational mind initiates this act of rebellion. Reason and instinct are at war throughout the novel, and when the narrator follows reason, he tends to sink deeper into his problems. When he allows improvisation and intuition to rule, he makes progress in his identity quest. For example, immediately after the money-scrambling scene, he is allowed to give the speech that will earn him the scholarship to a historically Black college. The speech is a straight imitation of one given by Booker T. Washington, historically known as "The Great Accommodator," and the college that the narrator attends is modeled after Tuskegee, the college that Washington founded and that Ellison briefly attended. The narrator mechanically attempts to recite his speech as he rehearsed it – "I spoke automatically" (30) – but as the drunken white men jeer, he finds himself altering the phrase "social responsibility" to "social equality" (31) without thinking about the divergent meanings of the phrases. The men sober up immediately and ask him to repeat the phrase slowly. He reverts to the original phrase and meekly explains his error: "I was swallowing blood" (31). Yet because of his unconscious slip, he understands something about the nature of power, especially as it pertains to language.

Such realizations are connected to the writings of Sigmund Freud whose ideas permeate the book along with allusions to countless other thinkers and literary works. The Battle Royal chapter ends with a Freudian flourish as Invisible Man narrates an ambiguous dream he had of his grandfather, a dream he attempts to reinterpret throughout the novel. His grandfather, who gave up his gun during Reconstruction and imparted confusing deathbed advice about how to succeed in the white world, appears in the dream with the narrator at a circus, refusing to laugh at the clowns. He instructs the narrator to open the briefcase he received at the Battle Royal containing the scholarship. The narrator finds inside an envelope full of smaller envelopes that represent "years," according to the grandfather, and finally one containing an embossed message: "To Whom It May Concern ... Keep This Nigger-Boy Running" (33). The grandfather breaks into mocking laughter and the narrator is left to wonder what it all means, but he mechanically follows the Dream script by rushing off to college without giving himself the chance to contemplate.

The Battle Royal is warm up for the marathon that is the rest of *Invisible Man*. Space constraints prevent as full an analysis as the novel merits, but a broad outline of the plot is worthwhile before exploring some of its thematic concerns. The narrator's experience at college is initially idyllic, but sours when he is instructed to drive a wealthy white donor named Norton during his visit. Norton asks Invisible Man to drive him to the poor Black part of town typically hidden from white visitors. The journey goes disastrously. The narrator and Mr. Norton listen at length to the story of a sharecropper named Jim Trueblood who narrates a horrifying tale of incest with his daughter. Norton, shaken, gives the man a hundred dollars and asks the narrator to find him a bar. They go to a dive called the Golden Day where shellshocked war veterans are taken once a week. Reenacting the narrator's unconscious rebellion against the drunken white man during the Battle Royal, the inmates lose all control and violently attack their caretaker (who, though Black, wears all white and is symbolic of the white world) and Norton himself. When the narrator returns the battered donor to the college, President Bledsoe promptly expels him, leaving him to wonder whether to follow orders from powerful people or to do what Bledsoe does and lie to them so he can remain "at the controls" (141).

Bledsoe sends Invisible Man to New York City with seven envelopes that are supposedly filled with recommendations for employment but are actually warnings to would-be employers not to hire him. They essentially carry the same message spelled out in the narrator's dream of his grandfather, to keep him running. After discovering the truth, he resolves to become more independent, but he initially doesn't get far. Following an explosion in a paint factory and subsequent shock treatment in a hospital, he feels as though his old self has died and he can begin a new life, and he makes a spontaneous sidewalk speech in support of an elderly Black couple being evicted from their apartment. The speech leads to a riot and the narrator flees the scene, but he is followed by a white man named Brother Jack who tells him how much he admired the speech and asks him to join the organization he leads.

The bulk of the rest of the novel is about the narrator's involvement with The Brotherhood, a Marxist organization in New York hoping to gain influence in Harlem. Invisible Man is groomed to be their Black spokesman. Here the narrator's confusion about the proper balance of planning and improvisation is challenged, for during his speeches he is sometimes praised for going off script and speaking from his emotions and sometimes denigrated for the exact same behavior. The more he tries to assert his influence over the Brotherhood's official messages, the more he understands he is controlled by invisible strings, illustrated in grotesque symbolism by a racist paper "Sambo" doll one of his former colleagues peddles on the streets. Brother Jack and other leaders purport to be his allies, but it becomes clear that they have manipulated his every move. Disillusioned, the narrator finds himself caught up in a massive Harlem riot, not knowing who his friends or enemies are, and eventually plunges into an open manhole that becomes his underground home while he figures out how to reenter society with a new role that will improve the conditions of his race without killing him.

This selective plot summary leaves out a great deal of the nuanced ideas that continue to be relevant in the Black Lives Matter era as public demonstrations against racial inequality clash with policing and other forms of social control. *Invisible Man* also addresses the root causes of social unrest, beginning with persistent poverty and the lack of opportunities perpetuated by racism. The novel scrutinizes philosophical ideas as much as social inequality, though. Invisible Man's story showcases a battle between fate and free will. All his attempts to develop himself into an Emersonian individual – to become "more human!" as he shouts during a key public speech (346) – are thwarted by American society's limiting control. The narrator is constantly in search of a wise mentor, or father figure, to enlighten him, but because of his deficient vision, he does not see how many of them – his grandfather, Bledsoe, and Brother Jack among many others – are false prophets who do him more harm than good.

When he arrives in New York, despite being ashamed of his expulsion, he is dazzled by opulence and blinded by the notion that he can grab his slice of the pie simply by working hard. When he sees Black couriers hurrying along with leather briefcases chained to their wrists, he thinks, "maybe they were chained to money. Perhaps the man with rundown heels ahead of me was chained to a million dollars!" (165). Focused entirely on getting ahead materially, he fails to see the possibility that these men, like him, are chained to the *idea* of money rather than to money itself, recalling the degradations he and his colleagues endured during the Battle Royal. Because of his American Dream-born notions of success, he overlooks some figures who might be the wisest in the book, but whom he regards as fools, or worse. Jim Trueblood, the scandal-ridden sharecropper who supposedly impregnated his own daughter, is someone the narrator despises not only because he has disgraced the Black race, but because he is somehow rewarded financially for telling the story to Norton; he thinks, "You no-good bastard! *You* get a hundred-dollar bill!" (69). Trueblood, though, is perhaps a trickster; at one point during the long story, the narrator says, "Trueblood seemed to smile at me behind his eyes" (61), suggesting that the repulsive story might not be true. Regardless, Trueblood converts sorrow into song, which is the heart of the Black vernacular tradition; he says,

I didn't think 'bout it, just started singin'. I don't know what it was, some kinda church song, I guess. All I know is I *ends up* singin' the blues. I sings me some blues that night ain't never been sang before, and while I'm singin' them blues I makes up my mind that I ain't nobody buy myself and ain't nothin' I can do but let whatever is gonna happen, happen. (66)

Trueblood's blues-inspired self is more accepting than the narrator's is at that moment and perhaps ever will be.

Another blues character the narrator initially denigrates is a singing, street-jive-talking drifter who calls himself Peter Wheatstraw, which was the stage name of William Bunch, a 1930s-era blues musician. Wheatstraw, significantly, is pushing a cartful of blueprints around the streets of New York when he runs into the narrator, and he tries to bond with our hero by asking him questions to stimulate their shared oral history: "is you got the *dog*?" (173). The narrator, mechanical and formal, tries to reason his way through this question and others, but he gradually realizes, "I liked his words though I didn't know the answer. I'd known the stuff from childhood, but had forgotten it; had learned it back of school" (176). Invisible Man only values what he had learned *in* school because he believes it will lead to success, but it amounts to accepted wisdom designed to keep him in his place, as opposed to what's learned "back of school" which might give him some tangible advantages in the world. When he dutifully declares, "You have to stick to the plan," Wheatstraw "looked at me, suddenly grave. 'You kinda young, daddy-o'" (175). Until he learns how to improvise like this bluesy street saint, he'll remain in his place of naïve optimism, and he'll remain invisible.

The key to overcoming invisibility is to embrace Black vernacular forms like jazz and the blues. In terms of Invisible Man's role, many readers have struggled to understand it because his position in the hole seems so passive: he fell into it during the riot and has not returned to society to take part in its reform. But he indicates his role as he meditates on the identities of some nameless African American youths who are doing nothing more than wandering down a subway platform, speaking "a jived-up transitional language" like Wheatstraw's. The narrator wonders, "who knew but that they were the saviors, the true leaders, the bearers of something precious? … . Perhaps each hundred years or so men like them, like me, appeared in society, drifting through; and yet by all historical logic we, I, should have disappeared around the first part of the nineteenth century, rationalized out of existence" (442). He connects with these youths though he never speaks to them, and he is concerned that he, like they, will live their lives unnoticed – invisible – and therefore be considered insignificant or dispensible. It is here that he realizes his role: "They were outside the groove of history, and it was my job to get them in, all of them" (443). He again hears the blues and wonders, "Was this the only true history of the times, a mood blared by trumpets, trombones, saxophones and drums, a song with turgid, inadequate words?" (443). Readers who wonder what the narrator is going to do next after the novel's conclusion perhaps overlook the fact that he has just done it: the narrative is his attempt to translate the blues into a novel, one that records the lives of those whom history ignores, one that preserves the survivalist magic of blues music, and one that converts "a song with turgid, inadequate words" into one of the most enduring works of American literature. The high achievement of art is far more important than succeeding in the path the narrator was following, from college, to a steady job, to middle-class respectability.

Invisible Man's history is tied to the legacy of slavery in America, but the racism that prevents him from attaining the Dream also applies to immigrants of African descent who are limited by discrimination. Barbadian American Paule Marshall's *Brown Girl, Brownstones* (1959), from its title on, understands how skin color affects identity. The protagonist, Selina Boyce, is dimly aware from early adolescence that her mother and other domestic workers from their home country constantly face racism: "Sometimes the white children on their way to school laughed at their blackness and shouted 'nigger,' but the Barbadian women sucked their teeth, dismissing them" (8). As she grows into a young woman, Selina does not face the same trials her mother's cohort faces, yet her outbursts of anger and violence are related. Lacking her mother's community and tough resolve, Selina elects to face adversity independently. The neighborhood contains characters who factor into her upbringing, women who gossip and form alliances and create adversaries as they go about their daily work. Selina briefly connects with all of them but primarily navigates her challenging adolescence and turbulent family life alone.

The challenges of fitting into America are evident in the novel's opening scene, a symbolic description of the brownstone rowhouses of the title. They are personified, "somber," "indifferent," resembling an "army." Closer inspection reveals that "each house had something distinctively its own" (1), offering the promise of individual identity in uniform America. The novel begins in 1939, and Selina senses the ghosts of the "Dutch-English and Scotch-Irish who had built the houses. There had been tea in the afternoon then and skirts rustling across the parquet floors and mild voices" (2). The presence of these past white residents is so vivid to Selina that she communes with them in her imagination, and even joins them in their genteel life: "Their white hands trailed the

Class, Race, and the Anti-Dream Narrative   129

banister; their mild voices implored her to give them a little life. And as they crowded around, fusing with her, she was no longer a dark girl alone and dreaming at the top of an old house, but one of them, invested with their beauty and gentility" (3). This instance of childish make-believe indicates some of the challenges to Selina's identity formation: her desire to connect with the affluent white world that she associates with beauty, grace, and civility indicates a fundamental dissatisfaction with her identity as a child of West Indian immigrants.

Her family life complicates her desire for a world that will never accept her except in her imagination. Selina scrutinizes a family photo that does not include her, though it includes a brother who died just before she was born. She feels guilt about her dead brother: in her mind, he died to make room for her. She even imagines herself staring from the womb through her mother's skin while the infant boy's body is being buried. There are no pictures of her. She feels unwanted. She bickers with her sister Ina to the point that they seem like enemies more than siblings. Her relationship with her father Deighton is sweet: he tells her stories of growing up in Barbados and suggests that the simple games he and his playmates made up are far better than the diversions American children indulge in, especially the movies. He is a doting father, but an unfaithful husband, causing friction in the household. The relationship that provides the tensest conflict of the novel is between Selina and her mother, Silla.

The turbulence of her family life centers around a central, contentious event. Deighton receives news that his sister has passed away in Barbados and left him land. He has romantic plans to build on that land, but Silla finds this notion foolish and wants to sell it in order to put money toward a house in America, a cornerstone of the Dream. Silla vows to her friends that she will find a way to sell the property in Barbados and claims that she will resort to anything, even the Barbadian spiritual practice of Obeah, to achieve her goal. Selina overhears this talk and confronts her mother and the others in one of the most dramatic scenes of the novel: Silla's friend Florrie says to Selina, "'Tell your mother that you's no more little girl, that you can hold your tongue like a woman ...' And as she spoke and laughed tenderly, her hand passed from Selina's shoulder through the wide neck of her middy blouse and, with a casual fleeting gesture, brushed one of her small breasts" (64). Self-conscious about her changing body and set on edge by her mother's betrayal of her father, she springs away from this assault, smashes a water glass, and brandishes it toward Florrie and her mother. She also burns with the secret she is supposed to keep, and eventually fails to keep it, telling her father about the whole plot to cheat him out of his dream.

Silla manages to sell the land through forgery and deception, and Deighton is left with a check for nine hundred dollars representing his wife's American Dream of homeownership rather than his own dream of repatriation. He leaves to cash the check, and returns with lavish, impractical gifts for his wife and daughters and a new trumpet for himself to fulfill his replacement dream to become a musician. His bitterness toward Silla is deep: after throwing the last of the gifts on the floor, he declares sarcastically, "'Is everybody satisfy? ... Good ... cause I well satisfy.' Walking close to the mother, he made an elaborate bow" (111). Silla has ruined his dream in order to follow the Dream script; his only satisfaction seems to be to seek revenge by refusing to comply.

Selina is witness to a difficult reality of immigrant life, namely that competition for success in the so-called land of opportunity divides families and communities. In another climactic scene, the wedding of a local Barbadian couple, she has a realization that spills over from her earlier encounter with Florrie: "To Selina, Florrie's glance was as loathsome as her hand had been on her breast. Again Selina felt the sharp sense of alienation. How could she have been born among people like Florrie Trotman with her bawdy stories? She wanted to leave the table. To leave them" (121). Essentially, she wants to sever ties with her community and family, which is not uncommon for teenagers, but it is greatly exacerbated by her conflicted set of loyalties, the bitter divide between her parents, and the stifling sense of obligation exerted by her immigrant milieu. If there is freedom in America, it is distant and inaccessible to Selina who already is plagued by "a sharp sense of alienation."

Deighton had tried to learn accounting through a correspondence course, but realized that he wouldn't be hired because of the color of his skin. He rejects the path to conventional success in America and joins an eccentric religion, claiming spirituality is what gives life meaning. His wife disagrees, telling him the meaning of life is "scuffling to get by. And having little something so you can keep your head up and not have these white people push you 'bout like you's cattle" (148). She points out that all their Barbadian neighbors have managed to put a down payment on American houses and that his newfound spiritual revelation is just another way to avoid hard work and determination: "It's that you was always looking for something big and praying hard not to find it" (149). Her unleashed fury reaches a crescendo when she blames him directly for the death of their infant son, and Deighton calmly informs the family that he's leaving. Silla reports him to immigration and he drowns during the boat voyage back to Barbados. Selina is left with her mother, the parent she "both loved and hated" (150) as opposed to her father, whom she only loved, if sometimes pitied.

Selina's father's death increases her feelings of loneliness and alienation. She resents her friends for merely following the path that is expected of them, yet her own path is unclear. At a party, Selina throws the first of multiple public tantrums in which she berates her former Barbadian friends for their blind adherence to conventional American success: work, relative wealth, homeownership, and duty to family. The community forms a civic group called the Barbadian Association devoted to improvement understood in financial terms. Their motto is, "It is not the depths from which we come but the heights to which we ascend" (188). At one of the Association's first meetings, a fellow member gives an inspirational speech, but Selina refrains from clapping and looks around in horror at her supposed community: "They were no longer individuals suddenly, but a single puissant force, sure of its goal and driving hard toward it" (190). She yearns for an alternative to the American Dream script reinforced by her mother and other Barbadian matriarchs, yet her choices are limited.

Against her mother's wishes, she begins a sexual relationship with a bohemian army veteran named Clive who offers a viable alternative to her prescribed path: he is intellectual, artistic, and worldly, prone to quoting T.S. Eliot and introspective lectures about how superficial the Barbadian Association is. Selina wants to escape with him away from her stifling milieu, and her plan becomes to ingratiate herself with the Barbadian Association in order to win their scholarship and use the money to flee. Her criticisms of her community are valid, but they don't leave her with any close connections. The racism she had long kept at bay rears its ugly head in a late scene that shatters her illusions of control over her claims to self-determination. Following a triumphant dance performance, Selina attends a party at a white friend's house to celebrate the evening. The friend's mother harangues her in the most condescendingly racist terms imaginable, and Selina is stunned into silence. The event becomes the central trauma of her life, replacing Florrie's physical assault and Silla's betrayal of Deighton that led to his watery demise: "Whenever she remembered it – all down the long years to her death – she was to stare helplessly, and every white face would be suspect for that moment" (246). It is a moment of discovery of America's essentially racist structure, but it is also a moment of disillusionment for a young woman who assumed that the world would accommodate her lofty dreams. She tearfully stares at her reflection, wrestling with her tragic epiphany, "crying suddenly because their idea of her was only an illusion, yet so powerful that it would stalk her down the years ... . along with the fierce struggle of her humanity she must also battle illusions!" (252). Her relationship with Clive fails because he refuses to prioritize her needs in the immediate aftermath, and although she wins the Barbadian Association's scholarship, she turns it down and admits that she had never been sincere in her intent to use the money for education.

There are echoes of *Invisible Man* in Selina's quandary and in the way she attempts to overcome it (joining an organization, deceptively using that organization to achieve her own ends, attempting to escape altogether). Like Ellison's narrator, it is sometimes tough to root for Selina because she is in the process of learning about herself, of discovering who she is while protecting her inner self. Both protagonists reject most of the institutions they encounter, and neither is sure how to proceed. One difference is that Selina at least partially reconciles with her mother, who puts the difficult question to her, "What it tis you want?" Selina fumbles over the answer, but eventually says, "Remember how you used to talk about how you left home and came here alone as a girl of eighteen and was your own woman? I used to love hearing that. And that's what I want" (265). This realization comes after she has firmly rejected the Barbadian Association's wealth, her mother's dream of property, and her sister's resignation to a conventional middle-class existence involving parenthood, all of which are foundations of the standard American success story. Instead, Selina recognizes the opportunity to explore her identity, and the real reward is the painful, often rough journey, not any pot of gold that lies at the end of it.

A recent novel, Imbolo Mbue's *Behold the Dreamers* (2016), alludes to the American Dream in its title but also to the so-called "dreamers" – immigrants or their children who faced deportation in the early twentieth century before the passage of the Deferred Action for Childhood Arrivals (DACA) act by President Obama in 2012. (The Trump administration attempted to weaken and overturn DACA in 2017 but it was fully reinstated under the Biden administration in 2022). Mbue's novel about immigrants from Cameroon takes place around the time of the financial crisis of 2008 coupled with the election of Obama, the first American president of African descent. In *Behold the Dreamers* the hope inspired by Obama's historic election clashes with the economic catastrophe of the financial crisis to illustrate the elusiveness of the American Dream for those who are poor, Black, or both.

Jende and Neni Jonga have migrated from Cameroon to America with the sole goal of climbing the ladder to wealth through hard work, determination, and a positive attitude. Their lives intersect with the Edwards family, fabulously wealthy white Manhattanites whose lifestyle resembles the opulence Jende and Neni have seen represented on television and in the movies. Clark Edwards, who works for Lehman Brothers – the investment bank primarily responsible for the financial collapse – hires Jende as his personal chauffeur and demands his absolute loyalty. Cindy Edwards later hires Neni as a domestic servant and nanny, a position Neni accepts as a lucrative alternative to the profession she is pursuing in health care. The Dream is referenced explicitly throughout the novel, and both Jongas believe in it so strongly that they are willing to struggle and sacrifice to claim their "share of the milk, honey, and liberty flowing in the paradise-for-strivers called America" (19). Much of the struggle they face is legal as Jende must go to extraordinary efforts to obtain work documents; when Clark first hires him, he dodges the truth about his work status as he waits for a green card.

Although the liberty the Jongas hope for eludes them throughout the novel, they're truly after the milk and honey. When Jende describes the Edwards' opulent apartment, Neni exclaims, "What would it be like to have a place like that? I'll jump and touch the sky every day" (27). Jende believes "a sweet mini-mansion" is "one of the many things that made America a truly great country" (82). Their belief in the greatness of America's opulence is unwavering. Clark occasionally hangs up his phone or folds up his laptop long enough to engage Jende in discussions comparing Cameroon to America. Jende declares, "To live in this country. Ah! It is the greatest thing in the world, Mr. Edwards ... . I stay in my country, I would have become nothing. I would have remained nothing. My son will grow up and be poor like me" (39). Instead, Jende hopes that in America, "my son will grow up to be somebody ... . I hope that one day my son will grow up to be a great man like you" (46). Nene shares this hope; she dissuades their son from his stated goal to be a chauffeur like his father, pushing him instead to be a doctor, a lawyer, or "a big man on Wall Street like Mr. Edwards ... . That'll make us so happy" (68). The Edwards' elder son Vince ironically drops out of law school and rejects the expectations that he will become like his father, whom he denigrates as "an absent provider who's going through the motions" (107). He renounces capitalism and vows to "unindoctrinate [Jende] on all the lies [he's] been fed about America," but Jende rejoins, "Nothing you or any man can say to me to make me stop believing that America is the greatest country in the world" (103).

The Jongas are hard-working and savvy about how to achieve prosperity and create opportunities for themselves and for their children. Like Alger's Ragged Dick, Jende realizes his suit is shabby and buys a new one even though the purchase eats up "a third of their savings" (31). Following Alger's blueprint, Neni and Jende create opportunities for lucky breaks, and they are the beneficiaries of largesse from the Edwards family and also from a local church Neni joins. When Cindy Edwards overhears Jende talking on the phone to a relative from Cameroon who needs money, she quietly slips him a check for five hundred dollars, and he accepts it gratefully but experiences a little guilt when he only sends the three hundred that had been requested and pockets the rest.

The transactional relationship between the two couples becomes more complex. Cindy reveals to Neni that she also grew up poor as a way of explaining why she is so demanding about domestic details: she feels constantly stressed in a world of socialites. Neni learns that Cindy copes with that stress through prescription pills and excessive amounts of alcohol at all times of the day. It seems that Cindy confesses her impoverished background to Neni as a way of bonding with her and reinforcing that the Dream is real for those who want it badly enough; she says, "I worked my way through college, got a job, my own apartment, learned how to carry myself well and fit effortlessly in this new world so I would never be looked down on again .... no one can ever take away the things I've achieved for myself" (124). There are clearly blind spots, though, as she boorishly claims, "Being poor for you in Africa is fine. Most of you are poor over there. The shame of it, it's not as bad for you" (123). As a way of making sure Neni won't say a word about her pills and booze, she gives her castoff designer clothes, toys her son never uses anymore, leftover catered food from her parties, and a monetary bonus; the narrator declares, "They had found a win-win solution" (125).

The solution is temporary, though. When Cindy suspects that her husband Clark has a secret of his own – an extramarital affair – Jende is put in an impossible situation. The truth is worse than Cindy suspects: Clark frequently hires prostitutes and has Jende wait outside hotels while he is with them. Jende warns Neni not to get involved with the Edwards' affairs; his stated policy is, "Make sure you only do what they say you do and exactly the way they say you do it" (110). This commitment to absolute obedience puts Jende in jeopardy, though; when Clark first hires him to be his chauffeur, he demands absolute loyalty and discretion, but Cindy also demands that he keep a detailed log of everywhere he drives Clark and she threatens him with the loss of a job and possible deportation if he does not comply. Jende's solution is to fabricate the log to indicate that Clark is just busy with work, following Clark's directive, "Continue doing as I ask you to do, and you won't have to worry about anything" (205). When the story of Clark's behavior hits the press, Cindy turns against Jende and forces Clark to fire him. It is clear, despite her earnest-sounding declaration of her own American Dream story, that she is still able to destroy the truly powerless.

Up until the point when Jende is let go, the Jongas remain positive and committed to the Dream narrative, but this unfortunate turn of events either causes or reveals a rift between them. Jende increasingly becomes furious with Neni's decisions and opinions, insisting that she obey him as she would have unquestioningly done in Cameroon. Various customs from their old country are not compatible with American culture: Neni is shocked when she sees a gay couple, Jende talks dispassionately about how Cameroonian children are beaten with a stick to obey, and there are stories of husbands abusing wives with impunity in the old country.

Neni, still enamored with America and not wanting to return to those ways, takes matters into her own hands and blackmails Cindy by showing her a picture she took when Cindy was passed out on drugs and alcohol. She understands the true relationship she had formed with her former employer: "She thought she could use us, stupid African people who don't know how to stand up for themselves. She thinks we're not as smart as she is" (272). Jende is furious with her and yet he takes control of the money she extorted. Tired of fighting the immigration courts and scrambling to make ends meet, he resolves to return to Cameroon, and though it seems like Neni will remain in America, she eventually agrees to repatriate with him for the sake of their children.

Neni clings to the hope for racial equality and opportunity she originally glimpsed on such fantasy-based television sit-coms as *The Cosby Show* and *The Fresh Prince of Bel-Air* which "had shown her that there was a place in the world where blacks had the same chance at prosperity as whites" (312). Jende is keen to remove her illusions by convincing her that "this country is full of lies" and "no longer has room for people like us" (332). Neni resigns herself to the idea that she is not an American woman who can tell her husband what to do; pathetically, "She buried her face in his shoulder and begged herself to be happy" (351). The feeling is thin, though; before long "she was back to despising him for taking her and her children away from America" (356). She realizes they will live much better in Cameroon than they would have if they had never come to America because they have returned with a good amount of money (including that which she extorted from Cindy), but she is also aware of how much her family – especially her children – will lose, including "the opportunity to grow up in a magnificent land of uninhibited dreamers" (361). Her continued belief in this narrative is at odds with Jende's succinct summary of his situation to Clark: "it's just not easy for a man to enjoy his life in this country if he is poor" (373).

There is no disputing the truth and authenticity of Jende's statement, and yet *Behold the Dreamers* also argues that wealth is no guarantee of happiness. The Edwards family is demonstrably more miserable than the Jongas. What unites the two families is that they don't question enough the script that they are following. Clark says to Jende during their parting conversation, "Family's everything ... I'm sure you know that already" (369). The statement rings hollow on multiple levels, especially since Clark then hands Jende an envelope full of money as if to show what speaks louder than family. Jende accepts it and bundles it up with the rest of the cash he brings back to Cameroon which will make him and the family "millionaires many times over" (352). The novel is unsettling and confusing because the material aspects of the Dream are all that remain even as we see two families – one rich and white, the other poor and Black – continue to be seduced by its twisted logic even as they are made miserable by it.

The anti-Dream novels considered in this chapter argue that the Dream is not available to those discriminated against because they were born poor, Black, or both. Characters who are prevented from achieving the Dream for these reasons are unfulfilled and often resort to desperate acts to change their circumstances. In some cases, as with Invisible Man or Jende Jonga in *Behold the Dreamers*, the natural conclusion is that the Dream was always a damaging fiction, but giving up their belief in it does not immediately yield an alternative. Those shut out from the Dream, according to the novel tradition, must seek a solution. Jende leaves the country and Invisible Man settles into a private hole apart from society, indicating that a clear-eyed understanding of the Dream's realities does not result in an automatic alternative that would accommodate the marginalized.

Further Reading

Cather, Willa. *My Ántonia* (1918)
Chute, Carolyn. *The Beans of Egypt, Maine* (1985)
Kennedy, William. *Ironweed* (1983)
Norris, Frank. *McTeague* (1899)
Petry, Ann. *The Street* (1946)
Sinclair, Upton. *The Jungle* (1906)
Ward, Jesmyn. *Sing, Unburied, Sing* (2017)

6 Multiethnic America

The development of the American novel tradition in the nineteenth century did not accommodate the voices of writers who were not of English or Scottish descent. The massive waves of immigration that initially crested in the early twentieth century would change that trend. It is often said that America is a nation of immigrants, and even though this cliché erases the history of Native Americans or enslaved Africans, it is true that the vast majority of American citizens can link their ancestry to the history of immigration. One distortion in the conception of this dynamic in the popular imagination is that Americans of British and Scottish descent are sometimes placed in another category altogether, as though the Puritan settlers weren't themselves immigrants, and as though seventeenth-century English colonists were not actively in competition with colonists from other European powers, including but not limited to Spain, France, and the Netherlands.

If there is a nod toward immigration in the story of English settlements in America, it is to claim origin. Even though Plymouth, Massachusetts was not the first settlement, to have ancestors who crossed the Atlantic on the Mayflower is akin to having royal blood. This historical/cultural phenomenon has been partly responsible for obscuring one of the main concerns of the American novel tradition, which is to negotiate the tensions between the pressure to assimilate and the desire to preserve aspects of distinct foreign cultures in the service of recognizing and enriching American multiculturalism. The Puritans are responsible for countless aspects of what is considered mainstream American culture, from language, to religion, to the American Dream that is the rudder of this study. American novels of immigration frequently follow the superficial outlines of the Dream script since the primary goal of many immigrants is financial prosperity. Distinct from other versions of this story, narratives of immigration and/or of the experience of protagonists from minority ethnic groups are complicated by the perceived need to sacrifice one's cultural heritage while chasing the Dream that silently demands assimilation.

DOI: 10.4324/9781003252863-7

Immigrant Stories: Losing My Religion/Accent/Name

American immigrant novels are frequently coming-of-age tales. The typical tribulations of growing up in America are heightened by perceptions of difference. For immigrants, difference often attaches to remnants of culture from their home country. Religion, language, food, and dress are persistent signifiers of difference that cause the protagonists of these novels to make difficult choices between preserving these remnants or purging them. Henry Roth's 1934 novel *Call It Sleep* is a coming-of-age narrative that reveals the tension between the desire to stick close to one's ethnic community for protection and the desire to transcend it for opportunity. The novel has many qualities of the *bildungsroman*. We can see autobiographical connections between Roth and his young protagonist David Schearl, both of whom immigrated from Austro-Hungary via Ellis Island around 1907 and learned about America through navigating the sometimes hostile, impoverished, overcrowded slums of the Lower East Side of Manhattan. Although it was critically well received, *Call It Sleep* fell into obscurity until it was revived in the 1960s and became a million-copy bestseller and a literary classic. Roth's novel earns that label not because it is beautiful, or perfectly constructed, or in full control of its energies, but rather for the opposite reasons: honesty, experimentation, and explosive, passionate storytelling.

Call It Sleep tells the story of a nervous, bright, self-conscious boy thrust into an unfamiliar world who must try to figure out how he might either fit in or develop survival strategies. He arrives at Ellis Island with his mother Genya to meet his father Albert who has preceded them to establish a toehold in the New World. The awkward reunion between David's parents indicates the conflicts in their relationship that persist throughout the novel:

> these two stood silent, apart; the man staring with aloof, offended eyes grimly down at the water – or if he turned his face toward his wife at all, it was only to glare in harsh contempt at the blue straw hat worn by the child in her arms, and then his hostile eyes would sweep about the deck to see if anyone else were observing them. And his wife beside him regarding him uneasily, appealingly. And the child against her breast looking from one to the other with watchful, frightened eyes. (11)

The tension and discomfort of this meeting is an overture for the novel's cacophonous symphony. Albert's discontentment with his wife manifests as persistent verbal abuse and escalates to physical violence, sometimes directed at his employers and sometimes toward David, especially in one brutal scene in which he beats him with a wooden clothes hanger.

Genya's attempts to protect her child are always compromised by the wary fearfulness she first displays in this scene. David is constantly worried about the ongoing war between them, hoping for peace, but often choosing exile as he realizes that there can be no harmony or freedom within their home. Framing the entire family drama is Albert's awareness of the regulatory watching eyes of other Americans.

The first section of the novel, "The Cellar," highlights David's anxious nature and his powerlessness. His father is the source of much of his angst, and he is happiest when Albert is at work, first as a printer and later as a truck driver for a dairy. Yet Albert's time spent at work does not provide a reliably safe buffer for his family. Unable to contain his bitterness, he is repeatedly fired for attacking his bosses and coworkers. When he sends David to collect his belongings and back pay from one job, the boss scorns Albert for sending a kid to do his dirty work and bluntly pronounces David's fate as he leaves: "Pretty tough for you" (27). With much trepidation, David delivers this money to his father and conceals the fact that his bosses and coworkers had spoken ill of him. In contrast to this small success, he often bungles the errands his father assigns him: when Albert sends him out for a Yiddish newspaper, he loses the change and ruins the paper by dropping it in a puddle. Later, when his father takes him out on a milk delivery run, he fails to protect the milk from thieves who claim they know Albert. His father's disappointment in him deepens as the novel continues, and his mother's attempts to protect him or comfort him are ineffective.

Albert's contempt for David stems from his suspicion that he is not his biological son. Albert's silent suspicion of Genya's infidelity is something David initially knows nothing about, but when Albert brings home Luter – his new boss and new best friend from the old country – David immediately senses something discordant. Luter flirts with Genya persistently and her responses are not necessarily innocent. David's fears shift from being alone with his father to leaving his mother alone with Luter. His anxieties increase as a neighbor girl attempts to "play bad" (53) with him, leading him into a closet and crudely explaining sex long before he is ready to understand. He tries to anchor himself by articulating his feelings toward Albert: "He didn't like his father. He never would like him. He hated him" (78). The simple clarity of this realization is complicated, though, as he has also begun to hate Luter's relationship with his mother, and his only confidant is Yussie, the brother of the girl who invited him to "play bad." The cellar of the section's title is a repository for all his psychological fears, including death, as it is connected in his mind to imagined buried bodies in the basement along with "the hordes of nightmare, the wobbly faces, the crawling and misshapen things" (92).

His only refuge is the city itself, a microcosm of impersonal, hostile America. In David's imagination, it becomes another living enemy: "Again a street as alien as any he had ever passed, and like the others, with squat, monotonous flanks receding into vacancy, slack with risen shadow" (98). This is but one of many naturalistic descriptions of New York in the novel that render it at best indifferent to David's well-being, and at worst a force bent on his destruction. He tries to fit in with schoolchildren, but they often bully him. At one point he fights back and believes he has killed one of them with a single blow. He runs away, becomes lost, and because he doesn't speak English well, he's unable to tell the police his address.

Differences between David's language and American English lead to battles that intensify throughout the novel. When Yussie notices that David's mother doesn't seem to be comprehending one of his stories, he turns to David and says, "Don' she wan' I sh' talk t' huh in Engklish?" (139). Except in moments like this one, readers can forget that speech in the novel has often been translated from Yiddish for our benefit. The street kids talk in the nonstandard idiom Yussie uses in the above passage. Later David enters a Jewish school where he is encouraged to imitate the sounds of Hebrew without being instructed explicitly as to their meaning. As with everything in this new world, language is something he must navigate on his own, without clear guidance from his elders or consistency from his peers. The scene in which he gleans inklings of his mother's infidelity and the possibility that he is not Albert's son is fascinating in this regard: he eavesdrops on his mother and her sister Bertha who are recounting the details of the affair, but they frequently lapse into the language of their youth, or, as the narrator puts it, they "[blot] out import under a screen of Polish ... . meaning scaled the horizon to another idiom, leaving David stranded on a sounding but empty shore. Words here and there, phrases shimmering like distant sails tantalized him, but never drew near" (196, 197).

David's informal education takes the form of connecting dots that don't seem to form a clear picture. Language is far from the only barrier he faces as he tries to adjust to American culture, and his growing awareness of subcultures within it complicates his thinking. His learning that his biological father was a Christian from the old country adds to his confused sense of identity. A boy named Leo embodies what David has unconsciously desired all along: freedom. Leo is confident, independent, and worldly, all the things David wants to be but is not. He is also Catholic, and this cultural difference proves to be both a source of education for David and a source of division. David had once denied he was Jewish when another kid asked him, but he stutters "Y-yea" when Leo asks him point blank, "You're a Jew, ain'tcha?" (303). Leo and David grill each other about their religious customs out of what seems like childish curiosity, including a good deal of comic misinterpretations: Leo, for instance, regards rosary beads as good luck charms, causing David to covet them as protection against the threats in his world. Underlying Leo's understanding of the differences between Christians and Jews are dangerous biases and stereotypes, though. In what might be the most significant plot point in a heavily plotted book, Leo encourages David to introduce him to his aunt's stepdaughter Esther for the purposes of engaging in a sex act, claiming "I like Jew-goils!" in one breath, then calling David a "sheen" and a "stingy kike" when he resists (326, 327). David is terrified and does everything he can to prevent the encounter, but Leo is forceful, and he promises David the magic rosary beads as compensation. Leo and Esther are caught, and Esther's sister calls him a "doity Chrischin" to which Leo responds with his own epithets, calling the sisters "jew hewhs" and "sheenies" (357). The event is so traumatic for David that he blurts out a wild version of his origin story to his rabbi, claiming that his mother is dead, among other falsehoods. The rabbi, David's aunt, and her husband converge on David's house to confront his parents about his behavior. Their resulting fight sends David careening out of his house one final time and he nearly dies from electrocution on a charged train track.

The novel modulates between two modes of literary fiction developing in the early twentieth century: naturalism and modernism. Part of what makes it such an enduring book is the author's willingness to combine these modes fluidly while telling an authentic story that features details of the Jewish-American immigrant story such as the gloriously inventive insults hurled at David and his peers by the rabbi and Albert, or the comic relief provided by Aunt Bertha in a novel that is otherwise relentlessly tense. The modernist strain of the novel goes deep into David's complex psychological state while the naturalistic elements provide a sociological survey of his world. After David is electrocuted, Roth pulls his camera away from David to allow us to hear the voices of everyone who witnessed the tragic event. They are all immigrants from different places, and their voices join together in a cacophonous roar of early twentieth-century urban America. The multitude of voices suggests that it is possible to withstand the pressure to assimilate, which is a significant note to end on as the reader imagines David's future.

Julia Alvarez's *How the García Girls Lost Their Accents* (1991) is an inventive variation on the immigrant coming-of-age narrative. As the title indicates, the theme is assimilation, there are multiple protagonists, and language is an important emphasis. Unlike *Call It Sleep* and many other novels about immigration, the García girls – Carla, Sandra, Yolanda, and Sofía – do not struggle against poverty: their parents immigrated from the Dominican Republic due to political upheaval rather than financial need, which is the more common catalyst for immigration, and which is the concrete connection between immigrant stories and the materialistic American Dream. Their father Carlos is a doctor who had helped engineer the overthrow of the Dominican Republic dictator Rafael Trujillo. We first meet the García girls as adults, and they are all professionals who have been privileged enough to attend private high schools and universities. In the absence of the pressure to put food on the table, the novel's focus is squarely on the nuances of what is lost in the process of assimilation.

How the García Girls Lost Their Accents is divided into chapters that read like standalone short stories, each of which focuses on or is narrated by one of the four girls, or occasionally their parents. It is further divided into three parts that move backward through time: 1989–1972, 1970–1960, and 1960–1956. Reinforcing this reverse chronology, the novel initially makes the reader work hard to figure out the birth order of the four daughters and their unique personality traits. Their mother Mami had associated each of them with a color when they were younger as though to impose an artificial distinction between them; the eldest daughter Carla, a developmental psychologist, believes "the color system had weakened the four girls' identity differentiation abilities" (41). This point is especially important as the novel illustrates that an emphasis on individual identity is one of the key differences between American and Dominican culture, the latter of which reinforces traditional gender roles and thus restricts opportunities for women. Although the protagonist is collective, we spend the most time with the third daughter, Yolanda, whose chapters are the first and last in the novel. Alvarez was a poet before this debut novel, and Yolanda is also a poet, suggesting that this perspective may be autobiographical.

The novel's backward movement through time causes the reader to continually revise impressions of the García girls. We learn as we reach 1961 – the year of their immigration – that although they came from wealth, their prosperity was something they had to reestablish in their early years after immigration, and that they went to private school partly because they were being discriminated against in public school. Even so, their father's motivation is to "smooth the accent out of their English in expensive schools" (36), and we learn how Yolanda in particular had to grow accustomed to unfamiliar customs – as well as the nuances of American English – in order to fit in. Sandi describes their mother's desire that, in preparatory schools, "we would meet and mix with the 'right kind' of Americans," but she adds, "we met the right kind of Americans all right, but they didn't exactly mix with us" (108). Unlike their parents, who are "heavy-duty Old World" (47) in their beliefs and attitudes, the girls are adolescents when they immigrate and thus are adaptable and eager to fit into their peer group; as Sandi says, "We began to develop a taste for the American teenage good life, and soon, Island was old hat, man. Island was the hair-and-nails crowd, chaperones, and icky boys with all their macho strutting and unbuttoned shirts and hairy chests with gold chains and teensy gold crucifixes. By the end of a couple years away from home, we had *more* than adjusted" (108–9). Assimilation has never sounded so easy or painless, but Sandi's narrative conveniently overlooks the girls' struggles, which come into focus as the book moves deeper into the past.

Much of their trauma involves adjusting to language and custom. In middle school Yolanda is asked to give a speech in English and works through it to the point of mastery: "She finally sounded like herself in English!" (143). Her father furiously rips up the speech, which he finds disrespectful toward authority. She snaps back, "This is America, Papi, America! You are not in a savage country anymore!" (146). Carla, the eldest, is tormented by her classmates who make fun of her English: they mock the way her "stop" sounds like "eh-stop" (153). She is approached by a pervert in a car, and she fumbles when describing him to policemen who are frustrated by her flustered attempts to describe the man and his vehicle: "'Can't she talk?' the gruff cop snapped" (161). The mean old woman in the apartment downstairs sums up the xenophobia they face: "The Garcías should be evicted. Their food smelled. They spoke too loudly and not in English" (170). At the end of that chapter, Sandi is disgusted by the drunken, boorish behavior of an American acquaintance who buys each of them a Barbie doll. The other sisters thank the woman in English, but Sandi offers "*Gracias*" in rebellion (191).

The contrast between the Dominican Republic and the U.S. is evident throughout the novel, but complex enough that there is no simple way to describe one as preferable to the other. Dominican culture is depicted as retrograde in terms of gender roles. Once the political situation on the island has stabilized, as Sandi reports, "we four girls would be sent summers to the Island so we wouldn't lose touch with *la familia*. The hidden agenda was marriage to homeland boys, since everyone knew that once a girl married an American, those grandbabies came out jabbering in English and thinking of the Island as a place to go get a suntan" (109). At the age of sixteen the youngest daughter, Sofía, is sent back for an extended period and becomes involved in a controlling, borderline abusive relationship with one of these homeland boys. Echoing the event that caused the family to emigrate, the other sisters stage what they call a "revolution" (122) and a "coup" (127) to rescue her from her macho oppressor, partly out of interest in her well-being, but also to resist the prescribed fate their elders are hoping for, "as if we've never been to the States or read Simone de Beauvoir or planned lives of our own" (119). Even their mother, who holds many traditional values, "did not want to go back to the old country where, [aristocrat] or not, she was only a wife and a mother" (143). The sexism of Dominican culture is only one of its tribulations. The final section takes place before the overthrow of the Trujillo government reveals it to be a dangerous, violent place, and some of those qualities persist when the girls return in the late 1980s, especially given their wealth, which makes them a target in a highly stratified class system. Still, Yolanda silently realizes while visiting the island, "she has never felt at home in the States, never" (12). Having lost not only her accent but much of her Spanish vocabulary, she is stranded between worlds.

America is no paradise, though. It is "a difficult place" (170) in which the García girls are called ethnic slurs and are subject to stereotyping even once they've entered college; one sexually aggressive boyfriend says to Yolanda, "I thought you'd be hot-blooded, being Spanish and all ... you're worse than a fucking Puritan" (99). Their Haitian maid had warned them: "You are going to a strange land ... . a bewitched and strange place" (223). Yet the maid also believes that the girls "have spirit in them" and "will invent what they need to survive" (223). This spirit is what enables them to overcome the challenges they face individually and collectively, but more importantly, it allows them to reinvent themselves. Some incidents from their childhood on the island are shameful: two sisters allow a cousin to convince them to expose themselves to him, one gets a maid fired by giving her a bank she had received as a gift, and one steals a kitten from its mother and causes its death. The process of losing their accents is a metaphor for the sacrifices associated with assimilation, and the costs are a diminishment of home and family ties, but the benefits are the opportunities to become independent women who follow their own paths to identity, if not unmitigated happiness.

The recurring dynamic of a protagonist at odds with American society seems to have a particular angle in novels of immigration, namely that the protagonist does not always resolve this crisis over the course of the novel. Just as David's parents in *Call It Sleep* are irreconcilably divided against one another, so too is David divided at the end of his narrative, and his experiences may have left him resilient, but there are scars that won't heal. His stubborn defiance can be seen either as a strength or a liability depending on whether the reader would be more relieved or more troubled by his willingness to follow cultural rules. Yolanda and her sisters in Alvarez's novel harbor a host of unresolved issues at the end, which is actually at the beginning given the novel's unorthodox structure. Another contemporary novel that displays ongoing tension and complexity of the pressure to assimilate is Jhumpa Lahiri's *The Namesake* (2003). Lahiri's work is shaped to some degree by her own life experiences. She immigrated with her parents from London to the United States when she was three, earned accolades (including the Pulitzer Prize for fiction for her debut collection of short stories) for her work as a writer who identifies as American, then emigrated to Italy in 2012. Her recent novels were originally published in Italian, her third language. This story of a writer who both immigrated to and emigrated from the U.S. is unusual, but perhaps reflects the reality of the lives of many migrants who are not also writers: the story does not always involve simply coming from an oppressed place to the Land of Opportunity and learning to fit into it as a way of finding a permanent home. The story may be another version of the familiar American story of changing one's identity, adapting, exchanging, sacrificing, and never finally arriving.

The Namesake focuses on Gogol Ganguli, a young man whose parents immigrated from India to Massachusetts. Their son's odd name is the result of a series of accidents. The novel flashes back to a moment in India when Ashoke, Gogol's father, is reading the great Russian author Nikolai Gogol when his train crashes. As rescue crews comb through the wreckage, a severely wounded Ashoke clutches a page of the book. An emergency worker sees the page in Ashoke's hand move, signifying that he is alive. Essentially, Gogol saves Ashoke's life, and when his son is born, he and his wife Ashima give him the name Gogol while they are waiting for the official name – determined according to tradition by the maternal grandmother – to arrive by post from India. The letter never arrives; the grandmother dies, and Gogol is stuck with a name he can't stand because it is so unusual.

What's in a name? In this novel, names encapsulate the entire story of the complex tension of American immigrants. Lahiri's narrator provides a small lesson on the specific distinction between "pet names" and "good names" in Bengali culture: "In Bengali the word for pet name is *daknam*, meaning, literally, the name by which one is called, by friends, family, and other intimates, at home and in other private, unguarded moments" (25–6). A good name, "*bhalonam*," is "for identification in the outside world" (26). Gogol gets what is essentially a pet name in place of a good name. This is just one indication in Gogol's life of the awkwardness of what it means to be born into two worlds separated by cultural misunderstanding. On the first day of Kindergarten, Gogol's parents attempt to invent a "good name" for the occasion – Nikhil, a Benghali nod to Nikolai Gogol's first name – but the five-year-old Gogol rejects this change. Since choice is a fundamental component of American identity, Gogol is put in the uncomfortable position of obeying his parents who insist he be called Nikhil or siding with his teacher who clearly disapproves of his parents' control. She says, "And what about you, Gogol? Do you want to be called by another name?" When he shakes his head, she triumphantly declares, "Then it's settled" (59) and asks him to write his name on a piece of paper, partly to test Ashoke's claim that his son is "perfectly bilingual" (58).

Lahiri highlights the conflicts of bicultural identity while still making it clear that there are benefits. The broader thematic concerns around Gogol's name have to do with fate and choice. Fate gives Gogol his name because of the train wreck and because the grandmother's letter never arrives, yet Ashoke and Ashima choose to name him Gogol, and they choose to rename him as he enters school. He rejects the name legally later in life. At the age of eighteen, he questions his parents' decision: "Why did you have to give me a pet name in the first place?" he cries, and his mother responds, "It's our way ... It's what Bengalis do" (99). His father is resigned to the fact that Gogol is not just Bengali, encouraging him to change his name legally if he wants: "In America anything is possible. Do as you wish" (100). Gogol pays the fee and visits a judge, apprehensive about the process. The judge asks him why he wants to change his name. At first, he mumbles, "Personal reasons," but when lightly pressed he blurts, "I hate the name Gogol" (101, 102), which is good enough for the judge. He legally becomes Nikhil at this moment, but characters and even the narrator continue to call him Gogol throughout the novel, indicating that a name change is superficial.

It's easy enough to observe that Bengali culture is rooted in tradition and American culture in change, but *The Namesake* is a complex enough novel to problematize this idea as well. Pointedly, Ashoke and Ashima are in an arranged marriage: they had not met before their wedding night. American culture dictates that partners choose one another, purportedly out of love rather than their families' determination that an arrangement is mutually beneficial to preserve culture and ensure financial stability. Much of the narrative involves Gogol's many courtships that lead to a single marriage which ends in pain and divorce. By contrast, his parents stay happily married until death parts them.

The trajectory of Gogol's life is away from his parents' culture's influence and into the American mainstream, and this is even more true of his younger sister Sonali, whose pet name Sonia "makes her a citizen of the world. It's a Russian link to her brother, it's European, South American. Eventually it will be the name of the Indian prime minister's Italian wife" (62). Gogol as a baby was subjected to the traditional Bengali "rice ceremony," occasioned by the first time a baby eats solid food. It involves presenting the baby with a pen, a clump of dirt, and a dollar bill to see which one it will choose, predicting whether it will grow up to be a scholar, landowner, or businessman, respectively.

Relatives egg him on to choose one of the three: "Gogol frowns, and his lower lip trembles. Only then, forced at six months to confront his destiny, does he begin to cry" (40). When he later learns about his namesake's particularly tragic life, he begins to wonder if in fact being named Gogol has doomed him to a lifetime of unhappiness. Sonia, by contrast, makes a mockery of her rice ceremony, refusing the food, playing with the dirt, threatening to put the dollar bill in her mouth. "'This one,' one of the guests remarks, 'this one is the true American'" (63). Gogol doesn't seem to fit into either culture.

And yet, even more than his parents, who are by many standards highly successful immigrants, Gogol does try to fit in. He follows classic American narratives – the hard-work-pays-off ethic of the Horatio Alger stories, or the you-can-become-anyone myth of *The Great Gatsby* – as he grows from an awkward kid into a successful, self-assured adult. School and career success come easily: he's bright and adaptable. As he moves further from his parents' influence, he consistently reinvents himself, especially to appeal to girlfriends who tend to be white, wealthy, and cultured. The mother of one of these girlfriends named Lydia repeatedly tells Gogol he's Indian, and her daughter corrects her: "Nick's American … . He was born here" (157). In this quotation Lydia even gives the person she knows as Nikhil a literal nickname in this insistence on his nationality, asserting her control. These long-term relationships with rich, white, American girls serve to provide Gogol with a more materialistic set of values, but the relationships don't last. After he breaks up with the final one, his mother suggests that he look up a girl named Moushumi, a Bengali friend Gogol had met at family parties when they were children, but "as much as he wants to make his mother happy, he refuses to let her set him up with someone. He refuses to go that far" (192). His fear is that it is too much like an Indian arranged marriage, and that he is expected to marry someone who shares his ethnicity. They do meet and the waiter asks if they are siblings: "'Oh, no,' Gogol says, shaking his head, laughing, at once insulted and oddly aroused. In a way, he realizes, it's true – they share the same coloring, the straight eyebrows, the long, slender bodies, the high cheekbones and dark hair" (203). Despite his resistance to his mother's matchmaking, he and Moushumi fall in love and marry.

Like Gogol, Moushumi is American in her independence. She keeps her last name, which silently disappoints Gogol: "Though he hasn't admitted this to her, he'd hoped, the day they'd filled out the application for their marriage license, that she might consider otherwise" (227). There is a cost to embracing American reinvention as the key to identity. Moushumi lived in France before their courtship, and when they visit

France together, Gogol is jealous of her past: "Here Moushumi had reinvented herself, without misgivings, without guilt. He admires her, even resents her a little, for having moved to another country and made a separate life. He realizes that this is what their parents had done in America" (233). This is one of multiple epiphanies Gogol has about the difference between his parents' lives and his. Increasingly he considers his own life inferior to theirs. At his wedding he reflects on how different an arranged marriage must be: "He thinks of his parents, strangers until this moment, two people who had not spoken until after they were actually wed. Suddenly, sitting next to Moushumi he realizes what it means, and he is astonished by his parents' courage, the obedience that must have been involved in doing such a thing" (222). To equate courage with obedience is to reveal the complexity of Gogol's divided world. His marriage fails even though he and Moushumi freely chose each other. The novel subtly suggests that the children of immigrants cannot expect to find happiness automatically either through clinging to tradition or rejecting it wholesale. Lahiri's characters are given ample choices to determine their own identity, but the ability to choose is not an identity trait, just context.

Negotiating Cultural Differences

American debates over immigration often correlate with economic or political trends that pit progressive politics against cultural conservatism. While the world's largest economy relies heavily on immigrant labor and on innovation that originates in other nations, Americans tend to demonize immigrants in times of crisis. The notion of American exceptionalism is often code for a brand of xenophobia that rejects misunderstood foreign cultures. Following a long period of peace and prosperity, the twenty-first century opened with the shocking terror attacks of September 11, 2001. The American mood swung rapidly, especially (but not exclusively) against Muslims. The Cold War appeared to be over, but 9/11 revealed a new geopolitical reality, one that led to prolonged American wars in Iraq and Afghanistan. Americans became suspicious and fearful as airports developed now-routine screening protocols. In the wake of the terror attacks, some novelists explored the new condition of fearfulness. Many of these works take place in New York City, the epicenter of the attacks: Jonathan Safran Foer's *Extremely Loud and Incredibly Close* (2005), John Updike's *Terrorist* (2006), and Don DeLillo's *Falling Man* (2007) are a few noteworthy examples. In the context of multiculturalism and immigration, Joseph O'Neill's post-9/11 novel *Netherland* (2008) is a narrative that seeks to understand the divisive realities of contemporary, multicultural America and to trace their origins. The novel simultaneously looks backward and forward while also looking beneath the surface of American reality.

All this looking is indirect because the novel's first-person narrator, Dutch-born Hans van den Brock, is both naïve and aware of his own shortcomings as an interpreter of his world. The other immigrant novels covered in this chapter tend to approach the subject in a binary way: a protagonist from a specific foreign country must negotiate with a monolithic American culture. In *Call It Sleep*, the narrator becomes dimly aware that America is made up of more than one set of immigrants, but Hans fully understands that multiple cultures combine to form American culture. Hans's hyperawareness of multicultural America as well as American history does not necessarily lead to a full realization of the complex relationship between subcultures. His struggle to see America and its place in the world clearly is an ongoing project.

The author, like his fictional narrator, has a unique vantage point from which to view the United States as he was born in Ireland and lived in Mozambique, South Africa, Iran, Turkey, and Holland before coming to America. Hans's background is slightly less global: the novel begins and ends in England where he lives with his wife Rachel and their son Jake, but Hans was born in Holland and spent his most memorable years in America, years which are the focus of the narrative. His time in New York was punctuated by the 9/11 attacks, which strained his marriage by causing Rachel to return with their son to her native England: "She had fears ... that Times Square, where the offices of her law firm were situated, would be the site of the next attack" (20). Hans, a stoic, does not share her fears, and despite his devotion to Rachel and their son, he remains in America and clings to his uninspiring job – investment banking in oil concerns – which he finds lucrative but not challenging or interesting. It's clear that the marriage lacks passion, and although Rachel is certainly unsettled by 9/11, she may also be using it as an excuse to separate.

Hans's personal story as well as the broad background of 9/11 are secondary to the novel's main storyline, though, which involves Chuck Ramkissoon, a Trinidad-born immigrant to America. In the novel's opening pages, we learn that Chuck has been murdered. The novel borrows the conventions of detective fiction: the mystery of who might have killed Chuck (and why) seems to be Hans's main concern. This dynamic of a self-effacing narrator and a colorful, mysterious, murdered protagonist led many reviewers to compare the novel to *The Great Gatsby*. Yet Hans reveals much more of himself than Nick Carraway does in Fitzgerald's novel, and Chuck is a very different figure from Jay Gatsby, even though both are victims of their romantic visions. In Chuck's case, his dream is not to reinvent himself in order to win back a lost love, but rather to sell America something that it does not know it wants. That something, the subject and metaphor of much of the book, is the British-born sport cricket.

The metaphorical potential of cricket is explored in great detail. On one level cricket represents the global influence of the British Empire, an empire which gave birth to America in the seventeenth and eighteenth centuries long before it collapsed in the twentieth. Hans meets Chuck on a cricket field in Staten Island and lists the countries of origin of his team – former British colonies – who are facing off against a team from another former colony, St. Kitts: "My own teammates variously originated from Trinidad, Guyana, Jamaica, India, Pakistan, and Sri Lanka" (10). Religion, an obvious source of ideological tension after 9/11, is as unimportant as race or ethnicity on the cricket field: Hans huddles with his teammates for a pre-match prayer "with arms around one another's shoulders – nominally, three Hindus, three Christians, a Sikh, and four Muslims" (11). There are many such litanies throughout the novel in which Hans not only connects with the foreign-born denizens of New York, but actively seeks them out. Cricket is a sport that exists in America, but as an underworld. The "netherland" of the title alludes partly to the cricket fields that most people don't see, a world beneath the visible surface that contains, as suggested in the quotations above, the possibility for multicultural and multiracial harmony despite the fierce competition of sport.

But cricket also reveals divisions, specifically the racial divide. Hans observes, "I was the only white man I saw on the cricket fields of New York" (10). Chuck, who describes himself as "very dark – like Coca-Cola" (18) – reinforces this perception. He is a natural teacher, and during one of his lectures, he tells Hans, "Every summer the parks of this city are taken over by hundreds of cricketers but somehow nobody notices. It's like we're invisible. Now that's nothing new, for those of us who are black or brown. As for those of you who are not ... you'll forgive me, I hope, if I say that I sometimes tell people, You want a taste of how it feels to be a black man in this country? Put on the white clothes of the cricketer" (16). Perhaps Hans's desire to understand the perspective of the racial other contributes to his willingness to forge a friendship with Chuck and with a host of others on America's margins, but his primary motivation for taking up cricket is nostalgia for his native Holland (where cricket is nearly as popular as soccer) and the sense that he is using the sport to distract himself from his failing marriage. He also wants to reconcile his immigrant identity: "I was determined to open myself to new directions, a project I connected with escaping from the small country of fog in which, at a point I could not surely trace, I'd settled. That country, I speculated, might have some meaningful relation to my country of physical residence" (38). Chuck and cricket offer a conduit to identity formation, and even salvation at a time when Hans admits to feeling "wretched" (31).

Cricket is not easily transplanted onto American soil, though. Part of Chuck's dream is to create a perfectly level cricket pitch, but America's wild landscapes don't easily accommodate it; Hans says, "By the standards I brought to it, Walker Park was a very poor place for cricket. The playing area was ... half the size of a regulation cricket field. The outfield is uneven and always overgrown ... . Large trees – pin oaks, red oaks, sweetgums, American linden trees – clutter the fringes" (7). This list of trees suggests American diversity but also variability. Chuck's utopian quest for a perfect cricket pitch – named Bald Eagle Park in honor of the avian symbol of the U.S. – indicates that he refuses to settle for anything third-rate. At the same time, Chuck and his fellow Caribbean- and Asian-born cricketers are willing to adapt, specifically to the baseball-like style of American cricket which involves hitting the ball in the air; Hans says, "They had grown up playing the game in floodlit Lahore car parks or in rough clearings in some West Indian countryside. They could, and did, modify their batting without spiritual upheaval. I could not. More accurately, I would not change" (49). The experience of a wealthy, white immigrant from Europe is markedly different from those who come from less affluent countries, easily identifiable by the color of their skin. Hans says, "To reinvent myself in order to bat the American way, that baseball-like business of slugging and hoisting, involved more than the trivial abandonment of a hard-won style of hitting a ball. It meant snipping a fine white thread running, through years and years, to my mothered self" (50). Note that the thread is white. Despite his seemingly egalitarian embrace of immigrants to America from all races and creeds, Hans reveals his privilege here and attributes it to stubbornness in the guise of purity. Other immigrants have little choice but to adapt to the American version of the game, a metaphor for assimilation.

Chuck is a striver and a hustler whose business dealings contain some shadowy corners. He wants to make it in America the traditional way, through entrepreneurship and tireless work. Hans, by contrast, makes loads of money with no effort whatsoever. Hans learns something of what it is like to be Black and relatively poor from Chuck, but Chuck also teaches Hans about the history of his own people, the Dutch who settled New York when it was New Netherland. He buys Hans a book of Dutch nursery rhymes from the colonial era and tacks a note to it: "You know that you are a member of the first tribe of New York, excepting of course the Red Indians. Here is something you might like" (58). The effect is immediate. As Hans journeys through the Hudson River Valley on business he is transported through time; he says, "I was startled afresh by the existence of this waterside vista, which on a blurred morning such as this had the effect, once we passed under the George Washington Bridge, of canceling out centuries .... I only have to look at New York forests to begin to feel lost in them" (59). As he name-checks towns that cropped up in the early years of American fiction – in stories by Washington Irving and novels by James Fenimore Cooper – we nearly expect him to bump into Rip Van Winkle in these disorienting woods. But what Hans is truly encountering, with Chuck's gentle mentorship, is the story of himself as an immigrant, the connection between the Old World and America that resides inside him, not just in the other immigrants he encounters.

Though he doesn't struggle the way most of his new friends do, Hans details what must be for many immigrants the maddening experience of American bureaucracy in the form of the Department of Motor Vehicles. In a detailed description wincingly familiar to anyone who has sat in a DMV, Hans waits in multiple lines trying to explain the fact that one of his forms of identification contains a typo. After hours of pleading, he speaks to a supervisor who, in a crass power move, directs him back to Immigration and Naturalization Services to obtain a new green card to correct the clerical error. When Hans asks the man if that's truly his wish, the response is a petty display of power: "'I don't want you to go there,' the supervisor said. Now he was pointing at my chest. 'I'm forcing you to go there.'" Hans's generally ebullient attitude toward the U.S. fades: "I was seized for the first time by a nauseating sense of America, my gleaming adopted country, under the secret actuation of unjust, indifferent powers" (68). In short, he gets a small taste of what it feels like to be Chuck Ramkissoon, pushed around by power-mad bureaucrats who don't particularly like immigrants.

Chuck's program to teach Hans something about American reality involves a dose of disillusionment, but Chuck also demonstrates the benefits of blending in. He wears a Yankees cap, for instance, as though claiming an inextricable connection to his city, but also to the word "yankee." (Hans even imagines that the title of Chuck's autobiography, if he were to write down the story of his immigrant life, would be *Chuck Ramkissoon: Yank* [133]). Chuck clearly studied for his citizenship exams more thoroughly than Hans did, giving him fodder for history lessons, including that "the word 'Yankee' itself ... came from the simplest of Dutch names – Jan" (154). He has thoroughly researched the demographics of immigrants in the U.S. and uses the statistics to convince Hans that his business aspirations are legitimate, even as he acknowledges the adversity he faces: "There's no way they're going to let a bunch of black guys take over prime Manhattan real estate," (79) he argues while driving

Hans to a remote area of Brooklyn where he plans to develop his perfect cricket pitch. He expands his business, changing the name from "Chuck Cricket Corp." to "New York Cricket Club" and revealing his growing ambitions as he argues that cricket is a "bona fide American pastime" that has been "in the American DNA" since 1770, before the Revolutionary War (101–2). The business involves much more than cricket, though. In partnership with Boris Abelsky – whom Chuck met in the Russian baths – they create such products as kosher sushi and get deep into real estate, all of which bear Abelsky's name because Chuck realizes his own is inscrutable in the largely Jewish New York marketplace.

As Hans journeys intermittently across the Atlantic in weak attempts to patch things up with Rachel, he also becomes suspicious that there may be a snake in Chuck's gleaming green cricket pitch. On one level he is impressed with the man who seems to be flourishing while America stumbles: "Chuck was making a go of things. The sushi, the mistress, the marriage, the real estate dealings, and, almost inconceivably, Bald Eagle Field: it was all happening in front of my eyes. While the country floundered in Iraq, Chuck was running" (163). Yet Hans's eyes do not always see clearly. There is truth in Rachel's assessment: "You never really wanted to know him … . You were just happy to play with him. Same thing with America. You're like a child. You don't look beneath the surface" (166). The comment stings Hans but causes him to consider his relationship with Chuck more critically. He reflects, "She has accused me of exoticizing Chuck Ramkissoon, of giving him a pass, of failing to grant him a respectful measure of distrust, of perpetrating a white man's infantilizing elevation of a black man" (166). Though he doesn't fully admit that she might be right, Hans experiences a mild epiphany.

Following Rachel's critical comment, Hans's twin crises are that he both needs to grow up and learn how to see his American world clearly. It is possible he ignores Chuck's flaws because he wants to believe in him, symbolically, the way he wants to believe in America. Just as he is disillusioned by America when he suffers in the underworld of the DMV, he gradually understands that there is an invisible imperfect side to Chuck, too. In some ways, Chuck is an overreacher who believes he is capable of manipulating America after identifying its faults. Reinforcing the theme of flawed vision, he tells Hans, "Americans cannot really see the world. They think they can, but they can't. I don't need to tell you that. Look at the problems we're having. It's a mess, and it's going to get worse. I say, we want to have something in common with Hindus and Muslims? Chuck Ramkissoon is going to make it happen" (211). Chuck's shortcoming is that he believes he can both run the game and win it. He tells Hans about a numbers-running game in Trinidad where the owner of the game, the "banker," announces the number, or "bursts the mark." "It's my game,"

(171) he confidently tells Hans, but Hans has witnessed the brutality and racism of Chuck's business partner Abelsky. The reader may never finally know how Chuck met his grisly end, but we are left to consider whether anyone can beat the house when the house is America. Chuck's romantic belief that America would easily give up its own national pastime to embrace cricket just because he sees things ordinary Americans can't is his downfall. One doesn't always have to play by the American rules, as Hans proves on the cricket pitch, but imagining that America will play by another set of rules is a dangerous game.

Netherland should leave the reader troubled about the costs of assimilation. Chuck, an individualist who tries to blend in as much as possible in America while quietly manipulating it, is murdered and leaves no meaningful legacy. Hans, who has more power based on his wealth and race, treats America as he treated Chuck, as a temporary playmate. He is back in London at the novel's conclusion, vaguely unsettled but not much wiser than he was at the beginning. Immigrants like Hans who are temporary migrants do not feel the same urgent need to assimilate into America. Hans's aim was never to become a jigsaw puzzle piece that might help complete the picture being assembled. Rather, the way his story intertwines with Chuck's indicates stubborn realities about late capitalism and race in the twenty-first century.

Seeking a Cultural Balance

Novels of immigration paint only part of the picture of multiethnic America. In other novels by minority authors, immigration may have occurred generations before the story, or it may be just an accepted fact of the lives of its characters rather than a process to be detailed and interpreted. Ethnic identity varies greatly in terms of the importance Americans attach to it. There are strong strains of genealogy in a host of great American works, from the family tree and "begat chart" that open John Edgar Wideman's Homewood Trilogy (1981–1983), to the digression into family history in Jeffrey Eugenides's *Middlesex* (2002), to Milkman's tireless efforts to piece together his fragmented family story, preserved in coded children's songs and folklore in Toni Morrison's *Song of Solomon* (1977). *How the García Girls Lost Their Accents* also begins with a family tree with diagonals and curvy lines, tracing the titular characters' ancestral connection to the Conquistadores. There are no dates on this tree, notably no date when the family moved to the United States. Multiethnic narratives are not just stories of immigration, in other words, but stories of origin and of the lasting effects of the experiences of ancestors – immigrants, enslaved people, or displaced Native Americans – on their descendants who might never have met them.

Maxine Hong Kingston rose to prominence with her 1975 memoir *The Woman Warrior*, the first chapter of which showcases the way she uses her imagination to fill in the details of a family story her relatives would not tell, a story marked by shame rather than pride. In her first novel, the wild and fantastic *Tripmaster Monkey: His Fake Book* (1989) she similarly tells the story of the lasting cultural effects of immigration on an unlikely hero, the impulsive and mercurial Wittman Ah Sing, a Beatnik pacifist in early 1960s San Francisco. Wittman's great-great-grandfather immigrated from China four generations earlier, so one would imagine that Wittman might be fully assimilated, especially given the fact that his namesake is one of the most iconic nineteenth-century American poets and that his last name ("Ah Sing") is an homage to "Song of Myself." Although he represents the Jeffersonian dream that immigrants labor so that their grandchildren can be poets, Wittman is far from assimilated. He is hyperconscious of his outsider status in American society based on his Chinese heritage. His worldview forms in reaction to the stereotypes of Chinese Americans that permeate American society, largely fueled by racist representations in the movies. The novel takes the form of the wandering hero going about his daily business without a plan, with a huge dash of fanciful imaginative digressions in the vein of Joyce's *Ulysses*. It would also be productive to compare it to an early work of Thomas Pynchon like *The Crying of Lot 49* (see Chapter 7) in which unpredictable and zany incidents make frequent incursions into the narrative, reveling in absurdity and entertaining the reader through plot tangents. Yet there is a serious core to the book. Whitman is a pacifist at a time when his country is escalating its military operations in Vietnam, and the particular way he is at odds with his country is intensified by the fact that the war is in Asia, his ancestral homeland. Late in the novel he realizes, "The dying was on the Asian side of the planet while the playing – the love-ins and the be-ins – were on the other, American side" (306). Playfulness is the impulse of the novel, the key to Wittman's understanding of how to reconcile his Asian roots with his American existence despite his disconnection from both.

"Play" has multiple connotations in the novel which builds toward an elaborate, extended dramatic performance. Wittman is a poet and a playwright who has struggled to find an audience for his art. He is determined not to sell out, but rather – like Chuck in *Netherland* – to give the people what they either don't necessarily know they want or have temporarily lost. The tradition of Chinese theater is one such loss. His mother and her friends were involved in a burlesque version of Chinese theater during World War II, and their playful artistic careers have been erased by history. Wittman realizes a distinctive quality of his Chinese forebears: "The difference between us and other pioneers, we did not come here for the gold streets. We came to play" (250). His own impulses toward playwriting and playing in general have been thwarted by the great American seriousness: the pressure to conform, to work professionally, to present oneself respectably, all of which are reinforced by his scolding mother despite her playful past. As a free spirit educated at Berkeley and inclined to the bohemianism of 1960s San Francisco, Wittman rejects the central tenets of Puritanical America. Like his poetic namesake, who famously loafs and invites his soul at the beginning of "Song of Myself," Wittman drifts, imagines, creates, and indulges in bodily pleasure while rejecting militarism, capitalism, and respectability, all of which are intertwined with the Dream script.

The first half of *Tripmaster Monkey* chronicles the specific ways Wittman rejects mainstream American society. He regards himself as the reincarnation of Monkey, or the Monkey King, a legendary Chinese trickster figure who signals his transformations by shouting the sound "Bee-ee-een!" (34). Whenever Wittman shouts this phrase, his transformation is generally toward chaos. When he brings a would-be girlfriend named Nanci Lee to his apartment to hear his poems, she unconsciously offends him, first by calling his poems "sweet and lovely" (opposite to the effect he wanted), then by suggesting they sound derivative of the proto-Black Arts Movement poetry popular at the time (31). When she tells him his work reminds her of the poet LeRoi Jones (later Amiri Baraka), Wittman reacts violently and chaotically: "He slammed his hand – a fist with a poem in it – down on the desk – fistful of poem. He spit in his genuine brass China Man spittoon, and jumped up on top of the desk, squatted there, scratching. 'Monkey see, monkey do?' he said. 'Huh? Monkey see, monkey do?' Which sounds much uglier if you know Chinese" (32). He leaps around the room causing destruction and denies that he is "freaking out": "I am really: the present-day U.S.A. incarnation of the King of the Monkeys" (33). This performance is related to his theatrical inclinations, but also represents a real yearning to be recognized for his own unique contributions to American culture without forsaking his Chinese identity; he laments, "Where's our jazz? Where's our blues? Where's our ain't-taking-no-shit-from-nobody street-strutting language? I want so bad to be the first bad-jazz China Man bluesman of America" (27). Nanci's pronouncement that his poetry sounds Black rubs a nerve: he wants his poetry to be recognized as a unique and important contribution, not unlike Black poetry or music, but not an imitation of it. On this level, *Tripmaster Monkey* is a quest novel, with the holy grail being Wittman's ability to produce original artistic work connected to his Chinese heritage but also to reproduce it in such a way that it benefits an audience.

The path to achieving this goal is not straight or smooth. Before achieving his artistic aims, he attempts to find his way in America conventionally, by working a respectable paying job. The results are hilariously disastrous. He cannot hold a retail job selling children's toys because he opposes the fact that so many of them are violent and ultimately contribute to the proliferation of war. During his stint at the toy store his chaotic monkey persona emerges: he simulates sex between a wind-up monkey doll and a Barbie doll in front of adult customers and their children. He is promptly fired. In addition to pacifism, he is sensitive to the pressure to conform to standards of beauty that are both impossible to achieve and Anglocentric; late in the novel he rants about Asian women who succumb to this pressure by surgically altering their eyelids.

These two early incidents – his explosion at Nanci and his job-destroying actions in the toy store – are the most heavily plotted chapters of the book, after which he is free to wander, which is the key to self-discovery and to contributing to his country. His wandering has him shuttling back and forth between the white world and Asian communities, and the fact that he doesn't fit comfortably into either is the source of his confusion. He finds himself at a corporate party and wonders, "What's wrong with him that he keeps ending up in Caucasian places? ... . Wherever I go, I do the integrating. My very presence integrates the place" (57). He is wary of being a cultural token just as he is wary of the essential conservatism of his parents' generation and of recent immigrants from China that he refers to as "F.O.B."s ("fresh off the boat"). His best friend is Lance Kamiyama, a Japanese American who is conventionally successful and who Wittman accuses of being a "conformist" and thus a "smug asshole" (118). Wittman is partially jealous of Japanese Americans because the history of the internment camps following World War II gave them a shared collective story that clearly defined their oppressed historical relationship to mainstream American society, parallel to the history of slavery for African Americans: as he puts it, "Executive Order 9066 has given to Issei, Nisei, Sansei their American history ... . And places ... . And righteous politics" (126). He doesn't romanticize or gloss over the group's painful history, but it contributes to his untethered feeling as Chinese Americans do not have a single, coherent story that is legible to others: they only have stereotyping to contend with.

Wittman meets a white girl named Taña at Lance's party and, following a weed-filled breakfast at the afterparty, they become lovers, but Wittman is wary that she might be a "freak for orientalia" (155). He tests her by asking her what Chinese feature of his turns her on and her answer passes the test: "Good. She did not tell him that she liked 'yellow' skin or 'slanty' eyes. She did not say he was 'mysterious'" (155). The new couple bump into a draft-evading drifter who has become ordained by a pop-up ministry. When the drifter asks if they want to be married so Wittman, "who had a principle about spontaneity" (163) can avoid the draft, he and

Taña assent and are instantly wed. The novel then parodies not only Wittman's inability to hold a conventional job, but also to follow the typical American rituals of courtship and domesticity. Their marriage is a joke, and they treat it as such, and yet they also seem to want to stick it out and see what happens. Wittman's disruptive monkey persona is a threat, though: when they go on a quasi-honeymoon at a fancy restaurant, he confronts a group at a nearby table who he believes are telling racist jokes and he makes a scene tempestuous enough to get them kicked out. But there are ways in which he treats the marriage seriously: he introduces Taña to his parents and brings her along in his search for a missing grandmother. Even in this ritual, though, he sees a difference between them: "They didn't have to worry about meeting Taña's family; white people don't have families. They're free" (176). Statements like these suggest that Wittman's perceptions of his world are uniformly clouded by his awareness of difference. His tirade that gets them kicked out of the restaurant and seemingly innocuous (if inaccurate) thoughts such as this one about white family relationships are related.

Wittman's conflict, then, is not limited to his minority status, but consistently filtered through it. His bohemian ideology separates him from mainstream American society, especially as the war in Vietnam escalates, but he is also enamored with facets of American culture and wants to be able to contribute to it. The resolution dominates the second half of the novel as Wittman figures out a way to unleash his chaotic monkey energy into a freewheeling dramatic performance. The first act involves everyone he knows, and it creatively reinvigorates Chinese drama in an American context, culminating in fireworks. The drama, which simulates warfare, is meant to purge the need for it: "Our monkey, master of change, staged a fake war, which might very well be displacing some real war" and replacing it with community, which "is not built once-and-for-all; people have to imagine, practice, and re-create it" (306). Wittman has created his community and it becomes a way to showcase his newly refined individual self. The novel concludes with a lengthy monologue in which his beliefs are both publicly exhibited and either accepted or challenged by the audience. The long, strange trip of the novel builds toward the ultimate Whitmanesque principle, the self that contains multitudes. In *Tripmaster Monkey*, this variation on the ultimate American theme – *e pluribus unum* – takes on a specific valence in the context of immigration and ethnic identity.

Although many examples of the multiethnic novel concentrate on the tension between the majority and minority cultures due to the pressure to assimilate, some focus on the way that pressure manifests within a minority community rather than dramatizing an overt culture clash. Rudolfo Anaya's *Bless Me, Ultima* (1972) is oriented toward the forces that both divide and unite a minority community, in this case Spanish-speaking residents of New Mexico in the mid-twentieth century. There are glimmers of the oppressive influence of the white Anglo world on this community such as the insistence on English in public schools and in religious education, but the novel is more overtly concerned with interrogating the divisive forces within the community.

There are many sources of division in *Bless Me, Ultima*, but the main one has to do with spiritual belief systems. Antonio, the protagonist and narrator, has been identified by his devout Catholic mother as the son who will become a priest. Antonio's three older brothers have followed the instincts of his father's side of the family and gone off to fight in the war. Antonio, almost seven at the beginning of the novel, is a sensitive visionary who is poised for success in education, so he seems a fitting candidate to fulfill his mother's dreams. He is not called, though, and many events in the novel distance him not only from the priesthood, but from belief in the Judeo-Christian God more generally. The most influential person who causes him to question his Catholic faith is the titular Ultima, an elderly woman regarded as a *curandera*, one who has magical powers and who uses natural cures to counter curses and spells within the community. Her connection to natural/pagan folkways makes her susceptible to charges of witchcraft.

Like other novels discussed in this chapter, Antonio's dilemma is tied to his parents' experiences. He asks Ultima why his mother's side of the family, who are farmers, are "strange and quiet" while his father's side, who are ranchers, are "loud and wild." She answers in terms of nature: "It is the blood of the Lunas to be quiet, for only a quiet man can learn the secrets of the earth that are necessary for planting – They are quiet like the moon – And it is the blood of the Marez to be wild, like the ocean from which they take their name" (38). Antonio's challenge is to learn to balance these forces within himself, but he also sees how such simple differences in personality or family origin can affect the larger community. Although the divergent orientations Ultima describes produce tension in Antonio's family with his own future in the balance, the real rift in the community is a blood feud between Tenorio Trementina and many other families, including Antonio's. Antonio's grandfather believes that Tenorio's daughters have cast an evil spell on one of Antonio's uncles. He hires Ultima to lift the curse, and her compliance cures Antonio's uncle but kills two of Tenorio's daughters.

Tensions escalate, mostly around belief systems. As an established midwife and curandera, Ultima is revered by those who honor traditional culture. The influence of the Catholic church is strong, though, and Tenorio uses that influence to rally a mob to kill Ultima as a witch, the traditional adversary of the Catholic faith. She passes a test that would have branded her a witch had she failed, but it remains clear that she possesses strong powers that cannot be rationally explained; Antonio says, "Was it possible that there was more power in Ultima's magic than in the priest?" (92). Further complicating this dichotomy is the rise of a new, pagan belief system in the community. Antonio's friend Cico introduces him to a community that believes in a deity from nature, the Golden Carp. Skeptical at first, Antonio eventually sees the majestic creature and confesses, "I could not have been more entranced if I had seen the Virgin, or God Himself" (105). Along with Ultima, the Golden Carp is yet another force pulling Antonio away from his mother's strong desire that he become a priest, a fate that intensifies as he excels in his religious training and all his classmates turn to him as a natural candidate for priesthood. His dilemma reaches the point of agony, and he appeals to Ultima to ask her what he should believe. She responds with wisdom that is not necessarily comforting to Antonio, but that will guide him better than any ideology: "As you grow into manhood you must find your own truths" (112).

This adage is a fitting summary of this and many other American multiethnic novels. American "truths" are actually products of a mainstream ideology that demands conformity, but it's not as though immigrants and their descendants are forbidden from discovering alternative truths. Gogol in *The Namesake* glumly conforms to the American Dream script and is disappointed with himself by the end of the narrative; Wittman in *Tripmaster Monkey* rebelliously pursues his own truths in the form of creative expression, and he is, by contrast, satisfied with his growth. American novels about immigrants and ethnic minorities are often connected to the American Dream story, but with an important variation as the goal, more than simply material prosperity, is a mature sense of identity that can accommodate America without completely yielding to it.

Further Reading

Cisneros, Sandra. *The House on Mango Street* (1991)
Diaz, Junot. *The Brief, Wondrous Life of Oscar Wao* (2007)
Eggers, Dave. *What Is the What* (2006)
Eugenides, Jeffrey. *Middlesex* (2002)
Hijuelos, Oscar. *The Mambo Kings Play Songs of Love* (1989)
Lee, Chang-Rae. *Native Speaker* (1995)
Ng, Celeste. *Little Fires Everywhere* (2017)
Okada, John. *No No Boy* (1957)
Puzo, Mario. *The Godfather* (1969)
Tan, Amy. *The Joy Luck Club* (1989)
Toíbín, Colm. *Brooklyn* (2009)

7 Old (and New) Weird America
Experimentation and Voices from the Margins

One of the many problems with the American Dream script is that it isn't authentically American. Though tied to "land of opportunity" myth in which prosperity is available to hard workers, the core idea of the American Dream is rooted in aspirational notions of class mobility articulated by European thinkers during the early Enlightenment. It's more accurate to say that the Puritans *imported* the American Dream rather than invented it. The New World just gave them the space to explore its possibilities. Immigrant groups after the English Puritans have not substantially altered the fundamental idea of the American Dream even as they adapted it to their individual circumstances. Put bluntly, the American Dream demands conformity. The true spirit of America, one hopes, ought to be considerably weirder.

I borrow the title for this chapter from the music critic Greil Marcus who employed it when writing about *The Basement Tapes*, a collection of spontaneously written songs recorded by Bob Dylan and the Band between 1967 and 1975. Marcus claims he got the rhythm for the phrase from the Beat poet Kenneth Rexroth who "was looking for a phrase to describe the country he thought lay behind Carl Sandburg's work … . Rexroth came up with 'the old free America." Marcus, saying the words made him dizzy, continues: "the idea, the words themselves, seemed all but natural, coded in the inevitable betrayals that stem from the infinite idealism of American democracy," and yet, "They cut Americans off from any need to measure themselves against the idealism – the utopianism, the Puritans' errand into the wilderness or the pioneers' demand for a new world with every wish for change – Americans have inherited. By fixing the free America, the true America, in the past, those words excuse the betrayals of those Americans who might hear them" (89). Crucially converting "free" to "weird," Marcus destabilizes the utopian spirit built into American thought, the mental straitjacket that unconsciously creates the sibling myths of the Great American Novel and the American Dream. Quite possibly, the path to freedom is weirdness, a variation on nonconformity.

Perhaps because our earliest prose traditions were nonfictional and thus wedded to reality, weirdness was a little slow to arrive in American literary history. The American novel had to establish itself before understanding that it had been too tame in both its topics and its methods. If we acknowledge that the American Dream script is formidable, we should also acknowledge that a tradition of domestic novels about families who strive to rise slightly above their station can only go so far before reaching limitations in terms of theme, plot, and character. Recognizing the American Dream script as a new form of tyranny, novelists had to be willing to cross boundaries and cultivate weirdness rather than fear it. The writers covered in this chapter flout or at least resist the formal conventions of realism – namely a carefully structured, chronologically organized plot that resolves an explicit conflict and recognizable characters who develop or fail to develop in conjunction with that plot – as a way of reimagining America. These writers explore topics and ideas that aren't primarily concerned with monogamous, heterosexual domesticity and middle-class respectability. Following Marcus's phrase, the weirdness of America is nothing new, but it was not always fully appreciated because it had been marginalized or buried.

To summarize the preceding chapters, the American Dream script dominates the tradition. Even the novels I have labeled "anti-Dream" in Chapter 5 are defined in terms of the Dream: they describe characters who chase the Dream but find it inaccessible because of their class and/or race. The novels of domestic discontentment by and about women in Chapter 3 are also tethered to the Dream as their protagonists are limited and defined by its silent mandate that women are expected to marry and to maintain domestic harmony. The immigration stories in Chapter 6 are largely mapped onto the Dream narrative as well, the point often being that ethnic groups on America's margins are encouraged to follow the script by assimilating even as they begin outside it due to language and custom, though in the novels at the end of that chapter by Kingston and Anaya we see alternative modes emerging. Chapter 4 on slavery and its legacies posits a different script centering on dreams of freedom and equality rather than prosperity, but as the chapter reinforces, the American Dream script depends on slavery while obscuring that relationship. The underpinning of the Dream script should be freedom, and yet a great many of our classic works stop short of fully exploring artistic or imaginative possibilities. For a country so obsessed with freedom, our novel tradition has been surprisingly constrained.

Nineteenth-Century Precursors to Modernism

Many of the novelists who escape the constraints of the American Dream narrative are willing to experiment with form. Students and critics of the rise of the novel in England note how its earliest practitioners dispensed with the illusion of realism, often calling attention to the artificiality of the nascent genre in metafictional ways. One noteworthy example is Laurence Sterne's *The Life and Opinions of Tristram Shandy, Gentleman* (1759–1767). Published when America was still a set of colonies, this brilliant, funny work and others like it (such as Henry Fielding's *Tom Jones* [1749]) weren't immediately transplanted in the soil of the New World, but their spirit of freedom and iconoclasm lingered somewhere in the collective imagination of our novelists, and that spirit would eventually run free in quirky works that were critically revered even if popularly overlooked. Sterne's book is famously digressive and meandering, the narrative moving backward through time more often than forward. Borrowing techniques from an even earlier novel, Cervantes's *Don Quixote* (1605–1615) – arguably the first novel in any language – *Tristram Shandy* is more playful than purposeful. That impulse took a while before settling into American novels which were long reluctant to be goofy or irreverent: if the witty but hardly playful Hawthorne is considered our first great novelist, that premise is clear enough. American novelists in the nineteenth century who were even slightly playful or experimental generally felt compelled to attach themselves to serious subjects or serious themes.

A way to break the spell of realism is to dispense with the illusion of verisimilitude by treating the novel as a miscellany rather than a continuous narrative with a uniform voice. One early writer who employed this technique was William Wells Brown in *Clotel, or The President's Daughter* (1853), the first novel by an African American author. It is a novel in the sense that it sustains a fictional narrative, but it experiments with the form by gathering various poems, short stories, newspaper accounts, and nonfictional slave narratives to produce a highly original work. Consistent with the experimental spirit of British predecessors like Sterne and Fielding, Brown varies his tone considerably, interspersing sentimental scenes with polemical passages and even humor. Like *Tristram Shandy, Clotel* is given to digression and doesn't always focus on the title character for extended periods. The fact that she dies prior to the novel's conclusion underscores that the novel is only partly interested in her character. Brown's willingness to experiment by mixing a variety of prose and poetic forms and his tendency toward self-consciousness as a purveyor of fiction make *Clotel* read like a novel from a century later when postmodernism flourished, yet as a novel concerned with the system of slavery while it was still in place, it obviously does not indulge in the zany humor of postmodernists like Pynchon, Barth, or Vonnegut.

The borderline between nonfiction and fiction is a repeated concern in *Clotel*. It's noteworthy that Brown earlier published an important slave narrative based on his experiences, *Narrative of William W. Brown, a Fugitive Slave* (1847), and he includes an abridged version of that work as the novel's introduction. This "sketch of the author's life" is cleverly written in the third person, a move that turns the traditional first-person subject of the slave narrative into a fictional character and also sidesteps the convention of having a white abolitionist's words frame the narrative. It begins, "William Wells Brown, the subject of this narrative, was born a slave in Lexington, Kentucky" (6). In rendering his own authentic experience in the third person, Brown shows his willingness to take full creative control. He also quotes himself in the initial sketch in *Clotel*, adding to the sense of playfulness and reliance on previously published material that defines this novel's unique characteristics.

Brown toys with the distinction between fiction and slave narratives throughout *Clotel*. One chapter is entitled "Truth Stranger than Fiction." After hearing of ill slaves being purchased for scientific dissection, one white character says to another, "I have often heard what I consider hard stories in abolition meetings in New York about slavery; but now I shall begin to think that many of them are true" (133). On more than one occasion the narrator says of an anecdote he has related, "This, reader, is no fiction" (148, 172), challenging readers to verify the story if they so desire, and even providing the source material should they care to do so, a technique later exploited for parodic purposes in Vladimir Nabokov's postmodern novel *Pale Fire* (1962), which is mostly footnotes. In the novel's conclusion, Brown writes, "I may be asked, and no doubt shall, Are the various incidents and scenes related founded in truth? I answer, Yes" (226). It is somewhat ironic that he should feel compelled to defend truthfulness in a work of fiction, but while *Clotel* marked a giant step away from the slave narrative genre and into the novel form, it also anchored its pivot foot.

Like other aspects of *Clotel*, the narrative voice is varied. It occasionally advances the kind of general pronouncements about slavery common to the slave narrative genre, made for the benefit of the unenlightened outsider, as in the following example: "In all the large towns in the Southern States, there is a class of slaves who are permitted to hire their time of their owners, and for which they pay a high price" (84). At other times the narrative voice is sentimental, as when Clotel parts from her lover Horatio: "Her voice was choked for utterance, and the tears flowed freely, as she bent her lips toward him. He folded her convulsively in his arms, and imprinted a long impassioned kiss on that mouth, which had never spoken to him but in love and blessing. With efforts like a death-pang she at length raised her head from his heaving bosom" (121). The narrator frequently turns the narrative over directly to his sources, reprinting newspaper stories verbatim, and even quoting from Thomas Jefferson's *Notes on the State of Virginia* as well as the *Declaration of Independence*, nonfiction documents written for the general populace that gain irony through the assertion that Jefferson is Clotel's father. Related to the miscellaneous nature of Brown's style, it is difficult to identify the main emphasis in his novel. As a result, *Clotel* is fresh and surprising nearly two centuries after its publication.

The same can obviously be said of Herman Melville's *Moby-Dick, or The Whale*, a novel that enchants and mystifies through its awe-inspiring breadth and depth of ideas as well as plot and character. The introductory nature of this volume prevents a full, original reading of *Moby-Dick* here – it is assumed that readers understand its importance to the tradition and can locate interpretations elsewhere – but a few words about the novel's willingness to experiment with form indicate how it represents and perhaps helps to define weirdness in the American novel tradition. "Define" is an apt word as Melville's ponderous classic begins with definitions, specifically with two pages of "etymology" followed by thirteen pages of "extracts" or quotations from previously published work attempting to define "the whale." This unusual opening is not intended to help the reader understand what a whale *is*, but rather what a whale *might mean*. This pursuit is the quest of the narrative, but the initial pages are a warning to the reader: you might have come to a novel in search of plot and character, but understand that the subject is broad, vague, and inscrutable. The novel's true subject is not the meaning of the whale, but knowledge itself. Dictionaries, maps, and other artifacts of human attempts to know their world and make a record of that knowledge must be put into conversation with a story.

Despite the seemingly helpful research that opens Melville's massive novel, everything about the narrative is meant to disorient the reader. The narrator Ishmael leads us right away out of what we thought was America – its principal city, New York – and into a watery world where nothing is easily knowable. He suggests he needs to get away from his countrymen periodically to avoid warring with them, and claims everyone feels this way, that "thousands upon thousands of mortal men [are] fixed in ocean reveries." The openness and freedom of the ocean is in contrast to their mundane lives consisting of "week days pent up in lath and plaster – tied to counters, nailed to benches, clinched to desks" (24). In contrast to the mechanical dullness of most work, the ocean is a space for meditation, as Ishmael quickly elaborates, that lures Americans from locations across the continent. It also represents freedom from the constriction of the routine work that funds the Dream but also inhibits creative free thinking.

Modernism's Radical Breaks

Clotel and *Moby-Dick* reveal a yearning for the nonconventional in nineteenth-century novels, but twentieth-century American writers took experimentation to new heights. The periods of literary history known as modernism in the early decades of the century and postmodernism which reached its peak in the 1960s through 1980s sought radically new methods of narration and new subject matter to accompany it. Thorough definitions and analyses of the two periods fill volumes of criticism and can only be glimpsed here. For our purposes, the impulse behind modernism involved a radical reconception of the nature of art and of the relationship between artists and audiences. The modern novel, consistent with other forms of literature and art more generally, sought to shock readers into a new way of thinking in order to put them in touch with the alienating complexities of modern existence. In an increasingly mechanized world in which the influence of longstanding institutions (notably formal religion) was weakened, modernist authors peered into the tormented inner selves of their characters, relying on new conceptions of the unconscious mind to produce works that were less mannered, less coherent, and more abstract than those of their predecessors. Postmodernists in the latter half of the century were less concerned with the depth of existence and more delighted with its endless surfaces. Postmodernists are also conscious of their place in literary history, aware that they have arrived after a movement (modernism) that thought of itself as the logical end of human cultural history. Postmodernists take art less seriously than their predecessors did. Postmodern novels call attention to their own artificiality, revealing their own fictional nature by breaking the spell of narrative altogether through techniques known as metafiction.

Though neither modernism nor postmodernism are uniquely American movements, both flourished in America. That said, American novelists contributed more robustly to postmodernism than they did to modernism, which flowed out of European currents of thought and thrived especially in Paris where many American artists became expatriates. (Djuna Barnes's 1936 modernist masterpiece *Nightwood*, for instance, does not fit comfortably into this study because even though the author is American, the characters and setting of the novel are mainly European). The pioneer of American modernism in the novel was Gertrude Stein who kept an eye on American culture even while living in Paris. Her doubly marginalized identity as a Jew in a mostly Christian country and a lesbian at a time when homosexuality was not widely accepted, spoken of, or understood helped Stein merge her unique perspectives with deep interests in art and psychology to create an innovative prose form that influenced the rising generation of fiction writers including Sherwood Anderson, Ernest Hemingway, and John Dos Passos. Her expatriation in Paris – which lasted much longer than that of earlier novelists Henry James and Edith Wharton or later novelists Hemingway, Fitzgerald, Richard Wright, Mary McCarthy, and James Baldwin – placed her at a further remove from mainstream American life and thus facilitated a further break from the conventions of American novels.

Stein's first published work *Three Lives* (1909) announced a new aesthetic that intrigued and puzzled readers simultaneously. The three women depicted in this triptych were unlikely subjects as their lives seemed mundane and/or devoid of the plot structure expected in novels. The style was deliberately repetitive (though as Linda Wagner-Martin points out, Stein "preferred to think of it as insistence rather than repetition" [Stein 11]). In the first portrait, "The Good Anna," for instance, we are told multiple times in single-sentence paragraphs that "Anna led an arduous and troubled life" (37, 39, 44). The narrator of each piece speaks factually and maintains a consistent distance from the three subjects, revealing them subtly and with an unusual blend of the specific and the general. The style of Stein's writing is so distinctive that it calls attention to itself more than to the traditional appeals of fiction (plot, theme, setting, and character). Even so, Stein's characters are primary to her work. They are rendered in such a way as to draw the reader's eye to the border between their inner and outer lives. Through repetition and subtle variation, Stein faithfully illustrates the surface of these lives while indicating – but not overtly declaring – what's underneath.

The first portrait, "The Good Anna," depicts a German immigrant to America whose life is outlined by her dedication to her work as a domestic servant, her deep attachment to pets, and her intense same-sex relationships, especially with the widow Mrs. Lehntman who was, we are repeatedly told, "the only romance Anna knew" (50, 53, 66). The nature of their romance is only hinted at: "Her affair with Mrs. Lehntman was too sacred and too grievous ever to be told" (61). Her involvement and gradual break with Mrs. Lehntman mirrors a pattern in her work life: she connects deeply to her employers and then moves on to other jobs, recognizing certain times as happy or unhappy, but generally keeping her head down and completing her tasks. In violation of a key principle of the American Dream script, she does not prosper because she ends up giving her savings to others who seem to need money more than she does: "She saved and saved and always saved, and then here and there, to this friend and to that, to one in her trouble and to the other in her joy, in sickness, death, and weddings, or to make young people happy, it always went, the hard earned money she had saved" (65). This is one of the facts of her life that readers will take away from the story even as specific details of Anna's employment in various households become less significant.

The "goodness" of the title, despite the fact that Anna seems a generally stern person who takes pleasure in scolding others for their behavior, indicates her essential kindness to pets and humans. She is independent and doesn't expect anything in return for her kindness. These simple truths are the outline of her simple life which ends abruptly in her death, as do the other two portraits in the triptych. We are not meant to feel a deep sense of loss at the end, just a factual understanding that the woman whose life has been described in detailed anecdotes is no longer: "Then they did the operation, and then the good Anna with her strong, strained, worn-out body died" (86). The suggestion that the medical operation might have been botched doesn't finally matter. The fact of her death, like the declarations and illustrations of moments both significant and insignificant, remain imprinted on the reader's imagination as incontrovertible artifacts of a lived life.

The same can be said for Stein's other two portraits of an African American protagonist in "Melanctha" and another immigrant from the working class in "The Gentle Lena." Stein's status as an outsider encouraged her to validate individual experience and drew her to the lives of women who were pointedly not like her, and yet with whom she felt solidarity. Consistent with her interest in painting, she accepted the portraitist's challenge of both rendering a character in terms of how they appear to the world and then choosing what subtle details might suggest a rich and unique inner life. The risk is that readers will only see the surface representation as perceived by an outsider, and Melanctha and other Black characters in her story are occasionally sketched in racially stereotyped terms. Through Stein's technique, the portrait of Melanctha's exterior becomes less meaningful as her inner life emerges with a focus on "the power she had so often felt stirring within her" (95). Melanctha initially locates the source of this power in her Black father rather than her white mother, but she grows over the course of her life: "In these young days, it was only men that for Melanctha held anything there was of knowledge and power. It was not from men however that Melanctha learned to really understand this power" (96). Instead, she learns to trust her intuition rather than accept wisdom from outside. Arising from a stereotyped portrait of her race and gender, Melanctha emerges as a consummate individual, unique, memorable, and intriguing.

In addition to power, the quest of Melanctha's life journey is wisdom, initially found not in traditional sources but in a rebellious, hard-living friend named Jane Harden. She observes Jane for two years, during which "Melanctha had come to see very clear, and she had come to be very certain, what it is that gives the world its wisdom" (101), wisdom being a word the narrator employs many times in quick succession without defining it. The rest of the narrative is subtly devoted to exploring what it is Melanctha understands as the world's wisdom which often comes from "wandering," a word that refers to her voracious appetite for understanding people through their actions and activities rather than their words, but also to a refusal to be tied down. She is courted by a doctor named Jefferson Campbell who criticizes Melanctha's friend Jane and who believes that happiness can be achieved by "being good and regular in life, and not having excitements all the time." By contrast, "Melanctha always had strong the sense for real experience" and "did not think much of [Campbell's] way of coming to real wisdom" (108). She tells him so in no uncertain terms and accuses him of not knowing himself and rejecting "real, strong, hot love"; she says, "You are just too scared Dr. Campbell to really feel things way down in you" (112, 113). Their relationship dominates her narrative and Campbell remains frustrated that Melanctha will not conform to his belief in the control of one's passions as a prescription for the broader success of the African American community. She returns to her "wandering" and leaves Campbell behind, proving both her independence and her refusal to conform.

Her life resumes the pattern of attaching herself to others, proving too spirited for them, and losing the attachment. Her moments of excessive excitement are balanced by periods when she feels "blue" and talks about committing suicide. After severing her relationship with Campbell, she becomes intensely friendly with Rose Johnson and her husband Sam, but Rose gradually becomes weary of Melanctha's "new ways to be in trouble" (169). One of those ways is by developing a romance with a gambler named Jem Richards, and her love for him is repeatedly said to make her "mad and foolish" (179). It is this intensity she lives for, though; it is connected to the power and wisdom she seeks through experiencing life with great passion, and it is the flip side of her blue moods. Rose Johnson scolds her, as Campbell had, for her behavior, saying things like "I don't see Melanctha why you should talk like you would kill yourself just because you're blue" (181). Melanctha finds herself in an especially dark place when both Rose and Jem break off their relationships with her at the end of the narrative, and the reader suspects that she will succumb to her suicidal tendencies. The narrator tells us that this was not her fate, though: "Melanctha never killed herself, she only got a bad fever and went into the hospital" (187). Like "the Good Anna," doctors are not able to save her and within two paragraphs she abruptly dies and her narrative ends.

The same pattern repeats in the final narrative, "The Gentle Lena," in which the titular character dies in childbirth in the last paragraphs. Her life, like Anna's and Melanctha's, had been characterized by struggle and by the ebb and flow of fulfillment and sadness. Stein's achievement in terms of breaking free from the tyranny of the Dream script is to advance a new kind of realism that is not predicated on such narrative tropes as cause and effect, or the resolution of conflict following a rising arc of complication. Melanctha's death due to consumption is random and unrelated to the rest of the tale except insofar as it concludes it. There is no moment of epiphany, and arguably no climax to any of the three narratives that comprise the novel. Moreover, though there are clear connections between these stories of women at the margins of American society, they are three distinct individuals who do not interact with one another though they inhabit the same city at the same time. In creating this structure, Stein writes a novel that is more like life than it is like other novels, and through her stylized use of ordinary language that flouts conventions of punctuation and capitalization, she further frees herself from the confinements of the American novel tradition while revealing the psychological complexities of characters whose experiences are authentically American.

Jean Toomer's landmark novel *Cane* (1923) borrows stylistic elements from Brown, Melville, and Stein, consciously or not. *Cane* is a mysterious marvel that stands at the crossroads of literary modernism and the Harlem Renaissance. Twenty-first-century readers might cringe at some of Stein's depictions of African American life in "Melanctha" even if they admire her attempts to explore daringly a demographic that had been largely absent from American fiction. Toomer's novel reflects a perspective on African American life that is based on experience as well as observation and is less likely to make current readers wince. Like *Three Lives*, *Cane* is divided into three main sections and like the nineteenth-century works discussed earlier in this chapter, it is more a miscellany of genres than a continuous narrative. Its experimentation produces a work that defies easy explanation or categorization and presents interpretive challenges even a century after its publication, making it an important contribution to the old, weird strain of American novels.

Like *Clotel*, *Cane* is a miscellany of stories, poems, and even a trio of ambiguous shapes – curved lines that precede each of the three sections arranged in different places on the otherwise blank pages that separate the sections. Stein's narrative distance, repetition, and stream-of-consciousness techniques are all present in Toomer's novel as well, and yet there are more than three lives represented here. The first section contains six stories, five of them titled after the first name of their female protagonists. As in Stein's novel, the reader seeks continuity through patterns that might connect them, emphasized by the poetry excerpts that appear in the beginning, middle, or end of each sketch. In the first section the themes are not unlike those of "Melanctha." Young African American women are pursued by men and have to work hard to assert their independence and avoid being at the mercy of masculine aggression. Karintha in the first sketch is a child who "carries beauty" and is thus relentlessly pursued: "This interest of the male, who wishes to ripen a growing thing too soon, could mean no good to her" (3). By the end of this brief tale, "Karintha is a woman" (4), a phrase that is repeated, and yet, her life does not end abruptly like the three women's lives in Stein's novel; before the poem that concludes the sketch, the narrator simply trails off: "Karintha ..." (4). The gap that opens up at the sketch's end indicates that Karintha's full story has not been told. Moreover, to fully understand the meaning of her tale, the reader must look carefully at the imagery Toomer employs rather than merely reading its minimal plot: the pine smoke and the color of dusk that saturate the story demand careful attention.

Even more than *Three Lives*, critics debate whether *Cane* is actually a novel or instead a collection. Such questions often hounded modernist novels; in his introduction to Barnes's *Nightwood*, T.S. Eliot defined a novel as, "a book in which living characters are created and shown in significant relationship" and went on to say, "prose that is altogether alive demands something of the reader that the ordinary novel-reader is not prepared to give" (xi-xii). Eliot's definition and observation could equally apply to *Three Lives* or to *Cane*. The pieces in Toomer's novel get longer as the book continues as though stretching toward the customary length of a novel, culminating in the third section, "Kabnis," a single sustained narrative that comprises roughly a third of the book. The reader is encouraged to see themes emerging from the novel's rich imagery, and in doing so to read the book as a continuous narrative even though the characters vary and do not appear in other sketches. (Location is also varied: the setting of the first and third sections are set in Georgia, emphasizing the sugar cane that lends the novel its title, but the settings of the second section are Washington, D.C. and Chicago).

The reader must accept that the protagonist of *Cane* is collective. The novel is largely about the struggle to understand the place of African Americans within American society, and each story is a variation on the struggle with no real reconciliation. However, the key to understanding *Cane*, as with Stein's work, is to become attuned to the forces of the irrational or unconscious mind that are at play. *Cane*'s surreal prose evokes the world of dreams, which is markedly different from the materialistic world of the American Dream. Ideas are expressed symbolically rather than literally. When the character Paul – the protagonist of the second-longest sketch titled "Bona and Paul" – has an apparent revelation about the possibility for interracial relationships, he expresses it this way: "I came back to tell you, brother, that white faces are petals of roses. That dark faces are petals of dusk. That I am going out and gather petals. That I am going out and know her whom I brought here with me to these Gardens which are purple like a bed of roses would be at dusk" (80). What might seem like a hopeful conclusion is dashed when he returns to find that his white would-be lover Bona is gone without a trace. As with "Karintha," the story is unresolved, though the conflict is clear, and the reader's imagination is recruited to fill in the gap that follows the conclusion.

Toomer was one of the first Black novelists to advance the idea that race was such a complicated topic in American society that it could not be addressed in a conventional narrative, and his novel is far from straightforward as a result. The theme of *Cane* might be found in its unusual form and style rather than in individual characters. Toomer sought to convey the absolute unknowability of the other, defined especially but not exclusively in terms of race. The ambiguity of each narrative and abstract nature of each image accumulate to create an overall effect of alienation, a hallmark of both modernist and Harlem Renaissance works. The reader enters the dreamworld of the novel in order to become disoriented rather than rationally enlightened. Even when a character like Paul believes that he has arrived at some new piece of wisdom, he can only express it indirectly, forcing the reader to become comfortable with a strong set of conflicting emotions rather than a coherent, rational idea.

The stream-of-consciousness technique and reliance on multiple narrators also characterize the work of Nobel Laureate William Faulkner, who had in common with Stein and Toomer a fascination with the tense state of race relations in early twentieth-century America. Faulkner was especially concerned with the shifting social order in the South, connected to other revolutionary social shifts in the modern era. Faulkner deliberately disrupts the artificial illusion of fictional realism by fragmenting his stories, not only alternating narrators – his signature technique – but by rearranging chronology and returning to significant moments to record them as impressions on human consciousness. *The Sound and the Fury* (1929) shows the author at the height of his stylistic powers, marking a significant moment in modern American novelists' willingness to experiment with form as a way of breaking free from convention.

The Sound and the Fury is divided into four distinct sections, reminiscent of the three each that Stein and Toomer use, but a difference is that Faulkner's four narratives and the characters within them are interconnected. Borrowing its title from a famous soliloquy in *Macbeth* about the absurdity of human existence, *The Sound and the Fury* is the story of the Compson family, southern landowners who have fallen on hard times as the South adjusts to a new post-slavery economy. Three of the narratives take place on three days in 1928: part one on April 7, part three on April 6, and part four on April 8. Part two takes us back to 1910 and has a different setting from the other three (Cambridge, Massachusetts where Quentin Compson attends college at Harvard). Faulkner titles each section with its date, underscoring the novel's thematic concerns with the relationship between time and memory. Part one is narrated by Benjy, Quentin's mentally challenged younger brother. His cognitive differences combined with a lack of chronological order and the fact that Benjy is obsessed with abstract topics and symbols challenge the reader. Extending Stein's technique, Faulkner demands that readers be patient with repetitions of incidents or objects that seem unrelated. One notable focus of Benjy's obsession is his sister Caddy, whom he says smells like trees or leaves, and whose dress once became wet, then muddy, from splashing in a river. We have to follow the disjointed clues of Benjy's narrative, then filter through his distorting language to understand that Caddy sexually "fell." Benjy understands her sexual behavior as a sin connected to the biblical fall from innocence, though he only expresses that understanding through symbols. Combined with the idea of the fall, the theme of Benjy's narrative involves a keen awareness of loss. Caddy is lost, the Compson family fortune is lost, and a character named Luster is perpetually in search of a lost quarter. The innocence of childhood is an especially poignant loss, especially as adults try to protect the Compson children from the knowledge of death. There are attempts to connect the past and the present out of a romantic desire to return to a lost past. One such attempt is to name or rename characters after ancestors: we later learn that Benjy was named after his Uncle Maury and that Benjy is a nickname. Caddy's daughter is also named Quentin after her brother, and these naming connections cause confusion rather than continuity between the family's prosperous past and a diminished present.

Benjy's narrative might come first in the novel because it is the perspective of a child, factual and undeveloped as well as emotionally needy. The later sections can be interpreted in terms of the stages of aging. Quentin's narrative, the second, is that of an adolescent, full of the chaotic energy of that turbulent stage in life, emotionally raw and intellectually risky. Quentin, on the verge of committing suicide, is inclined toward death and despair at a time when life should be carefree, but it isn't because he is aware of loss and fearful of adulthood. Though a Harvard student, Quentin's mind is in some ways just as disordered as that of his mentally challenged brother Benjy. Despite Quentin's conventional brilliance, his narrative is no more coherent, and he is just as obsessed with certain objects and incidents from his past. One object that transfixes him is his grandfather's watch. As he wanders around Cambridge preparing to drown himself, he is hyperconscious of its ticking, and eventually destroys it in a futile attempt to evade the ravages of time. He shares Benjy's obsession with his sister Caddy, whose "fall" is much more explicit here: she has become pregnant by an unidentified lover and marries a different man who sends her and her daughter away when he learns the truth. Quentin, plumbing the depths of his consciousness, expresses incestuous desires for his sister and suggests to his father that they had a sexual encounter, but his father understands he is lying. Quentin is left with the guilt and shame of his desire as well as the failure of his chivalrous attempts to protect his sister. In the middle of one lengthy stream-of-consciousness exchange between them devoid of standard punctuation and line breaks Quentin and Caddy say, "theres a curse on us its not our fault is it our fault/ hush come on and go to bed now/ you cant make me theres a curse on us" (100). Belief in this curse dooms the future of the Compson family even as it negates any lingering value associated with their past.

Quentin and Benjy's cynical brother Jason narrates the third section. He is materialistic in contrast to the emotional Benjy and the idealistic Quentin, and he clearly represents the irrevocable destruction of the Compson line. He disregards the past in favor of a present that he feels can restore the material worth the family has lost, and yet his narrative shows him running around pointlessly, the consummate modern man fleeing from the awful truth of how meaningless his life is. He is also dismissive of everyone who is not him and intolerant and crude; his narrative opens, "Once a bitch always a bitch, what I say" (113). He is unsentimental about the dissolution of his family since he is only concerned with his own fortune; he takes pride in the notion "that I was a different breed of cat from Father" (126). His mother desperately pleads that he look after his sister Caddy and her daughter Quentin, but it is clear he won't because of his extreme self-interest; he brags, "I'm glad I haven't got the sort of conscience I've got to nurse like a sick puppy all the time" (143). It's clear that he hasn't got any sort of conscience.

The fourth narrative, which takes place on Easter – ironically a holiday associated with rebirth – employs a third-person narrator but focuses mostly on a single character, Dilsey, the Compson family's Black servant. Like Benjy, Dilsey's emotional life is more developed than the other characters (especially Jason), but both Benjy and Dilsey are relatively powerless in this world. This day in the Compson household focuses on Dilsey's patient work and religious devotion which provide a stark contrast to the dissolution of the family. During the church service that day a car – a symbol of the modern world – passes by outside: "Dilsey sat bolt upright, her hand on Ben's knee. Two tears slid down her fallen cheeks, in and out of the myriad coruscations of immolation and abnegation of time" (183). This moment demonstrates how Dilsey's perseverance is likely to be a stronger force than all the sound and fury of the Compson family's past and present. There is no other way to avoid the many curses they endure, except for the female Quentin who runs away from her family on this holy day, a more hopeful escape than that taken by her namesake uncle who committed suicide.

The novel, like all of Faulkner's work, is infinitely more complex than this summary can indicate, but it should be clear that Faulkner was depicting a story far too chaotic and terrifying to be mapped onto a conventional model. Through a reliance on modernist techniques, he communicates indirectly that perspective is what matters most in the modern world, and that in a society marked by rapidly shifting values, we must seek meaning in new forms and new narrative arcs. Powerless characters like Benjy, Dilsey, and the female Quentin are allowed to frame the novel whereas the failures of the brothers Quentin and Jason represent a dying world order struggling (and failing) to preside. The fact that Jason's narrative most closely represents a straightforward realistic novel that follows the Dream template underscores the idea that only a break with convention will reveal deeper American truths.

Postmodernism and its Children

It should be clear that the modernist novelists, though devoted to experimentation, tended to cover brooding and serious subject matter like their nineteenth-century predecessors did. The old, weird America involving playfulness as well as spontaneity was identified in the mid-twentieth century when American novelists finally managed to shake off the purposeful seriousness of art that could be seen as a legacy of either the Puritans or the grim determination of westward-expanding pioneers in the nineteenth century. Jack Kerouac's *On the Road* (1957), initially denigrated by the literary establishment but embraced by the rising youth counterculture, represents a crucial turning point in the transition from modernism to postmodernism in the American novel. The story of the novel's composition has become the stuff of legend: Kerouac loaded an enormous roll of teletype paper into his typewriter and banged out the novel in a three-day frenzy fueled by coffee, cigarettes, and the amphetamine Benzedrine. Consistent with the Beat generation's "first word = best word" philosophy, he supposedly submitted the entire scroll to his publisher unrevised, though there are clear editorial differences between the published version and the scroll version. A thinly fictionalized account of some of Kerouac's cross-country journeys and encounters with colorful nonconformists, outlaws, hedonists, and drifters, *On the Road* became a sacred text for the countercultures of the 1950s and 1960s and, arguably, gave license to postmodern novelists to embrace the weirdest margins of American experience.

Kerouac names his fictional alter-ego Salvatore ("Sal") Paradise, indicating that his quest is to save the eroding paradise that is America, presumably by honoring its denigrated margins and drinking deep from the cup of experience. Many of his experiences on the road center on Dean Moriarty (modeled after fellow Beat Neal Cassady), a larger-than-life maniac with a criminal record who is extraordinarily adept at driving cars and seducing women. Sal's first solo hitchhiking excursion is a bust: he ends up cursing himself in the rain as he waits in vain for a ride from New York to Chicago. He had made the mistake of studying a map and planning on following a road that led across the entire country east to west. He laments, "It was my dream that screwed up, the stupid hearthside idea that it would be wonderful to follow one great red line across America instead of trying various roads and routes" (11). The method he needs to cultivate clearly involves spontaneity rather than rationality, experience over accepted wisdom, movement over stasis, and the road over the "hearthside." He also believes he needs a guru like Dean.

Missteps are just ways of fine-tuning Sal's quest, the object of which is not clearly defined from the outset. He declares, "Somewhere along the line I knew there'd be girls, visions, everything; somewhere along the line the pearl would be handed to me" (8). The girls are a clear enough goal, and though he does not come close to the number of sexual encounters Dean has, he does frequently renew the idea that his "girlsoul" (83) is somewhere to be discovered on his journeys. Visions are also recurrent features of his voyages, sometimes in the form of waking dreams and sometimes as a result of drugs and alcohol. "Everything" and "the pearl," though, are vague, and conventional language cannot articulate the ideas they represent. Sal employs his own idiom and often lets sentences full of neologisms run on for longer than a grammarian would allow, presumably in the belief that spontaneous prose is more likely to produce genuine, lasting insights than a more organized approach to writing can.

On the Road was a reaction to the dominant conservative mood of America in the aftermath of World War II. Kerouac and the Beat Generation were in search of spiritual values that were not easily found in the burgeoning American suburbs. The domesticity and material gain that define the American Dream were the polar opposite of the values the Beats sought, and the characters Sal latches onto would have been regarded as sexual deviants, shiftless vagrants, criminals, communists (in an era when that ideology was considered especially subversive) and drug-addicted hedonists by the American mainstream. Describing Dean and Carlo Marx – a character modeled after Beat poet Allen Ginsberg – Sal marvels how "their energies met head on" and describes how "I shambled as I've been doing all my life after people who interest me, because the only people for me are the mad ones, the ones who are mad to live, mad to talk, mad to be saved, desirous of everything at the same time, the ones who never yawn or say a commonplace thing, but burn, burn, burn like fabulous yellow roman candles exploding like spiders across the stars and in the middle you see the blue centerlight pop and everybody goes 'Awww!'" (5–6). Dean's madness is largely fascinating to Sal, but occasionally scary as he realizes, as others do, that Dean's affirmation of life (signified by ecstatic moments he calls "kicks" and emphasized through his oft-repeated word "Yes!") has a destructive counterpart: "I had a vision of Dean, a burning shuddering frightful Angel, palpitating toward me across the road, approaching like a cloud ... . Behind him charred ruins smoked" (259).

Nevertheless, Sal follows Dean across the country, in awe of his appetite for life. Here's a typical example: "'And dig her!' yelled Dean, pointing at another woman. 'Oh, I love, love, love women! I think women are wonderful! I love women!' He spat out the window; he groaned; he clutched his head. Great beads of sweat fell from his forehead from pure excitement and exhaustion" (140-41). This maniacal energy, which propels Dean to ever-increasing heights in jazz clubs and whenever he is driving a fast car on an open road, is what Kerouac tries to capture in the prose he's writing. Dean even provides the blueprint for this new approach to composition; watching Sal write he shouts, "'Yes! That's right! Wow! Man!' and "Phew!' and wiped his face with his handkerchief. 'Man, wow, there's so many things to do, so many things to write! How to even *begin* to get it all down and without modified restraints and all hung-up on like literary inhibitions and grammatical fears" (4). Sal's quest is to develop a new aesthetic that can adequately capture the experience of living life with a grand appetite for pleasure rather than for a gloomy search for meaning. Meaning lies in movement.

And yet, as becomes clear over the course of the narrative, the pursuit is not simple hedonism. The frenzy of the road and the sexual and alcohol/drug-fueled "kicks" Sal and Dean seek are balanced by true introspection and the desire to commune with one's spirit. There is a strong yearning for a new theology to replace or perhaps combine elements of Kerouac's Roman Catholicism, Ginsberg's Judaism, and the Buddhism all the Beats studied. Sal envisions himself as a visionary arriving to see his friends: "in their eyes I would be strange and ragged and like the Prophet who has walked across the land to bring the dark Word, and the only Word I had was 'Wow!'" (35). This is not the only time language is inadequate; at another point, Sal and his colleagues listen to Dean spout some incoherent wisdom: "There was nothing clear about the things he said, but what he meant to say was somehow made pure and clear. He used the word 'pure' a great deal. I had never dreamed Dean would become a mystic" (121). Most pointedly, Dean declares that a jazz saxophonist they saw performing "had IT ... . I wanted to know what 'IT' meant. 'Ah well' – Dean laughed – 'now you're asking me impon-de-rables" (207). They pursue the definition of "IT" during a hitchhiking trip in the back of a stranger's car, and they communicate their understanding (if not a definition) through stories from their youth filled with symbols, rocking the car with their ecstasy when they approach an articulation of IT; Dean cries, "we know what IT is and we know TIME and we know that everything is really FINE." He elaborates, pointing at the family in the front seat: "They have worries, they're counting the miles, they're thinking about where to sleep tonight, how much money for gas, the weather, how they'll get there – and all the time they'll get there anyway, you see. But they need to worry and betray time with urgencies false and otherwise, purely anxious and whiny, their souls won't really be at peace" (209). The manic revelation goes on, and it is clear that Sal has glimpsed his pearl, the "everything" he once sought in the ineffable "IT."

Their friendship waxes and wanes, develops, and eventually disintegrates when Dean abandons an infirm Sal in Mexico and Sal declares him "a rat" (302). Still, in the final words of the lengthy run-on sentence that concludes the novel, Sal lifts out one nugget of wisdom: "nobody, nobody knows what's going to happen to anybody besides the forlorn rags of growing old" and silently acknowledges the person to whom he owes this understanding: "I think of Dean Moriarty" (307). There isn't a whiff of conventional morality in this conclusion: Sal doesn't regret a moment of his experiences, even the moments when his hero disappoints him. Readers are much less likely to latch onto the meandering plot of *On the Road* than they are to remember its enthusiastic prose, its flashes of spiritual insight, its poetic language, and especially the journey on the road that never ends.

One important reader who was especially influenced by *On the Road* was the central figure in American postmodernism, Thomas Pynchon, who called it "one of the great American novels" (*Slow* 7). Famously reclusive and reluctant to give interviews or even to appear in public, Pynchon's minimal pronouncements of his aesthetic are derived almost entirely from his introduction to his collected early short stories, *Slow Learner* (1984), and he goes on to say that "Kerouac and the Beat writers" gave him and his cohort license "to see how at least two very distinct kinds of English could be allowed in fiction to coexist. Allowed! It was actually OK to write like this! Who knew? The effect was exciting, liberating, strongly positive. It was not a case of either/or, but an expansion of possibilities" (6–7). Pynchon and other high postmodernists – Donald Barthelme, John Barth, Robert Coover, Don DeLillo – took the artistic license offered by the Beat Generation and ran with it in new and unpredictable directions. In a self-deprecating way, Pynchon declares, "I thought I was sophisticating the Beat spirit with second-hand science" (14). Readers of Pynchon's first three novels for which he is best known – *V.* (1963), *The Crying of Lot 49* (1965), and *Gravity's Rainbow* (1973) – have found it essential to try to understand the science (particularly physics, more particularly thermodynamics) that undergird his complex, zany prose.

As suggested earlier in this chapter regarding *Moby-Dick*, an introductory volume like this one does not have the space to adequately cover a Pynchon novel or the broad movement of postmodernism it represents. A very brief engagement with his shortest novel *The Crying of Lot 49* will have to suffice to give a sense of how Pynchon and his ilk explored narrative experimentation in ways that both altered the trajectory of the American novel and departed from the standard American Dream script. In this way this cohort luxuriated in the old, weird America that thrives outside history books and platitudes. Pynchon's *V.*, for instance, explores the New York sewers which are supposedly rife with alligators that have been discarded as unsuitable pets. DeLillo's *Libra* (1988) considers the fuzzy border between truth and paranoid conspiracy theories that surround the assassination of President Kennedy. Barth's *Sabbatical: A Romance* (1982) focuses on the suspicious death of CIA operative John Paisley. Postmodernists are delighted with the instability of the truth caused by tendencies toward irrational beliefs, rumors, countertruths, and conspiracies. Their tendency toward hyper-intellectualism ironically does not seek to clarify the truth, but rather to exploit information, allusion, and authority to show how evasive the truth is. Given its emphasis on the instability of the truth in an age when information is manipulated by shadowy corporate and governmental organizations, the principle theme of postmodernism is paranoia.

In *The Crying of Lot 49* we find the truth slipping away every time we think we've taken a step closer. Taking a page from Kerouac and fellow Beat William S. Burroughs or their next-of-kin Joseph Heller and Ken Kesey, Pynchon's characters have absurd, jokey names like Pierce Invararity, Mike Fallopian, and Oedipa Maas, the novel's protagonist. Oedipa learns that her erstwhile lover Invararity has died and named her executor of his will. With no knowledge of how to perform this task, she sets out on a journey far more divorced from reality than the road trip in Kerouac's novel. Satirizing the Dream script, the novel starts with Oedipa returning from a Tupperware party but quickly has her engaging in drunken, kinky sex with a lawyer in a motel while a rock band called The Paranoids serenades them. It might seem that madcap scenes like that one are just attempts at absurd hilarity, and yet the postmodern reader, like Oedipa, becomes aware that there are other forces at play. Pynchon's encyclopedic mind produces allusions to both literature and popular culture while also employing the deep knowledge of physics alluded to above: the motel room scene illustrates chaos theory and entropy.

Oedipa, trying to fulfill her task of executing the will, stumbles into a vast conspiracy that ranges from a seventeenth-century Jacobean tragedy, to a postage stamp, to a mysterious corporation called Yoyodyne, to a hieroglyphic symbol she sees scrawled everywhere resembling a trumpet with a mute stuck in it. The symbol indicates the novel's theme of how communication is limited and controlled by invisible forces. The Jacobean tragedy, described at length, is one key to unlocking the mysteries all around her. Oedipa goes backstage to confront the play's director, claiming, "I want to see if there's a connection" (59) to the plot she's entangled in, underscoring the novel's inquiry into the tension between cause-and-effect and chaos. The director denies that anything is going on beneath the surface: "[The play] was written to entertain people. Like horror movies. It isn't literature, it doesn't mean anything" (60). Here Pynchon is playing with the assumption that some literary works are merely entertaining while more serious ones ("literature") contain meaning, encouraging his reader to delight in the outrageousness of his plots while leading us away from interpretation. When Oedipa asks to look at the script of the play, the director responds, "Why ... is everybody so interested in texts? ... . You can put together clues, develop a thesis ... . You could waste your life that way and never touch the truth" (61, 62-3). Oedipa is doing what the reader is doing, looking for a central truth that always slips just out of her reach. The director reiterates that the postmodern novelist – for which he is a stand-in – is at the controls: "I'm the projector at the planetarium" (62). In order to figure out the truth, then, Oedipa (again like the reader) has to become an active participant in rather than a passive recipient of art. She redraws the hieroglyphic symbol in her memo book and writes, "*Shall I project a world?*" (64). Her journey becomes a quest to separate the meaningful from the nonsensical without knowing where it will lead:

> Oedipa wondered whether, at the end of this (if it were supposed to end), she too might not be left with only compiled memories of clues, announcements, intimations, but never the central truth itself, which must somehow each time be too bright for her memory to hold; which must always blaze out, destroying its own message irreversibly, leaving an overexposed blank when the ordinary world came back. (76)

Although postmodernism is complex and impossible to summarize, this passage represents a succinct definition of how it regards art. The search for meaning in a postmodern novel is crucial, but far from straightforward, and the search may not produce anything like a lasting, coherent statement. More even than modernism, postmodernism creates active readers who must simultaneously believe in meaning and accept that it will likely always remain just out of reach.

After modernism and postmodernism shook the foundations of what the American novel was capable of, the Dream script lost its dominance in the tradition, though it certainly hasn't gone away as multiple examples of twenty-first-century novels in this study illustrate. Realism continues to flourish as the dominant mode of narration, but these experimental movements have given novelists license to vary the formula, if not a mandate to do so. The category of magical realism, which first flourished in South America, introduces fanciful elements to realism that expand possibilities, moving in the direction of the supernatural while remaining grounded in the familiar world of realism. (Examples can be found in this study in novelists like Toni Morrison, Octavia Butler, and Rudolfo Anaya). Science fiction, fantasy fiction, and dystopian future fiction have all become popular modes that stray further from both realism and its attendant American Dream plot while maintaining a connection to modern and postmodern themes and plots involving the way governments and corporations threaten and control individual will. The rise of graphic fictional narratives by artists like R. Crumb, Adrian Tomine, and Daniel Clowes exploit a multimodal genre to explore many other possibilities that demonstrate the American novel's possibilities in the twenty-first century.

In brief, since the high period of postmodernism in the 1960s through 1980s, even novelists who work primarily in realism have many options to depart from the main line of the tradition even while contributing to it. The spirit of weirdness can thus be merged with tradition to produce works with literary significance that are also free from the mandate to retell the same old story. From this vast, rich repository of significant works that are indebted to their experimental predecessors without being overly wedded to them or too easily categorized by the genres alluded to above, I've chosen Jennifer Egan's 2010 novel *A Visit from the Goon Squad* to complete this chapter. Though certainly not as experimental or outrageous as Pynchon or the other postmodernists, Egan's novel demonstrates how traditional narrative methods and an experimental attitude can and often do cooperate to produce novels that deviate from traditional American themes while exploring new ones.

Egan's novel shows an awareness of the methodology of both modernism and postmodernism. Like Julia Alvarez's *How the García Girls Lost Their Accents* (discussed in Chapter 6), the novel features a collective protagonist, the chapters employ a variety of narrative points of view, and the novel is not arranged chronologically. While Alvarez's novel moves back through time steadily, Egan's moves back and forth randomly, and the relationship between the protagonists of each story is fluid. The epigraph from Proust points us toward the theme of memory and aging. Without calling excessive attention to the historical events that sever past from present, the novel frequently returns to the disruptions to the American psyche presented by the terror attacks of 9/11; one character who had been incarcerated when the attacks occurred notes, "I go away for a few years and the whole fucking world is upside down .... Buildings are missing. You get strip-searched every time you go to someone's office" (94). Most changes characters face are personal, though, and it is only cumulatively that the novel engages with cultural loss.

The fact that there is no single protagonist causes the reader to look for connections and patterns between their individual stories, as in Stein's *Three Lives*. It could be argued that the central cast of characters is comprised of the male members of a high school punk band called the Flaming Dildos (Bennie Salazar and Scotty Hausmann) and their female groupies Jocelyn, Rhea, and Alice, but the novel is equally concerned with peripheral characters including the adult Bennie's record company assistant Sasha and a sleazy record producer named Lou who seduced Jocelyn when she was still in high school. We encounter all these characters (and many others even more peripheral to the rock band) at various points in their lives, and all are dealing with some kind of malaise linked to a significant transitional moment in their maturity. The novel opens with Sasha, a kleptomaniac who steals only from individuals rather than stores or corporations. While on a first date, she lifts a wallet from a random woman in the bathroom and reluctantly returns it to her without her date knowing what happened, apologizing and declaring to the woman, "It's a problem I have" (9). She keeps her stolen objects on a table in her apartment, and when her date asks her about them, she seduces him to avoid answering, then steals from his wallet while he is in the bathroom. This initial story unfolds as a back-and-forth dialogue with her therapist; she claims that the two of them together are "writing a story of redemption, of fresh beginnings and second chances. But in that direction lay only sorrow" (7). She later realizes, "Redemption, transformation – God, how she wanted these things. Every day, every minute. Didn't everyone?" (14). Rather than share this insight with her therapist, she demands silence and withdraws into herself as she feels minutes ticking away.

This is a recurrent theme in the novel: time and memory work together to prevent characters – and the narrative – from dwelling in the present, and silence is often as significant as noise. The novel occasionally swerves into future events, summarily telling the reader the fate of an individual character decades from the story's narrative present. Time is deterioration, and characters mark moments in which they are conscious of that fact, or they deny it. Rhea as a teen asks Lou if he remembers being the same age as her and Jocelyn whose adolescent life he is in the process of destroying, and he responds, "I *am* your age," adding "I'll never get old" (42). In a later chapter he is in fact old and dying in bed and Jocelyn, now recovering from the drug habit Lou forced her into, realizes the futility of her "lost time" (65). This once energetic man who gratified his furious appetites is a husk: "A man who turned out to be old, a house that turned out to be empty." She confesses to her childhood best friend Rhea, "It was all for no reason" (66). Rhea tries to comfort her with the fantasy of redemption and second chances, arguing, "You just haven't found the reason yet" (66). Through theme and variation, the novel argues that Jocelyn is right: we can't get back what we've lost.

As the novel delves deeper into this theme and many more, it becomes a miscellany of narrative styles even more varied than what we see in nineteenth-century precursors Brown and Melville. Egan employs first-, second-, and third-person narrators. One chapter is written as a parody of an entertainment magazine celebrity interview distracted by copious footnotes; another is presented as a PowerPoint slide presentation with arrows, graphs, and charts. Coupled with the back-and-forth movement across time, the multiple protagonists, and the intertwined plots, these techniques demonstrate the author's ability to play with the conventions of realism without dispensing with them. The traditional appeals of a realistic narrative remain intact while the reader must adapt to narrative changes without prescribed expectations.

Although the novel strays far afield from the main characters of the band plus Bennie's assistant Sasha and ranges over more than four decades, the intertwined plots all come together when the characters' lives either overlap or experience near misses and degrees of separation. Characters affect or even ruin each other's lives without realizing it. Moments that are framed as extremely significant in one character's life barely register in another's. We are left with the fragmented outlines of plots that the author has pieced together with significant questions hanging in the air: are there second acts in American life? Does time heal wounds, or does it combine with memory to make them worse? A significant number of characters either contemplate suicide, attempt it, or see it through, and these losses are the ultimate tests of how time and memory operate. Sasha's best friend in college – a troubled, closeted man named Rob – drowns semi-deliberately after blurting Sasha's deepest secrets to her then-boyfriend Drew. Years later we learn that Sasha has married Drew and that Rob's death haunts not only both of them but their twelve-year-old daughter Alison, as though memories are passed along to the next generation. Alison looks for wisdom in the efforts of her autistic brother Lincoln who is obsessed with the possible meaning of various pauses and silences in rock and roll songs. Her presentation of her story in the form of PowerPoint slides as well as the final chapter's emphasis on the way children use cell phones to communicate suggests that a rapidly changing technological world still wrestles with an ancient set of concerns.

Egan's novel breaks free from the Dream plot through narrative experimentation. It is more interested in the sometimes painful experiences of growing up than in the dull lives of grown-ups, but more, it is eager to connect the two. The triumvirate of youthful pursuits of happiness beginning in the late twentieth century – sex, drugs, and rock and roll – are framed differently here than they were in Kerouac's and Pynchon's novels, but in all cases they represent an attempt to explore a reality apart from the one that is presented as the conventional script. In one scene Jocelyn – high on cocaine and about to witness her best friend engaging in a frenzied sexual act at a rock concert – realizes, "I'm beginning my adult life right now, on this night" (38). Although she grows into a very conventional suburban mom with three kids, it is this moment that defines her most meaningful experience. Egan, like many writers who arrived after postmodernism, showcases the moments in American lives that are common to many but generally hidden, the peaks and valleys of experience that are either publicly devastating or privately buried away. Building on narrative techniques from modernists and postmodernists, twenty-first-century novelists embrace new ways of writing that keep the spirit of novelistic experimentation alive, using new technologies instead of regarding them as a threat.

Further Reading

Acker, Kathy. *Blood and Guts in High School* (1984)
Barnes, Djuna. *Nightwood* (1936)
Barth, John. *Giles Goat-Boy* (1966)
Burroughs, William S. *Naked Lunch* (1959)
DeLillo, Don. *Underworld* (1997)
Foer, Jonathan Safran. *Extremely Loud and Incredibly Close* (2004)
Heller, Joseph. *Catch-22* (1961)
Kesey, Ken. *One Flew Over the Cuckoo's Nest* (1962)
McCullers, Carson. *The Heart is a Lonely Hunter* (1940)
Nabokov, Vladimir. *Pale Fire* (1962)
Vonnegut, Kurt, Jr. *Slaughterhouse-Five* (1969)
Wallace, David Foster. *Infinite Jest* (1996)
Whitehead, Colson. *John Henry Days* (2001)
Wideman, John Edgar. *Philadelphia Fire* (1990)

8 Our Fragile Earth
Eco-Consciousness and the American Novel

In the fifteenth century, when European explorers first bumped into the shores of what later became the United States of America, the land seemed vast and laden with natural resources for the claiming. "Vast" does not mean limitless, though, and the "claiming" without replenishment has proven devastating. Two historical facts are noteworthy: one, Native Americans already inhabited this "new world," and despite many differences in customs, language, and ways of living across the tribes, one commitment they had and continue to have in common is stewardship of the earth. The second fact is that no group of immigrants who have made this land their home has demonstrated the same commitment to honoring or respecting American nature. The rise of industries and technologies that have led to American prosperity has simultaneously devastated our environment. As a result, glaring evidence of climate change in the twenty-first century is growing more apparent daily. A cultural tension is growing between those who despair that it might already be too late to save the planet and those who ignore the implications of the evidence. Even beyond climate change, which is a global phenomenon (though the United States has generated a disproportionate share of greenhouse gases), other disturbing issues sour the relationship between Americans and their natural surroundings, such as uneven access to clean water, shrinking greenspace, and threats to biodiversity through extinction.

The idea that our species is speeding up its own extinction certainly reframes the notion of the American Dream that anchors this study. Looked at through an ecological lens, the Dream itself is self-destructive given its emphasis on consumption rather than replenishment. One of the greatest prose works in our literary history that deeply examines this topic is not a novel: Thoreau's *Walden* (1854) is famously about one man's experiment in "living deliberately" by retreating from society and committing to understanding his place in nature without unduly disturbing its patterns. *Walden*'s influence on the American novel tradition is not always direct, but it is nevertheless felt. Twenty-first-century American

DOI: 10.4324/9781003252863-9

novels have become increasingly concerned with what is at stake if our relationship with the earth continues along its current path, but nature's fragility and humankind's potential for destruction have long been part of the American novelistic imagination.

American Nature and Broken Rituals

Leslie Marmon Silko's *Ceremony* (1977) is a fitting place to begin this inquiry because it sits at the intersection of a number of concerns both central to and tangentially related to the environmental crisis we are mired in. Silko's historical novel about a traumatized World War II veteran is inventively experimental in the way it interweaves a time-jumping third-person narrative with traditional Native American legends, and it remains urgently topical a half-century after its publication. The novel plays with time and memory as the story of its protagonist Tayo unfolds. War narratives – fictional and otherwise – are most often preoccupied with the senseless loss of human life and the psychological cost to soldiers who survive. Although those concerns are certainly at play in Silko's novel, the author is also concerned with the cost to the earth, especially insofar as traditional Native American beliefs seek to connect humanity and nature rather than regard them as adversaries.

World War II is an especially significant backdrop for *Ceremony* because the development and deployment of nuclear weapons signaled war's potential to cause widespread, irreversible ecological destruction on an unprecedented scale. After fighting in the Pacific Theater, Tayo returns to his native New Mexico, the site of the first nuclear test in the United States and the source of much of the uranium used in atomic bombs. The psychological devastation Tayo experiences is parallel to the broader devastation of the war. Throughout Tayo's journey toward healing, he is reluctant to see the war as an isolated event entirely responsible for causing damage to his world, though. The evil seeds had been sown long before in the form of greed and domination – referred to as "witchery" throughout the novel – which overwhelm the nobler attributes of humanity. An important scene occurs long before the war, when Tayo was a child hunting deer with his cousin Rocky whose death in the war becomes a key source of Tayo's mental anguish. Tayo feels empathy for the slain deer and just before they eviscerate it, he covers its eyes with his jacket. "'Why did you do that?' asked Rocky motioning at the jacket with the blade of his knife ... . Tayo didn't say anything because they both knew why. The people said you should do that before you gutted the deer. Out of respect" (51). Rocky is assimilated into and attuned to white culture, to the point that he doesn't honor the traditional beliefs of his people. He is eager to please his white coaches and teachers who tell him,

"Nothing can stop you now except one thing: don't let the people at home hold you back" (51). The ritual continues after the deer has gone cold: other hunters sprinkle cornmeal on the deer's nose to feed its spirit, and the carcass is laid out on a Navajo blanket where Tayo's Grandma further honors it by ornamenting it with turquoise beads. Rocky regards the ritual as "superstition" and is "embarrassed at what they did" (51, 52). Throughout the narrative, Tayo – whose father was white and whose mother was ostracized due to her relationships with white men – is pulled between traditional beliefs and the modern white world. It becomes clear that the former works toward growth and renewal while the latter is bent on destruction.

This scene from Tayo's memory shifts back to the present when Tayo is drinking in a bar. He and his buddies recall how he once lost control of his faculties and tried to murder a man named Emo in the same bar: "They all had explanations … . they blamed the liquor and they blamed the war." When a doctor reads Tayo a report advancing the theory that the war and drinking were responsible for an upsurge in violence, he responds, "It's more than that. I can feel it. It's been going on for a long time" (53). There are incidents from Tayo's personal past and his interactions with Emo that help explain the fight (which escalates into a feud as the plot progresses), but the memory of how the deer ritual was dishonored by Rocky and by the white world he yearns to join is emblematic of the erosion he points to.

Throughout Tayo's traumatic experiences during the war and after, nature is what calms and restores him. He realizes, "He had to keep busy; he had to keep moving so that the sinews connected behind his eyes did not slip loose and spin his eyes to the interior of his skull where the scenes waited for him" (9). The way to do this is to return to the pre-modern rituals of tending the farm, but it has become difficult: "The drought years had returned again, as they had after the First World War" (10). War is thus damaging both to humanity and to nature, and the growing separation between these realms is what threatens to destroy Tayo and his community as well as the livestock. Tayo also blames himself for the drought: while in the sodden jungles where he fought the war, "he had prayed the rain away" and this prayer, in his mind, caused the drought at home: "Wherever he looked, Tayo could see the consequences of his praying; the gray mule grew gaunt, and the goat and kid had to wander farther and farther each day to find weeds or dry shrubs to eat" (14). The fact that he was a soldier in a massively destructive war taints him and causes him to feel complicit. Moving back and forth across time and memory, Tayo connects the diminished condition of his world at home with the war-ruined landscape: "he cried at how the world had come undone, how thousands of miles, high ocean waves and green jungles could not hold people in their place" (18). He takes comfort from the animal world because, as his Uncle Josiah once told him, "only humans had to endure anything, because only humans resisted what they saw outside themselves" (27). The desired condition is to sense oneself as part of nature as other animals do.

Tayo feels alienated, but he is not alone, at least not if he learns to respect his Native elders as Rocky never did. Grandma recognizes that Tayo needs a medicine man rather than a white doctor and sends for old Ku'oosh despite "what the Army doctor said: 'No Indian medicine'" (34). At first Tayo resists the old man: "His language was childish, interspersed with English words, and [Tayo] could feel shame tightening in his throat" (34). He gradually changes his response, though, especially after Ku'oosh evokes strong memories of his childhood years when Tayo communed with crickets, bats, and snakes in a cave where he used to play. Ku'oosh acknowledges that Tayo might have been better off learning from him and the other elders "before you went to the white people's big war," then says, emphatically, "you know, grandson, this world is fragile" (35). The narrator elaborates:

> The word he chose to express 'fragile' was filled with the intricacies of a continuing process, and with a strength inherent in spider webs woven across paths through sand hills where early in the morning the sun becomes entangled in each filament of web. It took a long time to explain the fragility and intricacy because no word exists alone, and the reason for choosing each word had to be explained with a story about why it must be said this certain way. (35)

Tayo's narrative is part of this process of connecting language to story and story to meaning. Native American stories appear throughout the text, centered on the page, with line breaks like poems. One such piece that opens the book reads, "And in the belly of this story/ the rituals and the ceremony/ are still growing" (2). In this sense, the ceremony that will heal Tayo is a way of connecting the past to the crises of the present and of connecting his individual story to the legends of his people's past.

Tayo's journey toward healing depends on his developing ability to connect, like the recurrent figure of the spider in the novel. Silko's method of narration is deliberately fragmented, shuttling back and forth between key episodes over time, so that readers may participate in the same spinning and weaving process. At one point, Tayo instinctively rubs dust over his hands "the way ceremonial dancers sometimes did ... and then he knew why it was done by the dancers: it connected them to the earth" (104). This action unconsciously addresses the original, most fundamental rupture in a story full of ruptures: human separation from the earth itself.

Tayo must consistently listen to the stories told by his grandmother and the other elders who preserve their culture, stories that locate values in the animal world. As a boy, Tayo was once proud of himself for killing houseflies, but Josiah chastises him, telling him one of the old stories about how the greenbottle fly was responsible for asking the gods to forgive humans and thus ending an earlier drought. Such stories are ultimately more meaningful to Tayo than the science Rocky honors.

The idea that rituals, ceremonies, and stories are still growing explains not only the trajectory of Tayo's story, but its very existence. If the original healing ceremony conducted by old Ku'oosh were some kind of magical cure, the novel would not be able to advance its crucial argument that Tayo is partly responsible for his own healing, and for developing his own story. The novel emphasizes that the tools for healing are within him, that he has to access them and connect them to the ancient stories in his own way. Thus, he is led to a second medicine man, Betonie, whose spiritual powers seem even less plausible to Tayo. He lives in a rundown hogan filled with junk, and Tayo has a hard time understanding that the collection of what seems like garbage is actually Betonie's version of ritualized gathering that leads to healing. Tayo lashes out at the old man: "'Look,' Tayo said through clenched teeth, 'I've been sick, and half the time I don't know if I'm still crazy or not. I don't know anything about ceremonies … I just need help" (125). Betonie responds, "We all have been waiting for help a long time. But it never has been easy. The people must do it. You must do it" (125). Tayo is frustrated because he has internalized the individualism of the white world: "He wanted to yell at the medicine man, to yell the things the white doctors had yelled at him – that he had to think only of himself, and not about the others, that he would never get well as long as he used words like 'we' and 'us.' But … medicine didn't work that way, because the world didn't work that way. His sickness was only part of something larger, and his cure would be found only in something great and inclusive of everything" (125–6). This crucial epiphany allows him to open himself to Betonie's unique ceremony which involves a journey, a bloodletting ritual, and a hand-drawn map of the stars.

Combining Ku'oosh's and Betonie's ceremonies, Tayo's path to healing is set in motion, but he is not simply cured. His story becomes a quest for reconnection, and he repeats Betonie's wisdom at difficult junctures: "it has never been easy." The ultimate goal is to end the drought and to reclaim both the family's cattle that were stolen and the land that had been historically stolen by white people for the purposes of destruction. It also involves sexual healing with a woman named Ts'eh who also helps him reconnect with traditional ways and who joins him on a journey away from civilization and into nature where he has another epiphany:

"at that moment in the sunrise, it was all so beautiful, everything, from all directions, evenly, perfectly, balancing day with night, summer months with winter. The valley was enclosing this totality, like the mind holding all thoughts together in a single moment. The strength came from here, from this feeling. It had always been there" (235). This moment of perfect harmony and balance restores Tayo even as he comes to terms with the damage he has suffered. The earth's capacity for renewal despite the destruction of the "witchery" that has been unleashed upon it is hopeful, even if the recognition of it, as Tayo repeats, "has never been easy" (254).

Native American authors contributed heavily to the American novel tradition in the late twentieth century. In addition to Silko, authors like N. Scott Momaday, Gerald Vizenor, and Louise Erdrich enjoyed critical and popular success. In earlier periods Native American experience was often limited to novels by white writers. Both an awareness of the sanctity of the earth to Native Americans and a fear that nature will be destroyed if is not respected were central themes of one of the first novelists recognized for successfully transplanting the English novel tradition into American soil, James Fenimore Cooper. Although Cooper was not the first American novelist, he can be considered the first superstar in the tradition, remembered especially for his series *The Leatherstocking Tales* featuring the white pioneer Natty Bumppo and the Native American chief Chingachgook. Cooper's works emphasize his historical and anthropological intent in centering his novels on Native American and colonial encounters, yet in doing so he also reveals an urgency about the consequences of mistreating American nature. The same can be said of Catherine Maria Sedgwick's *Hope Leslie* (1827), another historical novel about the colonial era that emphasizes the animosity and warfare of Native American/colonist relationships but that also is concerned about the way the "wilderness" is treated as European settlers establish new colonies.

The great novels of the American Renaissance were primarily occupied with psychological and philosophical truths. *Moby-Dick* could be read through an ecocritical lens as it is on one level a novel about hunting a species that would become endangered, and Hawthorne's settings frequently involve forests as wild spaces where dark human urges can play out in a way they cannot in cities and towns, but neither of these writers approached nature the same way their contemporary Thoreau did, or with the same interest in the implications of contact between the spheres of humanity and nature. The late nineteenth-century realists mostly wrote socially oriented novels that might have been aware of fading nature to varying degrees, but except for Twain, their settings tended to be urban and their concerns mainly social. The regionalists and naturalists around the turn of the twentieth century began to shift their emphasis toward

American nature: writers like Sarah Orne Jewett, Jack London, Hamlin Garland, and Willa Cather depicted nature as both fragile and powerful, and perhaps more meaningful than it had been given credit for in earlier periods.

Ernest Hemingway is an important author to consider in this context. His outsized reputation as an adventurer, a big game hunter, a soldier, and an epicure would seem to position him as a writer unconcerned with the fragility of the earth, but the truth is more nuanced. His short stories in particular demonstrate a sensitivity toward and respect for nature that indicates a tremendous concern for the way humans treat the earth. *The Old Man and the Sea* (1952), his final short novel that has been the entry point to his oeuvre for many readers, is centered around the intense relationship between humans and nature's most powerful creatures. That theme recurs throughout Hemingway's work, including in his first (and many would say most enduring) novel, *The Sun Also Rises* (1926). It seems a novel preoccupied with human behavior, but nature is a crucial component of the novel's ethos. There is a grace and beauty in nature that is compromised when humans disrespect it.

Hemingway's beleaguered protagonist Jake Barnes is in search of tranquility throughout the novel, which is surprising given how he surrounds himself with boorish expatriates. In Paris in the novel's first section, Jake wants little more than to be left alone so he can concentrate on his writing, but the presence of hard-drinking friends and his one-time lover Brett Ashley distract him, to say nothing of the constant temptations and frenzied energy of the City of Lights. He repeatedly stares at churches and cathedrals, both from the inside and the outside, in an attempt to find the peace he craves, but as an atheist he does not find it in those spaces. He and Bill Gorton go on a private pilgrimage, breaking away from a train full of religious pilgrims to go fishing in the mountains above Bayonne. As they drive up and away from society, something shifts in Jake and he reverently admires the landscape: "away off you could see the plateau of Pamplona rising out of the plain, and the walls of the city, and the great brown cathedral, and the broken skyline of the other churches. In back of the plateau were the mountains, and every way you looked there were other mountains, and ahead the road stretched out white across the plain" (99). Here the feeling of the vast majesty of the mountains eclipses the attempts to recreate divinity in architecture: human efforts result in nothing more than a "broken skyline."

This description sets the scene for the next day when Bill and Jake hike into the mountains to fish. Although the setting is described in the classic Hemingwayesque factual way, it's clear that Jake experiences deep reverence and tranquility as he walks: "It was a beech wood and the trees were very old. Their roots bulked above the ground and the branches were twisted … . The trees were big, and the foliage was thick but it was not gloomy. There was no undergrowth, only the smooth grass, very green and fresh, and the big gray trees well spaced as though it were a park" (122). Bill ineptly remarks, "This is country" and Jake pointedly remains silent, continuing to notice details: "There were wild strawberries growing on the sunny side of the ridge in a little clearing in the trees" (122). The frenzied pace of Jake's milieu's debauchery in Paris and later at the fiesta in Pamplona is pointedly absent from this description in which Jake is in silent awe of nature's perfection.

One might argue that fishing, like the bullfighting that dominates the book's final chapters, is the opposite of reverence for nature, but the way Jake describes fishing rituals (when they are done properly) indicates a deep respect for nature that aligns Jake with Cooper's Chingachgook (who denigrates the wasteful ways of white colonists who hunt indiscriminately) and Silko's Tayo who engages in ancient rituals that honor slain deer. Jake first marvels at the beauty of wild nature: "As I baited up, a trout shot up out of the white water into the falls and was carried down. Before I could finish baiting, another trout jumped at the falls, making the same lovely arc and disappearing into the water that was thundering down" (124). He quickly euthanizes each fish he catches so they do not suffer. He then honors his catch by preserving their natural beauty:

> In a little while I had six. They were all about the same size. I laid them out, side by side, all their heads pointing the same way, and looked at them. They were beautifully colored and firm and hard from the cold water. It was a hot day, so I slit them all and shucked out the insides, gills and all, and tossed them over across the river. I took the trout ashore, washed them in the cold, smoothly heavy water above the dam, and then picked some ferns and packed them all in the bag, three trout on a layer of ferns, then another layer of ferns, the three more trout, and then covered them with ferns. They looked nice in the ferns. (124)

The minute attention Jake pays to his catch and the way he arranges them aesthetically even though no one else witnesses this beauty testifies to the fact that he regards hunting as a spiritual activity, not a nature-destroying ego trip. Later, during the bullfight, the same principles are initially advanced and then destroyed as Jake's thoughtless and ignorant cohort treats the fiesta in Pamplona as just another hedonistic orgy rather than as the sacred ritual it's supposed to be. Jake's inability to uphold the ritual's solemn meaning is a personal failure with broad implications. The other bullfighting aficionado in the novel, the hotelier Montoya, pointedly shuns Jake in the end, causing him to understand that he has violated and irrevocably corrupted the code he enacted on the fishing trip and at the start of the bullfighting.

Twenty-First Century Novels: Climate Change and Extinction

The awareness of the fragility and inherent value of nature that Silko, Cooper, Sedgwick, and Hemingway demonstrate in earlier periods of literary history reaches an unprecedented level of urgency in the twenty-first century due to heightened awareness of the ecological crisis we face. The power of nature has always been connected to beauty and majesty in the American imagination, and yet the power of humanity is increasingly rendered in antagonistic terms. If we are not careful stewards of the land that enables our dreams of prosperity, it will no longer support us, nor will it be allowed to support itself. For a novelist like Hemingway, whose aesthetic demanded especially careful reading in accordance with his famed "iceberg theory" in which 8/9 of the truth lurks under the surface of the sentences, any message about the earth's fragility might not be immediately apparent to his readers. Contemporary authors have begun to resort to less subtle methods of narration to ensure that the message is loud and clear. One such author is Barbara Kingsolver. Her 2012 novel *Flight Behavior* is both a realistic story of a dissatisfied housewife in an early midlife crisis and, more broadly, a parable of a planet in crisis, specifically (as she puts it in an author's note at the book's conclusion) "The biotic consequences of climate change" (415).

Dellarobia Turnbow's story begins as she is trekking up a wooded hillside on a remote segment of her in-laws' property. Her intent is to meet a would-be lover for a sexual tryst – one connotation of the "flight" of the book's title – but as she navigates the challenging terrain, she is arrested by a vision that she later compares to the burning bush in the Bible: "The forest blazed with its own internal flame" (14). She's not sure what she's seeing, but she calls it a "vision of glory" and notes that "it looked like the inside of joy" (15) in stark contrast to the boredom of her daily life. She sees it as a sign: "The burning trees were put here to save her … . It was a lake of fire, something far more fierce and wondrous than either of those elements alone" (16). (Fire and flood, connecting biblical prophecies to contemporary effects of climate change, are recurrent symbols throughout the novel). She abandons her romantic affair and returns to her quotidian world to ponder what she has seen. When her husband Cub tells her that his father has decided to clear-cut the timber on the property to pay off their mounting debt, she protests, saying they should all walk through the property before signing any papers, but acting mysteriously when Cub asks why she cares so much. She cannot tell him about the miracle she has witnessed because the admission might lead to the discovery of her aborted affair.

Dellarobia convinces the men of the family to walk the property with her and they discover the truth of her vision: the trees are covered with millions of Monarch butterflies. The water and fire imagery of her original vision recurs: "The density of the butterflies in the air now gave her a sense of being underwater, plunged into a deep pond … . Every tree on the far mountainside was covered with trembling flame" (52–53). The intensity of the experience causes Cub to believe – and later to testify in church – that Dellarobia experienced a vision and to argue that the migrating insects were sent by God and that the trees should be left alone. His belligerent father Bear, though, bluntly states, "We're going to spray these things and go ahead" (54–55), adding that he has a private stash of DDT, a pesticide banned because of the long-term damage it does to ecosystems. The plot then centers on a battle between those who see the trees as timber to be harvested and those who see them as a crucial habitat that demands preservation. The fact that the Turnbows and the region they live in are impoverished complicates the debate.

The family and the town become caught up in the unprecedented discovery. Dellarobia's difficult mother-in-law Hester grudgingly allows that it was a vision, and she sets up a system whereby members of her church can view the "miracle" for free, but others must pay for the privilege. Regional news stories promote the event with a focus on Dellarobia as a kind of oracle. She learns about Hester's scheme to profit from the butterflies when a family of Mexican immigrants – the daughter of which is a classmate of her son's – arrives at their house to see them. Dellarobia learns that the family was displaced from their hometown, Michoacán, when a flood destroyed the town which was where the Monarchs had migrated for centuries, a historically accurate event that occurred in 2010. She later learns that the flood was catalyzed by the same clear-cutting her father-in-law has planned.

A prominent lepidopterist named Ovid Byron arrives to examine the butterflies and pays Dellarobia to allow him and a team of postdocs to set up a field station in her backyard. She is initially self-conscious about her lack of education and lower-class status, but gradually bonds with this group and joins them on their fieldwork, learning more than she thought imaginable about the implications of the butterflies' appearance in Tennessee. Ovid tells her, "Every year that we record temperature increases, the roosting populations in Mexico move farther up the mountain slopes to find where it's still cool and moist." She naively responds, "Is that so bad? They're beautiful. We don't get a lot of bonuses around here" (147). He grimly allows, "We are scientists … . But we are also human. We like these butterflies … . But what we see here worries us" (148). She's disappointed that there are consequences to this rare beauty in her limited world – "Why did the one rare, spectacular thing in her life have to be a sickness of nature?" (149) – but part of her growth involves a deeper understanding of the world's broader needs, not just her individual ones.

The local weather becomes a crucial context for the plot as relentless rains ravage Dellarobia's Appalachian town. Dellarobia's community is skeptical of the realities and consequences of climate change because it is abstract, but as Dellarobia works more closely with Ovid and his team, she cannot deny the evidence. Though his vocabulary is specialized, he describes the situation in analogies she can understand. She finds herself doing similar translations within her community, and she also becomes more proficient in the language and methods of science, which are antithetical to her fundamentalist Christian upbringing. At times Ovid tells her the plain truth: "We are seeing a bizarre alteration of a previously stable pattern … . A continental ecosystem breaking down … . Climate change has disrupted this system" (228). One of his grad students expresses a cynical view of his fellow humans who deny climate change and blames the news media; he says, "every environmental impact story has to be made into something else. Sex it up if possible" (230).

Dellarobia finds herself the victim of this precise phenomenon. The media storms the family property and sets her up in a news story that distorts her interview and converts her image into a scantily dressed meme known as the Butterfly Venus. Although the tension between scientific and religious belief is constant throughout the novel, neither community is depicted as harshly as the media is. Dellarobia learns to avoid cameras, but late in the novel the same interviewer who turned the story into something "sexed up" arrives for a second interview. Dellarobia leads the camera to Ovid who refuses to answer the interviewer's questions in terms that might compromise his message and unleashes a diatribe that reveals the pent-up frustration of the scientific world. After soundly educating the newscaster about the realities of climate change and accusing her that she, like all journalists, is interested in the profit motive rather than the truth, he concludes, "Here is my full statement. What you are doing is unconscionable. You're allowing the public to be duped by a bunch of damned liars" (369). As Ovid's frustration approaches its peak, the conflict about logging the Turnbow land reaches a happy outcome as Bear, the taciturn patriarch, calls off the operation after being heavily lobbied by his wife, his son, and the church pastor.

Flight Behavior is carefully researched and includes a wealth of scientific information that is likely to enlighten readers in a way news journalism never can. Eco-conscious novels have an obligation to reveal and disseminate an accurate understanding of the scientific world, but they also are novels that tell stories about the struggles of individuals. Dellarobia's story begins with a desperate attempt to get away from an uninspiring marriage, and her growth leads to a much more reasoned and mature attempt to dissolve her marriage, with a separation from Cub and joint custody of their children. The broader drama of the butterflies is both the background to and the catalyst for this transformation. As inclement weather kills off butterflies who have had to flee their normal roosting colony, Dellarobia experiences her own challenging, painful, but necessary transformation. Her awakened curiosity about nature's systems precipitated by this random relocation will not go away when the butterflies expire. Speaking about herself, her marriage, and the compromised state of the planet all at once, she has her son Preston repeat the phrase, "It won't ever go back to how it was" (429). This is a clear-eyed acceptance that the earth we inhabit cannot be restored, and yet the novel's conclusion demonstrates hope. Dellarobia brings a stillborn lamb back to life based on a procedure she and Preston learned in a science book, and the two witness a new colony of butterflies after a devastating snowfall, an event she compares to "resurrection" (420). The novel suggests that it may be too late to return to a former Edenic state of environmental balance, but it is not too late to correct the path we are on, if people are willing to accept the truth and to take responsible action.

The appearance of the Monarch butterflies in Tennessee in *Flight Behavior* lures activists in addition to scientists and television crews. This dimension of the book is relatively muted: one activist asks people to sign a petition pledging to lower their personal carbon footprint. (Dellarobia ridicules him because he doesn't understand that people in her social class can't afford the behaviors this man wants them to modify, like air travel or dining at restaurants). Another group includes students and a professor from a local community college who end up helping Ovid and his scientists rather than continuing to carry their ineffective handmade placards. A third group includes women from England who knit butterflies and place them in the trees in a nod to the understated power of folk art. None of these protesters is what we would call radical. Ovid's stern warnings about the dire state of the world to the journalist and to Dellarobia constitute the strongest actions in the novel. Other contemporary writers lean more heavily into the more contentious dimensions of climate activism. One such novelist is T. Coraghessan Boyle whose short fiction and novels frequently scrutinize the intersection of human hypocrisy and the destruction of nature. Many of his novels illustrate this principle, but 2011s *When the Killing's Done* is especially focused. Set on the Channel Islands National Park off the coast of Santa Barbara – frequently referred to as "the Galapagos of North America" – the novel takes an unstinting look at the war between factions who differ on how to best preserve the earth.

When the Killing's Done pits two main characters named Alma Boyd Takasue and Dave LaJoy in an ongoing feud about animal rights. Alma is a biologist who works for the National Park Service and Dave is a local entrepreneur who has founded a radical organization called FPA, "For the Protection of Animals." The novel takes place in the first decade of the twenty-first century but opens in the 1940s when Alma's grandmother, pregnant, is stranded on one of the Channel Islands after her boat capsizes, killing her husband. She is left to scavenge on the island in a desperate search for food and water, "reduced to an animal, nothing more" (30), and eventually discovers four long-abandoned cabins containing lifesaving provisions. They also contain rats which Alma's grandmother chases off with instinctive fury before she is rescued. The history-minded narrator fills in details of how rats arrived on the island, an invasive species that has always benefited from the ability to stow away on the ships that transport human commerce.

Rats are the initial focus of the battle between Alma and Dave. She is leading an effort to use poison to eradicate rats from the island in the service of saving other species that live there including birds that face extinction due to the rats' appetite for their eggs. Alma delivers a lecture to inform the public of the plan, showing slides of adorable animals like foxes who are threatened by the demonic rats she shows in another slide, claiming, "Rats ... are responsible for sixty percent of all island extinctions in the world today" (59). Dave rudely disrupts the lecture, demanding a speedy leap to the Q-and-A and declaring Alma's words "Bull ... Propaganda and doublespeak" (59). His attempts to incite the crowd escalate quickly: "Nazis, that's what you are. Kill everything, that's your solution. Kill, kill, kill" (62). Asked to be civil, he rejoins, "I'll be civil when the killing's done" (62), providing the novel's title.

These two characters hold viewpoints that are each potentially valid, but irreconcilable, especially given Dave's unmeasured methodology. Although Alma is concerned with extinction, she does manipulate the audience by drawing a distinction between cute animals and the ones we loathe, and Dave points out this hypocrisy. Neither character is flawless in their initial introduction leading up to this battle, but the novel positions Alma as the protagonist and Dave as an angry psychopath rather than a committed activist. As Alma is finishing her lecture, Dave, who has been escorted out of the building, spray-paints racist and sexist words on her car. He is a reprehensible character: for instance, he verbally abuses restaurant workers and colleagues he recruits to battle the National Parks workers. His activism seems to come from a place of unbridled anger rather than from an altruistic dedication to animal rights. He is a definite type, a dreadlock-wearing white guy who drives a BMW and is intolerant of "bums," his preferred term over "homeless or less fortunate or needy or apartmentally challenged or whatever the phrase of the week is ... because his sympathies lie with the animals that *can't* help themselves" (69). It becomes clear that Dave is more a hater of humanity than a lover of animals, and he sees the world in those binary terms: "Is this a fundamental inconsistency: pro-animal, anti-human? Let it be, because it's no worse than the way the eco-cops see things" (69). Referring to Alma and others who work at the Park Service as "eco-cops" is consistent with his disgust for other authority figures, including judges and the police.

Boyle's novels, notably *Drop City* (2004), tend to view human behavior in terms of animal behavior: his characters are often rendered as predators, prey, parasites, or hosts. This dynamic is often reinforced by gender: *Drop City*, which takes place in the early 1970s, makes use of popular terms "cats" and "chicks" to refer to the predatory dynamic between young men and women, respectively, and *When the Killing's Done* reveals a similar dynamic, not limited to the two main characters. Dave is especially villainous as he is expressly described as a parasite (61) and demonstrates predatory behavior throughout the novel even as he claims to support helpless animals. Local media dubs him "Rat Lover" after his battle with Alma's crusade to rid a Channel Island of rats is fought in court: "*Rat Lover*. It's almost an oxymoron ... and yet still the word is getting out in a bigger way than he could have imagined. And that means money. Since the trial started, donations to FPA have gone through the roof" (133). Though he is evidently a success story when it comes to the American Dream narrative – a businessman who drives a luxury car, owns a boat, and can afford to retire young – his supposedly noble crusade is appallingly connected to capitalist greed.

This principle is clearly illustrated when Dave installs new sod at his house. "The whole operation has him conflicted – lawns are bad news for the environment, yes, but he's got to keep up property values, or his property value anyway" (210). His anger is triggered when raccoons invade his new lawn, digging holes in it in search of earthworms. When he contacts the local animal control bureau, they advise him to trap the raccoons and, rather than relocate them (which creates additional problems for both the animal and the habitat into which it is introduced), "dispose of them" (229), a solution that is antithetical to his principles. Yet for all his commitment to humaneness, he doesn't check his traps in a timely way. He discovers the raccoons with "eyes fixed on him, hands clutching the wire like prisoners in a penitentiary" (230). Worse, upon closer inspection, "What he sees is blood: the gray-gloved claws of both animals' forefeet are stippled with it ... . they've been clawing at the steel mesh since the door dropped down behind them, all night and into the break of day, tearing their own substance, in pain, bleeding" (231).

Although he regards himself as a "gifted predator" before this moment, he now understands himself to be a torturer, no better than the cosmetics manufacturers and factory chicken farmers who precipitated his commitment to animal rights in the first place. Dave has an easy time overlooking his flaws or contradictions while blaming others, though: he quickly finds a way to use the raccoons in his ongoing crusade rather than dwell on the pain he has inflicted.

The crusade moves onto a second island where Alma and her colleagues have undertaken the task of eradicating the island of another nonnative species, wild hogs. When Dave publicly questions why the hogs can't be captured and relocated, Alma points out, "The risk is just too great." The narrator elaborates: "The fact was that these hogs – Santa Cruz Island hogs – were a discrete population that had had no interaction with outside populations in a hundred and fifty years, and thus could carry leptospirosis, foot and mouth disease, mutations of common bacteria and viruses that could burn through the American hog industry and leave it twitching in the mud. So there was no choice but to euthanize them" (204–205). Simultaneously, Alma is leading a charge to capture and relocate golden eagles who are also predators on the island, threatening the extinction of the native foxes. This second phase incites Dave to again deface Alma's car (with the term "pig killer" [236]) and to renew his battle against her since he was unsuccessful in his rat crusade: the vermin were successfully eradicated from the first island.

Part of Dave's activism against the pig slaughter is to introduce another invasive nonnative species onto the island, namely the raccoons he trapped in his yard. His motivation is personal as he releases the creatures: "That would confound Dr. Alma, wouldn't it? A whole new race of animals out here on the island, and why not? Her precious foxes and skunks and lizards and the three types of snake had got here at random ... and it was nothing more than an accident of fate that raccoons hadn't been part of the mix ... . he – Dave LaJoy, citizen, homeowner, activist, defeated in court and ignored on the picket line – was the deliberate agent of release, nothing random about it. He was a life-giver, that was what he was, the rescuer of these creatures Animal Control had all but told him to eliminate" (265). His logic is clearly twisted and self-aggrandizing, and it escalates when he brings a small band of vigilantes to the island to cut through the fences segmenting the island into zones designed to facilitate the hog slaughter. He insists they press on despite unsafe conditions, and one falls to her death. Although he narrowly escapes manslaughter charges, donations to his organization dry up after the story breaks, and he becomes more desperate than ever. His final act is to bring two other species to the island – rattlesnakes and rabbits – and while he wrangles them belowdecks, a large container ship destroys his boat, killing everyone aboard as well as the animals he is transporting. Just before his death, he has a too-late epiphany: "he understands, for the first time, how wrong this is, how wrong he's been, how you have to let the animals – *the animals* – decide for themselves" (358).

Boyle's novel is a critique of human folly, but it also recognizes the troubled decisions humans must make constantly as they become aware of the earth's fragility. There is a strong emphasis on food in the novel, particularly centering around characters who are vegetarians or carnivores. (Both Alma and Dave are proclaimed vegetarians but decide it's okay to eat seafood and eggs). Alma wrestles with another dilemma when she becomes pregnant. She denies instinctive joy at this news; she and her partner Tim are "both committed environmentalists. Dedicated to saving the ecosystem, preserving what's left, restoring it. To bring a child into an overpopulated world is irresponsible, wrong, nothing less than sabotage" (283). This intellectual response is at odds with her feeling of maternal elation, "Because she's a living thing, that's why, and living things reproduce. The only discernible purpose of life is to create more life – any biologist knows that .... they have an obligation to pass their genes on if there's any hope of improving the species" (284). Her brain again tries to explain her natural feelings of joy. Tim does not share these feelings and summarily leaves her when she decides to keep the baby. Refusing easy conclusions, the novel continually reframes the dilemma of environmentally conscious Americans in the twenty-first century. It is impossible to be human without inflicting damage on the world, regardless of how hard we try. Alma accidentally hits a squirrel with her car, leaving it writhing and bloody but not quite dead; she wonders, "Why is she suddenly on the verge of tears?" (197) presumably given the fact that she is a scientist who has authorized the extermination of thousands of rats and hogs. As with her pregnancy, there is a difference between the abstract and the personal, and there are no easy solutions for saving what she calls "This skewed and doomed world" (107). There is some hope toward the novel's conclusion as a destructive monster like Dave is no longer alive to cause more trouble and Alma nurses her baby, but the novel ends ambiguously, with humanity nowhere in sight as a native fox and the invasive raccoon brought by Dave prepare to do battle on the island. It would seem like a natural battle, but it was manufactured by human behavior.

In his profound, sprawling novel *The Overstory* (2018), Richard Powers turns the personal crusade of a character like Dave LaJoy in Boyle's novel or Dellarobia Turnbow in Kingsolver's into an epic struggle shared by a host of characters over time. *The Overstory* considers the possibility that trees exhibit a type of sentience, shifting the focus from the other two novels from a primary concern with animal habitats. The scope and breadth of Powers's novel are expansive, indicating a growing need for stories of climate activism to be weighty and broadly applied. Powers employs multiple protagonists, spending the first part of the novel exploring their various backstories, all of which involve some mystical or symbolic connection to the world of trees. The novel is structured according to the growth cycle of trees: its four sections are labeled roots, trunk, crown, and seeds.

In the "Roots" section we are introduced to the nine protagonists at various stages of life in the 1970s. Their stories do not yet intertwine, but their chapters, named after the protagonists in what seem like distinct short stories, have common motifs. These characters tend to be lonely outsiders, often unconventionally brilliant, who suffer some sort of violent trauma. It is impossible to identify one main protagonist, but the first chapter traces the ancestry of Nick Hoel and he is also given the final scene at the end of the book, giving his story prominent status. Nick is an artist who emerged from a line of pioneers and farmers hailing from Norway and settling in Iowa. Their original immigrant ancestor planted a chestnut tree on the family property which became a local wonder because most chestnut trees died from disease in the early twentieth century. Without any stated reason for doing so, the patriarchs of the family enact a strange project to photograph the tree every month for decades starting early in the twentieth century while major historical events blur by in the background. The photographs eventually constitute "the oldest, shortest, slowest, most ambitious silent movie ever shot in Iowa," which might seem like a pointless exercise, and yet the sensitive viewer who flips through the photos can discern "the tree's goal ... stretching and patting about for something in the sky" (15), a clear parallel to the human search for a divine presence. The act of photographing the tree and scrutinizing the resulting artwork is also quasi-religious: the Hoel photographers can't say why they're undertaking this ritual, but the existence of the photos causes Nick to realize his purpose: "to spend his life making strange things" (19). He becomes an artist not for any commercial reason but to raise consciousness about the majesty and fragility of trees, which are frequently referred to as gods throughout the novel.

Nick's tree-focused art is in conversation with the science that other characters in the novel put their faith in, notably Patricia Westerford whose study *The Secret Forest* – originally ridiculed by the established community of dendrologists for its suggestion that trees are sentient and can communicate – eventually earns her an enormous following. Her rejection from the scientific community initially causes her to contemplate suicide, but she overcomes this urge and finds a fringe community of like-minded researchers who help launch her career, but more importantly, who aid in her mission to get others to care about the fragile ecosystems that are forests. Nick and Patricia are the model artist and scientist, respectively, because they are in no way motivated by ego or profit: they are purely devoted to a cause greater than themselves. Another main character, Neelay Mehta, can be said to merge art and science in the creation of a massive role-playing video game called *Mastery* that he developed in the 1990s. Neelay's game isn't really a game at all, but rather a simulation in which players cooperate to build a world, endlessly. Like the other two, Neelay has no regard for himself or for the material human world: he is obsessive, devoted, and committed to using emerging technologies to improve the state of the world. Consistent with the stories of other protagonists, Neelay has had spiritual interactions with trees. As a brilliant child, after his teacher accuses him of daydreaming when he is designing a prototype for his computer program, he storms off in frustration and climbs a tree. He falls and is paralyzed from the waist down for life, but he considers it a fortunate fall, or even believes "the tree dropped him" (105) so that he might experience the world as "a traveler in that country of surprise that he'll come to build, when machines are at last fast enough to keep up with his imagination" (103). His combining art and science enables him to realize his vision and to use it as a way to spread a message of salvation he believes was communicated to him by a forest of exotic trees on the campus of Stanford University. He becomes a devotee of Patricia Westerford, though they never meet.

Many of the other protagonists meet and directly interact in the central section of the novel, "Trunk." Nick meets Olivia whose brief story in the first section sees her electrocuting herself and temporarily dying after a series of impulsive decisions. Following her resurrection, she becomes a spiritual leader who can communicate with trees. Douglas, whose story inverts Neelay's in that he was saved by a tree that broke his fall after being shot out of the sky during a tour of duty in Vietnam, sees trees as his cause and salvation and spends years planting seedlings in a clear-cut forest. Mimi Ma, the daughter of Chinese immigrants who becomes a successful engineer, changes her life's trajectory when local authorities cut down a grove of trees that had been her only comfort in a work-laden life as well as the place where she felt she could communicate with her father who died from suicide at the foot of a mulberry tree. These four characters arrive in pairs at an encampment of eco-activists protesting the logging of giant redwoods in the Pacific Northwest in the 1990s. They are joined by Adam, a grad student in psychology who is studying the thought patterns of members of groups such as the one the other characters have joined, but he is lured into their cause. These five characters participate in protests that are originally nonviolent: Olivia and Nick spend weeks tree-sitting hundreds of feet above the earth to prevent loggers from cutting down a massive redwood, and Adam originally meets them there while conducting field research for his thesis. As the novel's rising action continues, these five along with their fellow activists escalate their tactics and suffer bodily harm in various clashes with law enforcement officials who resort to torture. This dimension of the plot reaches its climax when Olivia dies in an explosion meant to destroy logging equipment, and the remaining four activists must go underground to escape the federal authorities.

Much more complex and elaborate than can be glimpsed in that brief plot summary, *The Overstory* raises some key questions about how best to approach the ecological disaster humans have precipitated. Art, science, and activism (from peaceful protest to what has been labeled eco-terrorism) provide approaches that are distinct, but that can also be combined. Regardless of the approach readers find compelling, the repeated message of Powers's novel is that humans must recognize their place on the planet if they are to alter the legacy of the Anthropocene era. Human arrogance and individual egos must be vanquished if the planet is to survive. The folly of capitalist greed, political influence, and the will to dominate are all contexts for the stories of the main characters and those close to them, all of which involve death, which often occurs suddenly in the novel. Meanwhile, trees are frequently described in terms of their longevity showing their capacity or even their will to long outlast humans. The final sections emphasize the distinction between human time and tree time, the latter of which is patient and incomprehensible to most people. The photograph of the Hoel chestnut tree taken over many years is one of many examples of the vast differences between the way trees and humans age. Nick, for another example, lays down on the stump left behind after loggers cut down the tree where he and Olivia lived while protesting deforestation. The age of the tree is startling, measured by his body, "his head on a wadded jacket near the ring laid down the year Charlemagne died. Somewhere underneath his coccyx, Columbus. Past his ankles, the first Hoel leaves Norway for Brooklyn and the expanses of Iowa. Beyond the length of his body, crowding up to the cut's cliff, are the rings of his own birth, the death of his family, the roadside visit of [Olivia] who taught him how to hang on and live" (358). His lifetime is nothing compared to the lifespan of the tree, now a mere stump after it was senselessly cut down along with the other forest gods.

The stories of these characters might individually and collectively seem meaningless against the backdrop of ecological destruction, but Powers illustrates – with surprising optimism given how much misanthropy develops in his characters – that the human race is "beautiful" as Patricia says, as well as "doomed" (392). Her early contemplation of suicide renews itself late in life after her partner Dennis dies. Her life's work is divided between writing and lecturing on one hand and the creation of a seed bank on another, a repository that will presumably allow the last surviving humans to replant trees that would otherwise go extinct. At a public lecture, she meditates on the question, "What is the single best thing a person can do for tomorrow's world?" (456). The reader sees her planning to commit suicide as she pours a poisonous plant extract into her water bottle behind the podium, but at this crucial moment the narrative becomes ambiguous: "Down one branch" of the forking worlds of reality and the imagination, Patricia drinks the fatal water and dies, demonstrating that human extinction will preserve the planet. "Down another branch, this one, she shouts, 'Here's to unsuicide,' and flings the cup of swirling green over the gasping audience" (466). The phrase "this one" might indicate reality, or it might indicate the world of fiction that Powers has created. The narrative becomes deliberately ambiguous to show that the answers to the questions the novel has raised will not be easily resolved and that the point of novels may be to raise the consciousness of readers enough to be creative thinkers so that we may fully employ our brains to see our way out of our current crisis. As Neelay declares, "what do all good stories do? ... They kill you a little. They turn you into something you weren't" (412). This lofty goal can best be realized in a sophisticated complex novel such as *The Overstory*.

American Nightmares: Narrating Disaster

In the novels by Kingsolver, Boyle, and Powers, the focus is squarely on the consequences of environmental destruction. Other contemporary novels have alternative primary concerns, but an incident of environmental catastrophe is the catalyst for their narrative. In some cases, this scenario brings us into the realm of speculative or future fiction of the apocalypse or post-apocalypse, such as Stephen King's *The Stand* (1978), Ursula Le Guin's *Always Coming Home* (1985), Octavia Butler's *Parable of the Sower* (1993), or Matt Bell's *Appleseed* (2021). One enduring work of post-apocalyptic fiction is Cormac McCarthy's *The Road* (2006), the story of a father and son walking through a devastated American landscape hoping for little more than survival. We are never certain if the apocalypse was caused by human destruction or by some cosmic event, but the novel's dim view of humanity coupled with pointed anecdotes about human interaction with nature make it a valuable addition to the body of eco-conscious literature.

Whether the apocalypse that preceded the main action of *The Road* was caused by humanity or a natural disaster does not alter the fact that the landscape is ruined and that much of what humanity has produced during its reign amounts to rubbish. The unnamed boy and father trudge through this ruined world in search of the most basic needs: shelter, food, fuel, and water. They must immediately assess the few people they encounter on the road for trustworthiness: the father assumes everyone they encounter is malevolent but the boy hopes that everyone they encounter might be good so they can reconnect with a community. Evidence is on the father's side: the pair witness scenes of cannibalism (including of a baby), they are ambushed with arrows, and one man who asks for their help steals from them, an act punished by the father who makes him strip naked at gunpoint. They help one old man named Ely who claims to be ninety and who pronounces a grim truth: "Things will be better when everybody's gone" (172). The boy's innocent faith in humanity doesn't stand much of a chance against his father's cynicism, reinforced by pronouncements like this one.

Humanity as depicted in *The Road* is not just depraved in the way humans treat one another, but also in the way they treat nature. The senselessness with which people destroy nature is illustrated in one crucial scene the man remembers from his youth. He recalls watching a group of "rough men" who

> opened up the rocky hillside ground with pick and mattock and brought to light a great bolus of serpents perhaps a hundred in number. Collected there for a common warmth. The dull tubes of them beginning to move sluggishly in the cold hard light. Like the bowels of some great beast exposed to the day. The men poured gasoline on them and burned them alive, having no remedy for evil but only for the image of it as they conceived it to be. The burning snakes twisted horribly and some crawled burning across the floor of the grotto to illuminate its darker recesses. As they were mute there were no screams of pain and the men watched them burn and writhe and blacken in just such silence themselves and they disbanded in silence in the winter dusk each with his own thoughts to go home to their suppers. (188–189)

The men in this passage follow the broken logic of their foolish mythology by burning the animal that has long been associated with evil, but they reveal themselves to be the evil species, killing without purpose or cause. Their pointless, cruel act even begins with an assault on the earth itself which they "open up" with tools of destruction. The novel's concluding paragraph leaves aside all the vicious interactions between humans that have dominated the book and focuses instead on brook trout: "On their backs were vermiculate patterns that were maps of the world in its becoming. Maps and mazes. Of a thing which could not be put back" (287). This vision of "all things" that "were older than man" (287) suggests that Ely was right when he said, "things will be better when everybody's gone." The memory of the senseless slaughter of snakes indicates that humanity's destruction will lead to its own demise and that nature will endure. By the time we named "the Anthropocene," our era was nearly finished.

Postmodern novels as discussed in Chapter 7 illustrate many ideas, but one recurrent theme is human waste, often represented in ruined landscapes and garbage heaps. In one central postmodern text, Don DeLillo's *White Noise* (1985), the primary impulses may be satirical or parodic, but the novel is catalyzed by the appearance of a poisonous cloud that becomes known as the Airborne Toxic Event. DeLillo's novel centers on the melancholy experiences of Jack Gladney, a midwestern professor of Hitler Studies and family man who is overwhelmed by parenthood and baffled by a plot that involves his wife's infidelity and a mysterious drug called Dylar. The novel is rife with philosophical discussions and considerations of the discontentment of the postmodern age, particularly regarding consumerism. The reader joins Jack in his ongoing struggle to separate noise from signal, or to consider whether to believe in randomness or pattern, or to discern authentic, real experiences from simulation. All these inquiries are put to the test when the Airborne Toxic Event arrives without warning.

When the event first occurs, characters struggle to describe it before they are able to interpret it. Jack's son Heinrich tells him, "The radio calls it a feathery plume ... . But it's not a plume [but rather] a shapeless growing thing. A dark black breathing thing of smoke" (109). Jack is interested in what "the radio" calls it and also what "the movie" calls it as though official, disembodied voices of authority can illuminate what has happened. Heinrich tells him that we know that it was caused by a chemical called Nyodene D, which is known to be toxic, but the effects are unclear: "At first they said skin irritation and sweaty palms. But now they say nausea, vomiting, shortness of breath" (109). The radio voice adds more symptoms: "Convulsions, coma, miscarriage" (118). A mass evacuation follows with the urgent message, "Evacuate all places of residence. Cloud of deadly chemicals" (116). When the Gladney family reaches the evacuation encampment, Heinrich takes on the role of a wise leader since he seems to know more about the chemical than anyone else, or at least is able to articulate it; Jack listens to him as he preaches to a crowd, "it's basically simple. Nyodene D. is a whole bunch of things thrown together that are byproducts of the manufacture of insecticide. The original stuff kills roaches, the byproducts kill everything left over ... . no one seems to know exactly what it causes in humans or in the offspring of humans. They tested for years and either they don't know for sure or they know and aren't saying. Some things are too awful to publicize" (127). Later Jack suggests to Heinrich that the situation might not be dire, and his son snaps back, "If you came awake tomorrow in the Middle Ages and there was an epidemic raging, what could you do to stop it, knowing what you know about the progress of medicines and diseases? Here it is practically the twenty-first century and you've read hundreds of books and magazines and seen a hundred TV shows about science and medicine. Could you tell those people one little crucial thing that might save a million and a half lives?" (142–3).

It's a rhetorical question, of course. The Airborne Toxic Event comes and goes without adequate explanations of what caused it or how it could be prevented in the future; instead, it just leaves a swath of destruction. DeLillo's novel, consumed with questions of mortality, indicates that contemporary Americans must live with the prospect of random environmental catastrophe but without a clear idea of how to interpret, prevent, or cure it. Worse, technology has made us ever more immune to understanding or processing such events. A man in the evacuation encampment carries a TV and rants, "Does this kind of thing happen so often that nobody cares anymore? Don't those people know what we've been through? We were scared to death. We still are. We left our homes, we drove through blizzards, we saw the cloud. It was a deadly specter, right there above us. Is it possible nobody gives substantial coverage to such a thing? Half a minute, twenty seconds? Are they telling us it was insignificant?" (155). The irony here is that contemporary Americans measure the significance of something as catastrophic as the Airborne Toxic Event through television coverage. A faceless "they" control the media, the corporations, and the military, and the masses are doomed in their powerlessness. Jack realizes, "What people in an exodus fear most immediately is that those in positions of authority will long since have fled, leaving us in charge of our own chaos" (116). Given Heinrich's point that Jack would not even be able to offer guidance during the Black Plague of the Middle Ages, hope for the survival of the species is thin.

The novel that concludes this study connects the environment to a number of other thematic concerns in other chapters including the anti-Dream narratives that are inhibited by racism and class prejudice in Chapter 5 and the relationship between gender roles with regard to the Dream explored in Chapters 2 and 3. Jesmyn Ward's *Salvage the Bones* (2011) follows the challenging life of its narrator Esch Batiste and her brothers and father as they struggle to make ends meet in the essentially segregated fictional town of Bois Sauvage, Mississippi. Esch's mother died after giving birth to her youngest son and at the age of fifteen Esch is harried by the expectations that she should look after her "dead wild" (186) younger brother Junior and her hard-drinking father. She also learns that she is pregnant, and Manny, the boy who impregnated her, is not interested in accepting responsibility. Meanwhile, Hurricane Katrina – the 2005 storm responsible for the deaths of nearly 1,400 Americans in and around New Orleans – is bearing down on the community.

Deep connections between the human and animal worlds can be seen before the hurricane arrives about two-thirds of the way into *Salvage the*

Bones. The primary vehicle for this connection is dog fighting, the only form of entertainment available to the residents of the Black section of Bois Sauvage other than basketball. Esch's oldest brother Randall is gifted at the latter and hopes to attend college on a basketball scholarship, but her middle brother Skeetah does not have his brother's athletic prowess and devotes his life to training and breeding dogs for fighting. The practice of dog fighting is a felony offense in all fifty states because it is considered inhumane, but the novel does not engage in debates about the ethics of the practice, and the description of the fight staged in chapter eight is unstintingly gruesome, much more graphic than Hemingway's descriptions of bullfighting in *The Sun Also Rises*. Skeetah's devotion to dogfighting is just treated as a fact, though. The residents of Bois Sauvage get by using whatever means they can, including stealing if necessary: an exhilarating scene in the novel has Skeetah, Esch, and others raiding a farm in the white part of town to get medicine for Skeetah's dogs. Although the novel does not explicitly condemn Skeetah and others for training and breeding dogs for fighting, it does suggest that there are lessons to be learned from nature, but that humans are poor students.

The residents of Bois Sauvage – French for "wild woods" – are not careful stewards of nature. Esch says factually, "We dump our garbage in a shallow ditch next to the pit, and we burn it" (15). This practice is not uncommon in poor, rural areas, and its unsanitary implications are clear: "When there's good rain in the summer, the pit fills to the brim and we swim in it. The water, which was normally pink, had turned a thick, brownish red. The color of a scab" (15). Other images of decay are sprinkled throughout Esch's descriptions; she says, "Our house is the color of rust" (116). The woods, by contrast, are powerful and enduring: "The few dirt-scratched yards and thin-siding houses and trailers of Bois Sauvage seem a sorry match to the woods, like pitting a puppy against a full grown dog" (158). Reminiscent of *The Overstory*, Esch regards the trees as sentient (and superior) creatures: "There are oaks so big and old that their arms grow out black and thick as trunks … . all I can hear is the pine trees shushing each other, the oak bristling" (158, 159). Trees are personified throughout the novel and when the hurricane hits, trees are both instruments of salvation as the Batistes use them to escape once their house floods and weapons of destruction that the storm uses to pummel houses.

The more striking connections between humanity and nature have to do with the behavior of dogs, centering around Skeetah's beloved China who is seen giving birth in the novel's opening scene. Esch immediately compares the vivid description of the canine birth to her mother, who died after complications from giving birth to Junior: "Mama squatted, screamed toward the end … . What China is doing is fighting, like she was born to do" (2). Mama's death following childbirth foreshadows the death of multiple puppies from disease, from China's inability to provide food for all of them, and from the flooding after the hurricane. Esch describes sex between herself and her lover Manny in similar terms to the way she describes sex between China and another dog. Manny does not kiss her or look at her during sex and he "growls" (16) when he ejaculates. Randall later berates him for "dogging my sister" (201). Skeetah's relationship with his prize dog is frequently described as though they are lovers. He does not recognize a border between their worlds; he says, "some people understand that between man and dog is a relationship ... . Equal" (29). He has the unusual habit of storing razor blades in his mouth; Esch says, "Skeetah ate razor blades, sliding them between the pink sleeve of his cheek and tongue and back out of his lips so fast I thought I was imagining it. I asked him why he ate them once, and he grinned and said, *Why should China be the only one with teeth?*" (60). He sometimes sleeps in the shed to take care of China and her puppies and when the hurricane hits, he insists that the animals join them in the house despite Daddy's vehement protests. Though he wants to experience the brute power of animals and to see them as "equal," Skeetah also recognizes his responsibility to feed, train, and control, and to cure dogs when they're sick, or to mercy-kill them when they cannot be saved. The protective, loving relationship is complicated by his insistence that China fight, even when she is vulnerable in the aftermath of giving birth. His motivation for allowing this to happen is tainted by two things: his ego – he claims to have trained the top fighter in the region and to understand dogs better than anyone else does – and his possessiveness; he declares, "She's mine, and she fights" (175).

Although the novel doesn't explicitly weigh in on the ethics of dogfighting, the fact that one of China's breasts is irrevocably destroyed as a result of that decision links the novel's social critique to its concerns with the relationship between humanity and nature. Like China, the residents of Bois Sauvage are at the mercy of larger forces that limit their choices. Skeetah sees China's litter in economic terms. Each puppy can fetch two hundred dollars, and their fate is to do what their owners compel them to do: to fight until they die or are mortally wounded. In a painful scene, Skeetah loses his control over China and she kills one of her puppies because she doesn't want to feed it; at the same moment, Daddy loses three of his fingers in a tractor accident while trying to destroy a chicken coop so that he can prepare for the hurricane. Both Skeetah and Daddy yell "Don't do it!" "Stop!" and "No!" at the exact same time as the puppy and Daddy's fingers are lost (129). Both plaintively ask

"Why?" (130) immediately afterward. The residents of Bois Sauvage, like dogs bred for fighting, suffer because of the unavailability of material comforts, and they are pitted against one another. Having little choice, they do what is necessary to survive. The community is fractured as a result, and fistfights are as common in the novel as dogfights.

Although hurricanes are nothing new on the Gulf Coast, the novel emphasizes that the magnitude of extreme weather events is increasing. Esch's Daddy declares, "News is right: every week it's a new storm. Ain't never been this bad" (6–7). Esch thinks he is "obsessed with hurricanes this summer" and believes "that the Gulf coast would be a new tornado alley" (46). He knows why the storms are increasing in number and magnitude: "the water so hot" (90). Despite his obsession and eagerness to prepare for the impending storm, he has no idea that Katrina is capable of flooding the community to the point that water would rise up from below, and the family barely escapes through the roof as the deluge hits. As Esch puts it, "Katrina surprised everyone with her uncompromising strength, her forcefulness, the way she lingered; she made things happen that had never happened before" (248). The remaining puppies do not survive, and though Skeetah clings to hope that China survived and is wandering around looking for him in the storm's aftermath, the other characters in the book and the reader don't share his optimism. "I failed her," he admits (238). When Esch weakly offers comfort with the standard line "It's going to be all right," nature provides a mocking retort: "The hurricane laughed" (238). We can no longer expect comfort from nature. Thinking of her own absent mother, China's murder of one of her own puppies, and the Greek myth of Medea that she alludes to throughout the novel, Esch fashions the hurricane as "the mother that swept into the Gulf and slaughtered" and adds, "Katrina is the mother we will remember until the next mother with large, merciless hands, committed to blood, comes" (255).

Although the community does come together in the wake of the storm, any hope at the end of this novel is tempered by the bleak realities Esch articulates. There is no real value in simply hoping for a better future when the forces that can destroy it are understood. The author, who lived through Hurricane Katrina, says, "if I was going to assume the responsibility of writing about my home, I needed narrative ruthlessness. I couldn't dull the edges and fall in love with my characters and spare them" (266). The American novel tradition in general depends on a similar willingness to face realities. Delusions such as the Dream narrative or the fantasy that our planet is not in peril will not suffice. Our novelists, for centuries, have troubled our national mythology rather than created it. As Hollywood continues to produce fantasies of superheroes who fight to conquer evil, our novelists will need to summon even more narrative ruthlessness so that the tradition can continue its vital, unfinished business. As Adam Appich, one of the protagonists of *The Overstory* puts it, "The best arguments in the world won't change a person's mind. The only thing that can do that is a good story" (356). Unless novelists stop believing that idea, the tradition will continue to flourish.

Further Reading

Bell, Matt. *Appleseed* (2021)
Butler, Octavia. *Parable of the Sower* (1993)
Erdrich, Louise. *Love Medicine* (1984)
King, Stephen. *The Stand* (1978)
Le Guin, Ursula. *Always Coming Home* (1985)
Momaday, N. Scott. *The Way to Rainy Mountain* (1969)
Owens, Delia. *Where the Crawdads Sing* (2018)
Stegner, Wallace. *Angle of Repose* (1971)
VanderMeer, Jeff. *Southern Reach Trilogy* (2014)

Works Cited

Alger, Horatio Jr. *Ragged Dick*. Hildegard Hoeller, editor. 1868. Norton, 2008.
Alvarez, Julia. *How the García Girls Lost Their Accents*. 1991.Algonquin, 2010.
Allison, Dorothy. *Bastard Out of Carolina*. Penguin/Dutton, 1992.
Anaya, Rudolfo. *Bless Me, Ultima*. Quinto Sol, 1972.
Baldwin, James. *Another Country*. 1962. Vintage, 1988.
Baldwin, James. *The Fire Next Time*. 1963. Vintage, 1991.
Baldwin, James. *Notes of a Native Son*. 1955. Beacon, 1984.
Barnes, Djuna. *Nightwood*. Intro. T.S. Eliot. 1937. New Directions, 1961.
Bloom, Harold. *The Western Canon*. Harcourt Brace, 1994.
Boyle, T. Coraghessan. *When the Killing's Done*. Viking, 2011.
Brown, William Wells. *Clotel, or The President's Daughter*. Robert S. Levine, editor. 1853. Bedford/St. Martin's, 2000.
Butler, Octavia. *Kindred*. Beacon, 1979.
Chopin, Kate. *The Awakening*. Sharon M. Harris, editor. 1899. Bedford/St. Martin's, 2008.
Cooper, James Fenimore. *The Leatherstocking Tales*, Vol. 1. Library of America, 1980.
Crane, Stephen. *Maggie: A Girl of the Streets (A Story of New York)*, Kevin J. Harris, editor. 1893. Bedford/St. Martin's, 1999.
de Crevecoeur, St. Jean. "What Is An American?" Hutner, pp. 5–11.
De Forest, William. "The Great American Novel." Hutner, pp. 155–159.
DeLillo, Don. *White Noise*. Penguin, 1985.
Editorial Board, *The New York Times*. https://www.nytimes.com/interactive/2023/06/20/opinion/nyt-columnists-culture.html
Egan, Jennifer. *A Visit from the Goon Squad*. Knopf, 2010.
Emerson, Ralph Waldo. *The Complete Works of Ralph Waldo Emerson: Essays* (first series, vol. 2). Library of America, 2010.
Faulkner, William. *The Sound and the Fury*. David Minter, editor. 1929. Norton, 1994.
Fuller, Margaret. "American Literature." Hutner, pp. 37–47.
Hawthorne, Nathaniel. *Letters of Hawthorne to William Ticknor, 1851-1864, Vol. 1*. Carteret Book Club, 1910.
Hemingway, Ernest. *Green Hills of Africa*. Scribner's, 1935.
Hemingway, Ernest. *The Sun Also Rises*. Scribner's, 1926.
Herrick, Robert. "The American Novel." Hutner, pp. 168–176.

Hurston, Zora Neale. *Their Eyes Were Watching God*. 1937. Perennial, 1998.
Hutner, Gordon, editor. *American Literature, American Culture*. Oxford UP, 1999.
Johnson, James Weldon. *The Autobiography of an Ex-Colored Man*. 1912. Macmillan, 2022.
Karl, Frederick. *American Fictions 1940-1980*. Harper and Row, 1983.
Kerouac, Jack. *On the Road*. 1957. Penguin, 1976.
Kingsolver, Barbara. *Flight Behavior*. Harper Collins, 2012.
Kingston, Maxine Hong. *Tripmaster Monkey: His Fake Book*. 1989. Vintage, 1990.
Klein, Marcus, editor. *The American Novel Since World War II*. Fawcett, 1969.
Lahiri, Jhumpa. *The Namesake*. 2003. Mariner, 2004.
Larsen, Nella. *Passing*. Thadious M. Davis, introduction. 1929. Penguin, 1997.
Lauter, Paul. *Canons and Contexts*. Oxford UP, 1991.
Marcus, Greil. *The Old, Weird America: The World of Bob Dylan's Basement Tapes*. Picador, 1997.
Marshall, Paule. *Brown Girl, Brownstones*. 1959. Echo Point Books, 2015.
Martin, Wendy and Sharone Williams. *The Routledge Introduction to American Women Writers*. Routledge, 2016.
Mbue, Imbolo. *Behold the Dreamers*. Random House, 2016.
McCarthy, Mary. *The Group*. Harcourt, Brace, and World, 1963.
Melville, Herman. *Moby-Dick, or The Whale*. 1851. Bobbs-Merrill, 1964.
Minter, David. "A Cultural History of the Modern American Novel: Introduction." *The Cambridge History of American Literature*, Sacvan Berkovitch, editor. Cambridge UP, 2002, pp. 1–9.
Morrison, Toni. *Beloved*. 1987. Vintage, 2004.
Norris, Frank. *The Responsibilities of the Novelist*. Grant Richards, 1903.
Olney, James. "'I Was Born": Slave Narratives, Their Status as Autobiography and as Literature." *Callaloo* 20 (Winter, 1984), 46–73.
O'Neill, Joseph. *Netherland*. Vintage, 2008.
Perry, Thomas Sergeant. "American Novels." Hutner, pp. 160–167.
Powers, Richard. *The Overstory*. Norton, 2018.
Pynchon, Thomas. *The Crying of Lot 49*. 1965. Harper Perennial, 1999.
Pynchon, Thomas. *Slow Learner*. 1984. Back Bay Books, 1995.
Roth, Henry. *Call It Sleep*. Intro. Alfred Kazin. 1934. Farrar, Strauss, and Giroux, 1991.
Roth, Philip. *American Pastoral*. Vintage, 1997.
Rowson, Susanna. *Charlotte Temple*. Cathy Davidson, introduction. 1794. Oxford, 1986.
Sedgwick, Catharine Maria. *Hope Leslie*. Mary Kelley, editor 1827. Rutgers UP, 1987.
Seed, David, editor. *A Companion to Twentieth-Century United States Fiction*. Wiley-Blackwell, 2010.
Silko, Leslie Marmon. *Ceremony*. Penguin, 1977.
Smiley, Jane. *Thirteen Ways of Looking at the Novel*. Knopf, 2005.
Stein, Gertrude. *Three Lives*. Linda Wagner-Martin, editor. 1909. Bedford/St. Martin's, 2000.
Stowe, Harriet Beecher. *Uncle Tom's Cabin*. 1852. Library of America, 1991.
Strout, Elizabeth. *Olive Kitteridge*. Random House, 2008.
Toomer, Jean. *Cane*. 1923. Darwin T. Turner, editor. Norton, 1988.

Twain, Mark. *The Adventures of Huckleberry Finn*. 1885. John Seelye, introduction. Penguin, 1985.
Updike, John. *Rabbit, Run*. 1960. Fawcett, 1982.
Updike, John. *Hugging the Shore*. Vintage, 1983.
Walker, Alice. *The Color Purple*. Simon and Schuster, 1982.
Wegelin, Christof, editor. *The American Novel: Background Readings and Criticism*. The Free Press, 1972.
Wharton, Edith. *The Age of Innocence*. 1920. Regina Barreca, introduction. Signet, 1996.
Wharton, Edith. "The Great American Novel." Hutner, pp. 177–182.
Whitehead, Colson. *The Underground Railroad*. Doubleday, 2016.
Williams, Sherley Anne. *Dessa Rose*. Harper Collins, 1986.

Index

Adventures of Huckleberry Finn, The (Twain) 10, 14, 21, 27–29, 31, 93–95, 100
Age of Innocence, The (Wharton) 28–29, 69–72, 77
Alcott, Louisa May 3, 68
Alger, Horatio 2, 9, 10, 41–42, 48, 57, 60, 113, 132, 147
Allison, Dorothy 10, 119–122
Alvarez, Julia 10, 82, 141–144, 154, 181
Always Coming Home (Le Guin) 204
American Pastoral (Roth) 56–60
American Renaissance 3, 6, 15, 17, 24, 190
American Revolution 16, 64, 153
An American Tragedy (Dreiser) 7, 29, 115
Anaya, Rudolfo 10, 158–160, 162, 181
Anderson, Sherwood 167
Another Country (Baldwin) 8, 19, 32–34
Appleseed (Bell) 204
assimilation 137, 141–142, 144, 151, 154, 162
Awakening, The (Chopin) 66–70, 73
Autobiography, The (Franklin) 7, 16, 41
Autobiography of Alice B. Toklas (Stein) 82
Autobiography of an Ex-Colored Man, The (Johnson) 50–53
Autobiography of Miss Jane Pittman, The (Gaines) 96

Baldwin, James 2, 8, 19, 30, 32–34, 88, 99, 167

Baraka, Amiri (LeRoi Jones) 156
Barnes, Djuna 166, 171
Barth, John 30, 164, 179
Barthelme, Donald 30, 179
Barthelme, Frederick 115
Bastard out of Carolina (Allison) 119–122
Beat Generation (*see also* Kerouac, Jack) 37, 155, 161, 175–179
Behold the Dreamers (Mbue) 132–136
Bell, Matt 204
Bellow, Saul 30
Beloved (Morrison) 15, 31–32, 86, 96–99, 103
Bennett, Arnold 23
Biden, Joseph 132
Black Arts Movement 99, 156
Black Lives Matter Movement 111, 126
Bless Me, Ultima 158–160
Bloom, Harold 1
Bondwoman's Narrative, The (Crafts) 92
Boyle, T. Corraghessan 11, 198–200, 204
Bradley, David 96
Brown, Charles Brockden 3, 16
Brown Girl, Brownstones (Marshall) 128–132
Brown, Rita Mae 73
Brown, Sterling 77
Brown, William Hill 15
Brown, William Wells 11, 92, 163–166, 170, 183
Burroughs, William S. 179
Butler, Octavia 10, 100–103, 109, 181, 204
Byron, George Gordon Lord 21

Index

Call It Sleep (Roth) 138–141, 144, 149
Cane (Toomer) 170–172
canon wars 5–6, 8, 11, 26, 77
Carver, Raymond 119
Catcher in the Rye (Salinger) 7
Cather, Willa 82, 99, 191
Ceremony (Silko) 186–190
Cervantes, Miguel de 163
Chaneysville Incident, The (Bradley) 96
Charlotte Temple (Rowson) 15, 63–66, 78, 82
Chesnutt, Charles 21, 49–50
Chopin, Kate 9, 21, 66–70, 73
Cisneros, Sandra 31
Civil Rights Movement 18
Civil War 18, 19, 28, 43, 86, 87, 91–93, 96, 99
climate change 18, 77, 185, 193–211
Clotel, or The President's Daughter (Brown) 92, 163–166, 170
Clowes, Daniel 181
Cold War 18, 148
Colored Museum, The (Wolfe) 88
Color Purple, The (Walker) 80–82
communism 36, 118, 125, 175–176
Confessions of Nat Turner (Styron) 87, 99, 103
Confessions of Nat Turner, The (Turner) 87
Cooper, James Fenimore 3, 11, 16, 19, 152, 190, 192–193
Coover, Robert 179
Crafts, Hannah 92
Crane, Stephen 10, 113–116, 118–119
Crumb, R. 181
Crying of Lot 49; The (Pynchon) 155, 178–181, 184
Cullen, Countee 53

de Balzac, Honoré 20
de Beauvoir, Simone 144
de Crevecoeur, J. Hector 41
Deerslayer, The (Cooper) 190, 192–193
DeLillo, Don 2, 11, 30, 148, 179, 206–207
Defoe, Daniel 16
De Forest, William 19–24
Dessa Rose (Williams) 103–109

Dickens, Charles 16, 20
Dickinson, Emily 3, 17
Didion, Joan 31, 73
Don Quixote (Cervantes) 163
Dos Passos, John 29, 167
Douglass, Frederick 16, 87, 90
Dreiser, Theodore 7, 23, 29
Drop City (Boyle) 198
DuBois, W.E.B. 50, 52
Dylan, Bob 161

Egan, Jennifer 11, 82, 181–184
Eisenhower, Dwight 36, 39
Eliot, T.S. 131, 171
Ellison, Ralph 2, 4, 7, 10, 30, 32, 99, 122–128, 131–132, 136
Emerson, Ralph Waldo 3, 4, 7, 8, 17, 126
Erdrich, Louise 31, 190
Eugenides, Jeffrey 154
"Everybody's Protest Novel" (Baldwin) 88
Extremely Loud and Incredibly Close (Foer) 148

Falling Man (DeLillo) 148
Fanshawe (Hawthorne) 16
Faulkner, William 11, 97, 99, 172–175
Fear of Flying (Jong) 73
Feminine Mystique, The (Friedan) 73
Fern, Fannie 3, 73
Fielding, Henry 21, 163
Fienberg, Leslie 82
Fire Next Time, The (Baldwin) 32–33
Fitzgerald, F. Scott 2, 7, 9, 15, 29–31, 46–49, 56, 59, 147, 149, 167
Flight Behavior (Kingsolver) 193–198, 200
Flight to Canada (Reed) 100, 103
Foer, Jonathan Safran 148
Ford, Richard 31, 119
Franklin, Benjamin 7, 16, 41
Franzen, Jonathan 31
Freud, Sigmund 124
Friedan, Betty 73
Fuller, Margaret 3–4, 17

Gaddis, William 30
Gaines, Ernest J. 96, 100

Galsworthy, John 23
Garland, Hamlin 29, 191
Gates, Henry Louis Jr. 92
Gilded Age 44, 46
Gilman, Charlotte Perkins 66
Ginsberg, Allen 176–177
Giovanni's Room (Baldwin) 32
Gogol, Nikolai 145, 147
Goodbye, Columbus (Roth) 56
Go Tell It on the Mountain (Baldwin) 32
Grapes of Wrath, The (Steinbeck) 29–30, 115–118
Gravity's Rainbow (Pynchon) 7, 30, 179
Great American Novel 2, 7, 8, 14–34, 35, 88, 122, 161
Great Depression 18, 29, 73, 115, 118, 122
Great Gatsby, The (Fitzgerald) 7, 15, 29, 31, 46–49, 56, 59, 147, 149
Great Migration 18
Group, The (McCarthy) 73–77, 80

Haley, Alex 96, 100, 104
Harlem Renaissance 49, 51, 53, 170, 172
Harper, Frances Ellen 73
Hawthorne, Nathaniel 3, 5, 16–21, 27, 62, 163, 190
Heller, Joseph 179
Hemingway, Ernest 2, 11, 14, 28–30, 167, 191–193, 208
Herrick, Robert 23–25
Highsmith, Patricia 82
Holmes, Oliver Wendell Sr. 19
Hope Leslie (Sedgwick) 65–66, 190
House of Mirth, The (Wharton) 5, 25
Howells, William Dean 2, 9, 21, 42–46, 48–49, 56, 59, 115
How the García Girls Lost Their Accents (Alvarez) 141–144, 154, 181
Hughes, Langston 9, 53
Hurston, Zora Neale 2, 9, 77–80, 84

Incidents in the Life of a Slave Girl (Jacobs) 87
Infinite Jest (Wallace) 7, 30
Invisible Man (Ellison) 4, 7, 30, 122–128, 131–132, 136

Iola Leroy (Harper) 73
Irving, Washington 3, 16, 19, 152

Jacobs, Harriet 16, 87
James, Henry 21, 23, 28–29, 87, 167
Jazz Age 46
Jefferson, Thomas 5, 92, 155, 165
Jennie Gerhardt (Dreiser) 115
Jewett, Sarah Orne 191
Johnson, Charles 96, 100
Johnson, James Weldon 9, 50–53, 122
Jong, Erica 73
Joyce, James 155
Jubilee (Walker) 99

Karl, Frederick 4–5
Kennedy, John F. 58, 60, 179
Kerouac, Jack 11, 21, 30–31, 37–38, 175–179, 184
Kesey, Ken 179
Kindred (Butler) 100–103
King, Stephen 204
Kingsolver, Barbara 11, 193–198, 200, 204
Kingston, Maxine Hong 10, 155–158, 160, 162
Klein, Marcus 5

Lahiri, Jhumpa 10, 31, 145–148, 160
Larsen, Nella 7, 9, 53–56, 122
Lauter, Paul 5
Lee, Harper 82
Le Guin, Ursula 204
Lewis, Sinclair 25
Libra (DeLillo) 179
Lincoln, Abraham 87, 92, 100
Little Women (Alcott) 68
Locke, Alain 77
London, Jack 29, 115, 191
Longfellow, Henry Wadsworth 4
Lowell, Robert Trail Spence 19–20

Maggie: A Girl of the Streets (Crane) 113–116, 118–119
magical realism 181
Mailer, Norman 30
Main Street (Lewis) 25
Making of Americans, The (Stein) 7

Man in the Gray Flannel Suit, The (Wilson) 37
Marcus, Greil 161–162
Marrow of Tradition, The (Chesnutt) 50
Marshall, Paule 10, 128–132
Martin Eden (London) 115
Marxism (*see* communism)
Mason, Bobbie Ann 119
Mbue, Imbolo 10, 132–136
McCarthy, Cormac 11, 31, 204–205
McCarthy, Mary 9, 30, 73–77, 80, 167
McTeague (Norris) 115
Melville, Herman 7, 11, 16–18, 20, 22, 27–31, 165–166, 170, 179, 183, 190
metafiction 166
Metalious, Grace 37
Middle Passage (Johnson) 96
Middlesex (Eugenides) 154
Mitchell, Margaret 99
Moby-Dick (Melville) 7, 16–17, 27–29, 31, 165–166, 179, 190
modernism 37, 69, 141, 163, 166, 170, 172, 175, 181
Momaday, N. Scott 190
Morrison, Toni 2, 10, 15, 31–32, 86, 96–100, 103, 109, 154, 181

Nabokov, Vladimir 164
Namesake, The (Lahiri) 145–148, 160
Narrative of the Life of Frederick Douglass, American Slave 87, 90
Native Son (Wright) 29–30, 115, 117–118
naturalism 29, 42, 113–115, 140–141, 191
Naylor, Gloria 82
Netherland (O'Neill) 148–155
Nightwood (Barnes) 166, 171
Norris, Frank 14, 21, 29, 115

Oates, Joyce Carol 31
Obama, Barack 132
Octopus, The (Norris) 115
Old Man and the Sea, The (Hemingway) 191
Olive, Again (Strout) 82–85
Olive Kittredge (Strout) 82–85

O'Neill, Joseph 10, 148–155
On the Road (Kerouac) 21, 30–31, 37–38, 175–178, 184
Our Nig (Wilson) 92
Overstory, The (Powers) 200–204, 208, 211

Pale Fire (Nabokov) 164
Pamela (Richardson) 63
Parable of the Sower (Butler) 204
Passing (Larsen) 7, 53–56
Perry, Thomas Sergeant 22–24
Petry, Ann 82
Peyton Place (Metalious) 37
Play It as it Lays (Didion) 73
Poe, Edgar Allen 3
Portrait of a Lady, The (James) 28–29
postmodernism 37, 100, 163, 166, 175–176, 178–184, 206
Powers, Richard 11, 31, 200–204, 208, 211
Price of Salt, The (Highsmith) 82
Puritans 15, 17, 27, 137, 144, 156, 161, 175
Pynchon, Thomas 2, 7, 11, 30, 155, 164, 178–181, 184

Rabbit, Run (Updike) 8, 37–40, 42, 46, 56
Ragged Dick (Alger) 9, 41–42, 48, 60, 113, 132
realism 11, 21–22, 37, 42, 109, 115, 162–163, 170, 172, 175, 181, 183, 190
Reconstruction 124
Reed, Ishmael 10, 30, 100, 103
Revolutionary Road (Yates) 37
Rexroth, Kenneth 161
Richardson, Samuel 63
Rise of Silas Lapham, The (Howells) 42–46, 48–49, 56, 59, 115
Road, The (McCarthy) 204–205
Roots (Haley) 96, 101, 104
Roth, Henry 10, 138–141, 144, 149
Roth, Philip 9, 30, 56–60
Rowson, Susanna 3, 9, 15, 63–66, 78, 82
Rubyfruit Jungle (Brown) 73
Ruth Hall (Fern) 73

Sabbatical: A Romance (Barth) 179
Salinger, J.D. 7
Salvage the Bones (Ward) 207–211
Sand, George 20
Sandburg, Carl 161
Scarlet Letter, The (Hawthorne) 16, 27
Scott, Sir Walter 16
Sedgwick, Catharine Maria 3, 16,
  65–66, 190, 193
September 11th Terror Attacks
  148–150, 182
Shakespeare, William 21, 173
Silko, Leslie Marmon 11, 186–190, 192
Simms, W. Gilmore 19
slave narratives 87, 90, 92, 163–164
slavery 17–19, 28, 31, 49, 86–112,
  113, 128, 163–164, 173
Smiley, Jane 1, 7, 31
Song of Solomon (Morrison) 31, 154
Souls of Black Folk, The (DuBois) 50
Sound and the Fury, The (Faulkner)
  172–175
Stand, The (King) 204
Stein, Gertrude 7, 11, 82,
  166–173, 181
Steinbeck, John 2, 10, 29–30, 115–119
Sterne, Laurence 163
Stone Butch Blues (Feinberg) 82
Stowe, Harriet Beecher 10, 20, 22–23,
  25, 27–28, 51, 63, 87–92, 94–95,
  97, 100, 104
Strout, Elizabeth 9, 82–85
Styron, William 87, 99, 103–104
Sun Also Rises, The (Hemingway)
  28–29, 191–193, 208

Tan, Amy 82
television 18, 36–38, 58, 96, 101, 135,
  198, 207
Terrorist (Updike) 148
Thackeray, William 21
Their Eyes Were Watching God
  (Hurston) 77–80, 84
Thoreau, Henry David 3, 7, 8, 16–17,
  185, 190
Three Lives (Stein) 167–171, 181
To Kill a Mockingbird (Harper) 82
Tomine, Adrian 181
Tom Jones (Fielding) 163
Toomer, Jean 11, 170–172

Transcendentalists (*see* American
  Renaissance)
Tripmaster Monkey (Kingston)
  155–158, 160
Tristram Shandy (Laurence) 163
Trollope, Anthony 20–21
Trump, Donald 132
Turner, Nat 87, 99, 103
Twain, Mark 9, 14, 21, 27–29, 44,
  93–95, 100, 190

Ulysses (Joyce) 155
Uncle Tom's Cabin (Stowe) 10, 20, 23,
  25, 27–28, 51, 63, 87–92, 94–95,
  97, 100, 104
Uncle Tom's Children (Wright) 88, 115
Underground Railroad, The
  (Whitehead) 109–112
Underworld (DeLillo) 30
Updike, John 30, 37–40, 42, 46,
  56, 148
Up from Slavery (Washington) 49

V. (Pynchon) 179
Vietnam War 58, 155, 157–158, 202
Visit from the Goon Squad, A (Egan)
  181–184
Vizenor, Gerald 190
Vonnegut, Kurt Jr. 30, 164

Walden (Thoreau) 8, 16, 185
Walker, Alice 9, 31, 77, 80–82
Walker, Margaret 99
Wallace, David Foster 7, 30
Ward, Jesmyn 11, 207–211
Washington, Booker T. 49, 124
Wegelin, Christof 5
Wells, H.G. 23
Wharton, Edith 2, 5, 9, 21, 23, 25–28,
  30, 69–72, 77, 167
Wheatley, Phillis 5
When the Killing's Done (Boyle)
  198–200
Whitehead, Colson 10, 31, 109–112
White Noise (DeLillo) 206–207
Whitman, Walt 3, 17, 155–156, 158
Wideman, John Edgar 30, 154
Wilson, Harriet 92
Wilson, Sloane 37
Wieland (Brockden Brown) 16

Williams, Sherley Anne 10, 103–109
Wolfe, George C. 88
Woolf, Virginia 97
World War One 18, 187
World War Two 18, 36, 46, 115, 155, 157, 159, 176, 186–188

Wright, Richard 10, 29–30, 32, 77, 88, 115, 117–119, 167

Yates, Richard 37
"Yellow Wallpaper, The" (Gilman) 66

For Product Safety Concerns and Information please contact our EU representative GPSR@taylorandfrancis.com Taylor & Francis Verlag GmbH, Kaufingerstraße 24, 80331 München, Germany

Printed and bound by CPI Group (UK) Ltd, Croydon, CR0 4YY
06/06/2025
01896215-0006